Gospel Light's

BIG BOOK
OF DISCIPLESHIP BASICS

CD-ROM INCLUDED

Reproducible!

Gospel Light

GUIDELINES FOR PHOTOCOPYING PAGES

Editorial Staff

Founder, Dr. Henrietta Mears • **Publisher,** William T. Greig • **Senior Consulting Publisher,** Dr. Elmer L. Towns • **Senior Managing Editor,** Sheryl Haystead • **Senior Consulting Editor,** Wesley Haystead, M.S.Ed. • **Senior Editor, Biblical and Theological Issues,** Bayard Taylor, M.Div. • **Associate Editor,** Veronica Neal • **Art Director,** Samantha A. Hsu • **Designer,** Zelle Olson

Adapted from Gospel Light's Preteen Curriculum *The Edge*.

Contents

How to Use This Book 5

Getting Started with Small Groups 6

Keep the Kids Talking! 8

Leading a Student to Christ 10

Accepting Jesus

Lesson 1: The Problem of Sin 13

Lesson 2: The Sin Solution 17

Lesson 3: Light in a Sinful World 21

Becoming a Disciple

Lesson 1: Get to Know God 25

Lesson 2: Obey All the Way 29

Lesson 3: Depend on God's Wisdom 33

Building Relationships God's Way

Lesson 1: Faithful Friends 37

Lesson 2: Live Honestly 41

Lesson 3: Who's Your Neighbor? 45

Lesson 4: Tongue Control 49

Lesson 5: Be Angry, But Sin Not 53

Lesson 6: The Gift of Forgiveness 57

Depending on Jesus

Lesson 1: Living Water 61

Lesson 2: Bread of Life 65

Lesson 3: The Good Shepherd 69

Lesson 4: The Way 73

Lesson 5: The Vine 77

Getting into God's Word

Lesson 1: Doers of the Word 81

Lesson 2: The Great Temptation 85

Lesson 3: The Fruit of God's Word 89

Growing in Faith

Lesson 1: Hungry for Goodness 93

Lesson 2: Love Is God's Law 97

Lesson 3: Faithful Habits 101

Lesson 4: Faith That Leads to Obedience 105

Growing Together in the Church

Lesson 1: Love and Pray for God's Family 109

Lesson 2: One Spirit 113

Lesson 3: Accept Each Other 117

Knowing God

Lesson 1: The Only True God 121

Lesson 2: God's Faithfulness 125

Lesson 3: Ever-Present Power 129

Lesson 4: Everlasting Love 133

Living Clean

Lesson 1: Learn from Your Sin 137

Lesson 2: Make It Right 141

Lesson 3: A Fresh Start 145

Living Confidently

Lesson 1: Trust in God 149

Lesson 2: Handling Fear 153

Lesson 3: My Future 157

Lesson 4: Tough Times 161

Lesson 5: God Is Good 165

Reaching Out

Lesson 1: The Great Commission 169

Lesson 2: Taking Action 173

Lesson 3: Know and Tell the Good News 177

Lesson 4: Witness with Love and Respect 181

Talking to God

Lesson 1: Teach Us to Pray 185

Lesson 2: A Song of Praise 189

Lesson 3: Confess Your Sins 193

Lesson 4: A Grateful Heart 197

Lesson 5: Ask the Lord 201

Using My Gifts

Lesson 1: Here I Am, Lord 205

Lesson 2: Serve with God's Strength 209

Lesson 3: Rely on God's Strength 213

Lesson 4: Parable of the Talents 217

Indices

Bible Study Index 221

Bible Verse Index 222

How to Use This Book

If you are the children's pastor,

1. Look at the Contents to get an idea of the discipleship topics presented in *The Big Book of Discipleship Basics*.

2. Read through any lesson to gain an understanding of the three main components in each lesson: Get Started, Get It Together and Get Going. Note the Get Real student worksheet that can be completed in class or at home.

3. If *The Big Book of Discipleship Basics* will be used as an ongoing discipleship program, you may want to recruit a coordinator several months before the program begins. Provide the coordinator with this book and plan regular check-ins with him or her. Be available for practical support and encouragement.

4. If teachers will use these lessons to supplement an existing curriculum, provide them with copies of each lesson.

Lesson Schedule

Get Started

5-15 minutes

Introduce students to the lesson topic through hands-on activity.

Get Together

20-30 minutes

Lead students in Bible study and discussion that helps them to develop an understanding of the lesson topic.

Get Going

20-30 minutes

Using a student worksheet, guide students to plan and pray about ways to apply the lesson topic in their own lives.

If you are the coordinator,

1. Look at the Contents to get an idea of the discipleship topics presented in *The Big Book of Discipleship Basics*.

2. Read through any lesson to gain an understanding of the three main components in each lesson: Get Started, Get It Together and Get Going. Note the Get Real student worksheet that can be completed in class or at home.

3. In conjunction with the children's pastor, recruit the appropriate number of small-group leaders needed. (One adult for every small group of no more than 10 children is recommended.)

4. Prepare ahead of time the materials needed for the Get Started activities and photocopy the Get Real worksheets for students.

If you are a teacher or small-group leader,

1. Look at the Contents to get an idea of the discipleship topics presented in *The Big Book of Discipleship Basics*.

2. Read through any lesson to gain an understanding of the three main components in each lesson: Get Started, Get It Together and Get Going. Note the Get Real student worksheet that can be completed in class or at home.

3. Prepare and lead lessons to supplement your existing curriculum, or as assigned by program coordinator.

Getting Started with Small Groups

Small Groups Help Preteens Develop Relationships with Their Peers

Relationships are key to long-term spiritual growth and involvement in church life for the emerging adolescent. Kids who do not have friends at church do not enjoy themselves and do not keep coming back.

For preteen ministry to be successful, the ministry leader must account for the socialization needs of the preteen child that are central to this developmental stage. Preteens feel social acceptance is their number one concern. For leaders to accomplish their instructional objectives, the church program must provide for activities that meet students' socialization needs. Because of that socialization need, small groups must be incorporated into the preteen ministry in as many ways as possible. It is through small groups that early adolescents can get to know one another and build the friendships they need.

Small groups are a pivotal point between children's programs and youth programs and an essential ingredient to any complete preteen ministry. Although younger children certainly want to belong and to have friends, the need for relationships becomes central in preteen years. Within a small-group setting, it is much more likely that students will get to know a significant adult and a group of peers. Both are necessary to the healthy development of the preadolescent.

The great news about small groups is that any church can do them. They do not require finances or church facilities. They require only loving adults who are willing to give up a few hours each week to lead preteens.

For the small-group ministry to be healthy, it must be a positive and encouraging environment. The early adolescent longs for a group of peers in which he or she can develop trust and find caring. Where these elements are built, the small group will flourish. Once the relationships and trust are built, then the small group becomes a wonderful environment for teaching biblical truths.

For preteens, small groups are essential for both education and discipleship. Educationally, small groups lend themselves naturally to one of the most effective means of teaching preteens—cooperative learning. Spiritually, discipleship relationships within the context of the small group allow for several kids to be mentored at once and for deeper relationships than are usually created in the typical Sunday School setting.

Occasionally Mix the Group Members to Maximize the Small-Group Experience

There are several ways to purposefully expose kids to more potential friendships:

■ **Have assigned small groups that change quarterly.** Keep track of your students' attendance and evenly distribute regular attenders and infrequent attenders among the various small groups you form. This will help each group have a core of students. Three months will allow your small-group leaders to get to know the group members well enough to give you feedback on who should or should not be grouped together for the next quarter.

■ **Each month or so, offer kids an alternative affinity group.** Once each month group students according to their common interests or hobbies. They may choose from computers, service projects, discipleship, art and recreation activities. The leader of each group weaves the Bible study into his or her specialty and the kids get to meet others who are interested in the same topic or activity, but who are not necessarily in their regular small group. Also, have special activities so that kids can choose to do something different once each month or so.

■ **Have "upset basket" Sundays when no one is in his or her regular group.** As each preteen arrives, hand him or her a square of colored paper at random. Have each small-group leader dress in that color for the morning or wear a name tag made of paper of the same color. Kids will complain and ask if they can switch, but in the end they will enjoy the experience of working with a new adult and some peers they may not have spent much time with previously.

The Importance of Small-Group "Families"

The most important goal of small groups within your preteen ministry is to establish healthy relationships between students and adults in which mentoring and discipleship can take place. The small-group leader's goals must include helping each early adolescent feel significant and valued as a member of the group.

■ **Emphasize the importance of small-group leaders being present to greet each member of the small group as he or she arrives.** Remember that preteens are very self-conscious. The first minute after they arrive in the room is critical. The more welcome and secure they feel, the better their whole morning will go.

■ **Emphasize the importance of being genuine, real and transparent for the kids.** This may be the most important quality of the preteen small-group leader whose goal is to mentor and disciple their students. Such positive and enriching contact with adults is priceless.

Preteens are in the process of leaving the family and at the same time are desperately looking for another "family" to belong to. They need to build relationships with adults who can help them grow spiritually and help them learn how to live the Christian life. Consistency in both the leadership and membership of small groups is very important for providing an atmosphere in which strong bonds of friendship can be formed.

The adult who wants to disciple a small group of preteens must be willing to invest much of his or her time encouraging them and supporting them.

The leader must invest in genuine, caring relationships with the kids. The leader can build relationships with kids in so many ways. Just do things with the kids that are important to them:

■ Attend their sporting events.

■ Be there when they receive awards at school or badges in Scouts.

■ Let them telephone you to tell you about hurt feelings or bad grades.

■ Take them to McDonald's for sodas when they do well on tests.

■ And maybe easiest, but most effective, invite them to hang out with you at your house, doing what you would be doing anyway, seeing you in action with your family, eating your food, watching your TV and learning what differences being a Christian makes in your everyday life.

Of course, in today's world, the preteen leader must be smart about the ways he or she chooses to spend time with kids. Make sure that you take necessary precautions to keep yourself above reproach. That means, don't be alone with a child, and avoid being too touchy. While with a group of kids and adults, just spend some one-on-one time with kids.

Should Small Groups at This Age Be Coed or Single Gender?

Here are the advantages of each approach.

The Advantages of Separating Boys and Girls for Small Groups

■ In single-gender small groups, young men or young women are able to develop close relationships with role models of the same gender.

■ Preteens have a developmental need to have close friends of the same gender.

■ Same-gender groups may initially be easier to bond, since some activities will be naturals for each gender.

■ Since preteens are only beginning to show interest in the opposite gender and girls generally reach this point earlier than boys, many kids would initially prefer to be with only their own gender.

■ Some hot topics can be discussed more appropriately in single-gender groups, like physical changes and sexuality, which are so much on the minds of some early adolescents.

The Advantages of Combining Boys and Girls in Coed Small Groups

■ Young men and young women both need male and female role models. Coed groups led by a married couple are ideal because they also show preteens a picture of the value of Christian marriage and family life.

■ Preteens are becoming aware of the opposite gender and need healthy guidance in developing appropriate friendships. The small-group context is ideal for this training.

■ Coed groups allow for activities that may be considered traditionally male or female to be shared and experienced by both genders, allowing for a broader appeal to nontraditional kids!

■ Oftentimes in coed groups, boys tend to be less aggressive and girls tend to be friendlier. The mixture seems to bring out the best in both genders.

■ Some spiritual topics can be more fruitfully discussed in coed groups because a variety of opinions might be shared.

Keep the Kids Talking!

Children like to speak their minds! The challenge is to keep the discussion focused on the lesson, to involve all children and to prevent distracting chatter. Children's learning will be much more effective when they are involved in the process of learning through discovery and discussion rather than through sitting and listening.

Good Preparation

Write good questions before class. Good discussions occur when the teacher knows what questions to ask. Study the class material thoroughly (even if it's a familiar Bible story) and think through the discussion questions provided in this book. Think of additional questions to ask as well. Avoid questions with obvious one-word answers. Discussion grows out of questions that ask for opinions, ideas, reactions, etc., not just repeating factual answers. (This means you must begin preparation well before your group meets!)

Minimize distractions. Children are naturally curious and are interested in everything that goes on—whether it's the lesson activity at hand or not! Evaluate the distractions in your classroom by asking the following questions: Is there noise in the classroom from the choir warming up next door? Are people walking through the hallway? Are there toys or items scattered around the classroom that the children will want to play with? Are cell phones ringing? Do parents arrive long before the class ends and stand around outside the room?

Then consider these solutions: If outside noise is a problem, play a music CD or cassette as background to cover outside noise. Toy shelves can be turned to face the wall to help children avoid the temptation of playing with the toys. Arrange chairs so children are faced away from distractions. Remind teachers (and children!) before class begins to turn off cell phones. Keep in mind, however, that your reaction to distractions is the biggest factor. If you respond in a matter-of-fact manner, children will, also.

Limit the discussion. Children are not able to remain interested during long times of discussion. Children's physical requirements for movement need to be met. It's better to end the discussion time before children grow restless. Most discussions should be tied to some physical activity, either as an introduction to the activity, as a break during the activity or as a summary after the activity.

Involve everyone. Try to involve all children in a discussion. Start by asking several easy, low-threat questions that all children are capable of answering. Seek to involve the potentially disruptive child right at the start. Children are less likely to be disruptive when they're occupied. If a child looks restless, call him or her by name and ask a question. Also ask questions of children who have been quiet. Be sure not to ask a difficult question they may not know. One reason children may not participate is that they feel they don't know the answer and don't want to be embarrassed in front of their peers.

Handling Interruptions

Get back on track. Despite the best plans, a discussion may veer off course. First, determine if the new topic is valid. Perhaps one child is overly focused on a small detail (such as how Joshua could make the sun stand still when in reality Earth moves) but the rest of the class is not interested. Acknowledge that the new topic is interesting and can be discussed at another time, and then return to the original topic. Restate the last question and if children do not respond, try another question.

If a child deliberately wants to get off the topic, use humor to return to the topic. If the children digress because they don't understand the topic or the question, use a simpler question or take time to explain the topic.

Discussion off the topic is not always cause for alarm. Sometimes a child needs to discuss a topic not on the agenda or finds an unexplored point in the topic. If the new topic will help children apply Bible truth to everyday life and will benefit the

entire class, stay with it. If a child needs to discuss a special need, such as a death in the family, make time at the end of the activity for the class to offer support and prayer.

Go with the flow. Interruptions will happen. If the interruption is minor and the children are not unduly distracted, then ignore it and continue. Some interruptions require the teacher to stop and take care of matters: a child needs to leave early, an adult arrives to make an announcement or the air conditioner needs to be adjusted. Try to get the class back on track. If the class has grown too distracted, move on to another activity.

Be prepared for silence. Sometimes children will respond to a question with silence. This can be good if the children are pondering a deep question. It can be fatal if this is due to lack of understanding, embarrassment or boredom.

Give children a few seconds to think about the question. Ask for a visual signal (thumb up, fist on chin, etc.) when students think they may have at least part of the answer. Rephrase the question in case the first question was not understood. If children still are unable to answer, you might share the answer you would give and then move on to another question.

Sometimes children do not respond when the questions are too easy (Who are Jesus' parents?), too obvious (Does God want us to help our neighbors?), too personal (What sins have you committed this week?) or too difficult (According to legend, what are the names of the three wise men?). After class, revise the questions that failed to get a good response and use the improvements as a model for writing good questions for the next class.

Sometimes children will give the answer they think the teacher wants to hear. Write open-ended questions that are more challenging: How would you feel if you had been a shepherd who was off-duty the night the angels appeared? What do you think the blind man did after Jesus healed him? How can you defend your friend from a bully?

Leading a Student to Christ

Many adult Christians look back to their elementary years as the time when they accepted Christ as Savior. Not only are children able to understand the difference between right and wrong and their own personal need of forgiveness, but they are also growing in their ability to understand Jesus' death and resurrection as the means by which God provides salvation. In addition, children at this age are capable of growing in their faith through prayer, Bible reading, worship and service.

However, children (particularly those in early elementary grades) can still be limited in their understanding and may be immature in following through on their intentions and commitments. They need thoughtful, patient guidance in coming to know Christ personally and continuing to grow in Him.

1. Pray.

Ask God to prepare the children in your class to receive the good news about Jesus and prepare you to effectively communicate with them.

2. Present the Good News.

Use words and phrases that children understand. Avoid symbolism that will confuse these literal-minded thinkers. Discuss these points slowly enough to allow time for thinking and comprehending.

a. "God wants you to become His child. Do you know why God wants you in His family?" (See 1 John 3:1.)

b. "You and all the people in the world have done wrong things. The Bible word for doing wrong is 'sin.' What do you think the Bible says should happen to us when we sin?" (See Romans 6:23.)

c. "God loves you so much, He sent His Son to die on the cross for your sin. Because Jesus never sinned, He is the only one who can take the punishment for your sin. On the third day after Jesus died, God brought Him back to life." (See 1 Corinthians 15:3-4; 1 John 4:14.)

d. "Are you sorry for your sin? Tell God that you are. Do you believe Jesus died to take the punishment for your sin and that He is alive today? If you tell God you are sorry for your sin and tell Him you do believe and accept Jesus' death to take away your sin—God forgives all your sin." (See 1 John 1:9.)

e. "The Bible says that when you believe in Jesus, God's Son, you receive God's gift of eternal life. This gift makes you a child of God. This means God is with you now and forever." (See John 1:12,13; 3:16.)

As you give children many opportunities to think about what it means to be a Christian, expose them to a variety of lessons and descriptions of the meaning of salvation to aid their understanding.

3. Talk personally with the child.

Talking about salvation one-on-one creates opportunity to ask and answer questions. Ask questions that move the child beyond simple yes or no answers or recitation of memorized information. Ask what-do-you-think? kinds of questions such as:

"Why do you think it's important to . . . ?"

"What are some things you really like about Jesus?"

"Why do you think that Jesus had to die because of wrong things you and I have done?"

"What difference do you think it makes for a person to be forgiven?"

Answers to these open-ended questions will help you discern how much the child does or does not understand.

4. Offer opportunities without pressure.

Children are vulnerable to being manipulated by adults. A good way to guard against coercing a child's response is to simply pause periodically and ask, "Would you like to hear more about this now or at another time?" Lovingly accepting the child, even when he or she is not fully interested in pursuing the matter, is crucial in building and maintaining a relationship that will yield more opportunities to talk about becoming part of God's family.

5. Give time to think and pray.

There is great value in encouraging a child to think and pray about what you have said before making a response. Also allow moments for quiet thinking about questions you ask.

6. Respect the child's response.

Whether or not a child declares faith in Jesus Christ, adults need to accept the child's action. There is also a need to realize that a child's initial responses to Jesus are just the beginning of a lifelong process of growing in the faith.

7. Guide the child in further growth.

Here are three important parts in the nurturing process:

a. *Talk regularly about your relationship with God.* As you talk about your relationship, the child will begin to feel that it's OK to talk about such things. Then you can comfortably ask the child to share his or her thoughts and feelings, and encourage the child to ask questions of you.

b. *Prepare the child to deal with doubts.* Emphasize that certainty about salvation is not dependent on our feelings or doing enough good deeds. Show the child verses in God's Word that clearly declare that salvation comes by grace through faith (i.e., John 1:12; Ephesians 2:8-9; Hebrews 11:6; 1 John 5:11).

c. *Teach the child to confess all sin.* "Confess" means "to admit" or "to agree." Confessing sins means agreeing with God that we really have sinned. Assure the child that confession always results in forgiveness (see 1 John 1:9).

The Problem of Sin

Get Started ■ 5-15 minutes

Action: Identify problems people face because of sin in our world.

Without Circles

What You Need

Paper, pencils.

What You Do

1. Distribute paper and pencils to students.

2. Students draw pictures of things that would be different if circles didn't exist (donuts, baseballs, basketballs, the sun, people, cars, etc.). After several minutes, invite students to describe their pictures.

3. Ask these questions.

■ **Would a world without circles be easier or more difficult? Why?**

■ **What are some of the problems we might have without circles?**

■ **It's fun to think about how just one change in our world could affect so many things. But there's something that did completely change the world and has created countless problems ever since. What do you think it might be?**

■ **How do you think the world changed after the first sin?**

■ **What are some problems we have because of sin?**

4. Conclude the activity by saying,

■ **Let's see why sin caused lots of problems in a world that had been perfect.**

Bonus Idea

Divide group into two teams and give each team a large sheet of paper. Teams compete to see how many things they can write or draw that would be different if circles didn't exist. After several minutes, call time. Teams compare items to see who has the most ideas that don't match.

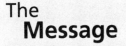

The Message

Sin separates us from God.

The Bible Basis

Genesis 2; 3:1-19; Romans 3:23; 5:12; 6:23

From the time of Adam and Eve's sin, God began to show a way for sin to be forgiven.

The Scripture

"For the wages of sin is death, but the gift of God is eternal life in Christ Jesus." Romans 6:23

Get It Together ■ 20-30 minutes

Action: Realize that because sin separates us from God, we all need His forgiveness.

Genesis 2; 3:1-19; Romans 3:23; 5:12; 6:23

What You Need

Bibles.

What You Do

Lead students to read and discuss the Bible verses listed. Extend the discussion with the questions and comments provided.

Introduction

It's hard to imagine what life might have been like if sin had never happened way back in the beginning of the world. Let's talk about what really happened.

A Perfect World

■ Read Genesis 2:8-9 to find the description of the place where Adam and Eve first lived.

■ What did God provide for Adam and Eve?

■ What do you think Adam and Eve's relationship with God was like?

God created a beautiful perfect world. Then He created two people, a man and a woman—Adam and Eve. God provided EVERYTHING Adam and Eve needed. In this perfect world, Adam and Eve were loved and cared for by God. Their relationship with God was one of friendship and happiness.

One Rule

■ Read Genesis 2:16-17 to find the one rule God asked Adam and Eve to follow.

■ Why do you think they had only one rule?

■ How many rules do you have in your family or in your school classroom or in our city?

■ What would happen if Adam and Eve broke the rule?

Wouldn't it be nice if we lived in a world where only one rule was needed? That one rule, however, had a stiff penalty. If Adam and Eve ate fruit from the tree of knowledge, they would die! Dying was something that had never happened before in God's creation.

The Bible doesn't say why God made this rule. Some people think God's rules are intended to keep us from enjoying life. However, as we see from the rest of this story, God's rules are really to protect us and to keep us from doing things that hurt ourselves or other people.

Satan's Temptation

■ Read Genesis 3:1 to find what Satan first said to Eve.

■ What was wrong with Satan's words?

■ What did Satan say in Genesis 3:4-5 to tempt Eve to disobey God?

■ What are some times when people today do what they think is right instead of what God says is right?

Things were going along very well for Adam and Eve, until one day, Satan, God's enemy who is sometimes called the devil, came visiting. He was disguised as a serpent. Satan planned his words to confuse Eve and cause her to doubt what God had said.

Satan lied. He wanted Adam and Eve to disobey God by choosing to do things their way instead of God's way.

14

The Results of Sin for Adam and Eve

■ How do you think their sin made Adam and Eve feel?

■ Read Genesis 3:15 to find what God promised.

When Adam and Eve ate fruit from the tree of the knowledge of good and evil, they sinned by disobeying God. By that one disobedient act they caused sin to become a part of the world. Now everyone born after them would have a desire to sin and disobey God. They felt so guilty and ashamed that they hid from God.

Because of their sin, Adam and Eve no longer had a perfect life. They no longer had a close relationship with God and with each other. They couldn't live in the beautiful garden anymore. Their work, instead of being something they enjoyed doing with the abilities God gave them, became a difficult struggle of trying to survive! Eventually, their sin resulted in their deaths.

But even in this sad situation, God gave them hope—the promise of someone who would take away their sin. God promised that one of Eve's descendants would someday defeat sin and Satan.

The Results of Sin for Us

■ What does Romans 5:12 say was the result of Adam's actions?

■ How does Romans 3:23 describe the results of our sin?

■ How does Romans 6:23 contrast the wages of sin with God's plan to defeat sin?

Many centuries later, Paul, a follower of Jesus, wrote how sin changed the world and our relationship with God.

Sin entered the world, and sin brought death.

Because of our sin, we are separated from God and from experiencing His love.

"Wages" is another word for what we earn. Instead of receiving the punishment our sins have earned—death—God gives eternal life because of Jesus Christ.

Conclusion

Romans 6:23 tells us that the result of sin is death. (Read verse aloud.) But because Jesus came to live as a human, He was able to defeat the sin problem we have had since the time of Adam and Eve. As a result of what Jesus did, when we believe that Jesus paid the price for our sin, we can receive God's forgiveness. God's gift to us every day is forgiveness! (Lead students in prayer, thanking God for His forgiveness and for sending Jesus. Then talk with interested students about becoming members of God's family, referring to "Leading a Student to Christ" on pp. 10-11.)

Get Going ■ 20-30 minutes

Action: Privately list, and then pray about, reasons he or she needs God's forgiveness.

Distribute Get Real (p.16) to students. Invite students to tell or write answers to the questions. End the discussion by completing Get Connected with students. (Optional: Students complete page at home.)

GET REAL

- If Adam and Eve hadn't sinned, do you think the world would still be perfect today? Why or why not?

- Do you think people today feel like Adam and Eve felt after they sinned? Why or why not?

- Though feelings and attitudes are not good or bad in themselves, why do you think it is important to base our actions on something other than our feelings?

- When are some times kids your age might sin by disobeying God?

- What can you do to remind yourself of God's gift of forgiveness?

Get to Know

"For the wages of sin is death, but the gift of God is eternal life in Christ Jesus."
Romans 6:23

Get Connected

Think about reasons you need forgiveness from God. Then pray, asking God for forgiveness and thanking God for showing His love by sending Jesus to Earth and by forgiving your sins.

The Sin Solution

Get Started ■ 5-15 minutes

Action: Discover and discuss examples of the principle "Reap what you sow."

Reap What You Sow

What You Need

Ingredients, equipment and utensils for snack you choose (see ideas below).

What You Do

1. Students make and eat one of the snacks below.

■ Snack 1: Spread softened cream cheese over rice cakes or minibagels. Sprinkle colored sprinkles on cream cheese.

■ Snack 2: Slowly add 1½ cups milk to ½ cup peanut butter. Blend until smooth. Add one small package instant vanilla or chocolate pudding. Beat slowly until well mixed. Let stand five minutes. Spoon pudding into ice-cream cones and serve immediately. (Serves 10 students.)

2. While students are eating, ask these questions that encourage students to think about the consequences of different actions.

■ **What were the results of your work? When are some other times that you have done something that produced a good result?**

■ **What are the results of some wrong actions of kids your age?**

■ **What might be the results of studying hard in school? Practicing the guitar?**

3. Conclude the activity by saying,

■ **Getting the results of something you have done is often called reaping what you sow. When a farmer sows, or plants, seeds, he hopes he will reap, or get the result of, a good harvest.**

■ **Today we'll be talking about the results, or consequences, of sin—doing things our way instead of God's way. We'll also see how God planned to deal with the results of sin.**

Bonus Idea

Divide the group into pairs. Pairs create multiple-choice quizzes that describe different situations or actions with four possible consequences. Pairs switch quizzes with other pairs in group and choose the matching consequences for the situations described. Pairs may score and discuss quizzes with each other.

The Message

Sin brings death, but Jesus gives life.

The Bible Basis

Leviticus 9; 16:21-22; Hebrews 7:23-28; 10:1-4

The sacrifices offered by the priests temporarily paid the penalty for the sins of the people, but Jesus' sacrifice paid the penalty forever!

The Scripture

"This is how we know what love is: Jesus Christ laid down his life for us." 1 John 3:16

Get It Together ■ 20-30 minutes

Action: Understand that the Old Testament sacrifices could not be a permanent solution to the problem of sin.

Leviticus 9; 16:21-22; Hebrews 7:23-28; 10:1-4

What You Need

Bibles.

What You Do

Lead students to read and discuss the Bible verses listed. Extend the discussion with the questions and comments provided.

Introduction

All of our actions have results—some good and some bad. Sometimes these results make a big difference in our lives. That's how it is with sin.

Results of Sin

■ What is the most important result of sin?

■ What happens to our relationship with God when we sin?

When we disobey God, our relationship with God is interrupted. Sin separates us from God, and we aren't able to experience the benefits of knowing and loving Him.

Sin is serious business! In fact, the Bible says the ultimate result of sin is death—separation from God now and forever! The good news is that from the very first time people sinned, God had a plan for dealing with sin.

A Temporary Solution

■ Read Leviticus 9:7-8 to find out what God wanted His people, the Israelites, to do in order to be forgiven for their sins.

■ What were they to bring as a sacrifice?

Moses, one of the great leaders of the Israelites, told his brother, Aaron, that the Lord had commanded the Israelites to make sacrifices at the altar.

As a way of paying for their sins, the Israelites sacrificed the best animals from their flocks or herds. These animals took the punishment for the Israelites' sins. The religious leaders of the Israelites, called priests, led the people in sacrificing the animals to God.

In Bible times, animals were raised to provide food and clothing. The animals in a family's herd were valuable. They were like money on legs! Leviticus 9:7 says that taking something precious they owned—a perfect animal of the herd—and giving it to God was how the Israelites were to make atonement for their sins.

Atonement for Sins

■ What do you think the word "atonement" means?

■ How might a person today try to make up for a wrong action?

"Atonement" means to make up for the wrong things you have done, to restore things back to the way they were before. A good way to remember this explanation is to break the word into parts: "at-one-ment"—bringing back together what has been broken apart.

Sometimes a person accepts punishment for the wrong action, or sometimes a person tries to fix the problem caused by the wrong action. But the only way in Old Testament times to restore a broken relationship with God was through the sacrifice of a perfect animal—one not sickly or blemished in any way.

All through the Old Testament, the priests acted as the go-between or mediators between God and the Israelites. But this solution to the problem of sin was only a temporary one. Something MORE had to be done. Let's find out why.

The Problem

■ Look in the New Testament part of your Bible to find Hebrews 7:23. What does this verse say was the problem with every one of the high priests?

■ Why were the animal sacrifices only a temporary solution? Read Hebrews 10:3-4 to find the answer.

Jesus' Sacrifice

■ Who did God send as the perfect go-between, or bridge, between Himself and people?

■ Read Hebrews 7:27 to find out why Jesus was better than the priests and animal sacrifices in the Old Testament.

■ How is Jesus different from the priests of the Old Testament?

■ What was God's plan for dealing with sin?

Because they were human, the priests eventually died! The priests, being human, weren't any more perfect than the people themselves. It was clear that a better priest was needed—someone who was perfect and who would live forever!

The blood obtained through the death of animals reminded people of their sin but could never COMPLETELY take away sin because an animal cannot fully substitute for a human being.

So now we come to the really good news in God's plan for dealing with sin.

Jesus, God's Son, is perfect! Because He had no sin, He didn't need to offer sacrifices. The priests were not perfect, but Jesus is perfect and lives forever. Only the sacrifice of someone as perfect as Jesus would be good enough to take away people's sins completely.

Jesus died on the cross to take the punishment for our sins and to bridge the gap created by our sin. Because Jesus never sinned, He was the perfect and final sacrifice. And because Jesus came back to life again and is alive today, we know that we can be forgiven and live forever with Him.

Conclusion

Even though the people in the Old Testament didn't know the story of Jesus' birth, they showed faith in God by offering the animal sacrifices God required. Because of their faith, their sins were forgiven. The animal sacrifices were a picture of Jesus' much greater sacrifice. Now, after Jesus lived on Earth and died to take the punishment for everyone's sins, we can show our faith in God by admitting our sins to God and asking for His forgiveness.

First John 3:16 tells us the love God had for us by sending Jesus to die for our sins. (Read verse aloud.) Jesus was God's gift of life to us—the perfect solution to the problem of sin. (Pray with students, thanking God for the gift of life in Jesus. Talk with interested students about becoming members of God's family, referring to "Leading a Student to Christ" on pp. 10-11.)

Get Going ■ 20-30 minutes

Action: Think about Jesus' sacrifice for their sin, and thank God for sending Jesus to take away sin.

Distribute Get Real (p. 20) to students. Invite students to tell or write answers to the questions. End the discussion by completing Get Connected with students. (Optional: Students complete page at home.)

- What are some ways people might try to get rid of the problem of sin?

- Why is it important that God sent Jesus to Earth?

- What's the most important thing kids your age need to know about God's plan for dealing with sin?

- How would you describe God's plan for dealing with the problem of sin in the world?

- When you think of God's plan to deal with the problem of sin, what can you thank Him for?

Get to Know

"This is how we know what love is: Jesus Christ laid down his life for us."
1 John 3:16

Get Connected

What difference does it make to you to know about Jesus' death on the cross? What would life be like if Jesus had not died on the cross? Thank God for showing His love by sending Jesus to Earth and by forgiving your sins.

Light in a Sinful World

Get Started ■ 5-15 minutes

Action: Explore uses of light.

Turn On the Light!

What You Need

Black construction paper; gel pens, gel markers or chalk; tape.

What You Do

1. Distribute black paper. Ask the questions below.

■ **Imagine a world as dark as this paper. What are some things that would be hard for you to do without any light?**

■ **What are some things that help people who can't see?**

■ **What do you think would be your hardest adjustment if you no longer could see?**

2. Students use gel pens, gel markers or chalk to draw pictures of things people usually need light in order to do (read, draw, play sports, etc.). Encourage students to draw as many pictures as possible and then tape the pictures to a door or window in your classroom, attempting to fill the area with pictures.

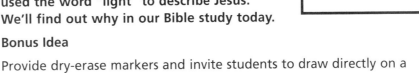

3. Conclude the activity by saying,

■ **We use light for many things. Even if we couldn't see at all, light would still be important to us. Without light, we would not be able to grow food to eat!**

■ **A long time ago, a writer in the Bible used the word "light" to describe Jesus. We'll find out why in our Bible study today.**

Bonus Idea

Provide dry-erase markers and invite students to draw directly on a clean window. Be sure to erase drawings immediately after class.

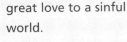

The Message

Become part of God's family by accepting Jesus.

The Bible Basis

Luke 2:22-40

The birth of Jesus demonstrated the light of God's great love to a sinful world.

The Scripture

"Everyone who believes in him receives forgiveness of sins through his name." Acts 10:43

Get It Together ■ 20-30 minutes

Action: Realize that Jesus is like a light, helping us to see and receive God's love.

Luke 2:22-40

What You Need

Bibles.

What You Do

Lead students to read and discuss the Bible verses listed. Extend the discussion with the questions and comments provided.

Introduction

Usually we only talk about Jesus' birth at Christmastime, but His birth changed history in such a dramatic way that it's important to think about it at other times of the year, too.

A Temple Visit

■ What's something parents often do after a baby is born?

■ According to Luke 2:22-24, why did Mary and Joseph take Jesus to the Temple?

Forty days after Jesus was born, Mary and Joseph took Jesus to the Temple in Jerusalem. The law of Moses—the Law God gave to Moses on Mount Sinai in the book of Exodus—said that the firstborn child was to be dedicated to God. Dedicating the baby showed that the child would serve God. The law also said that a woman had to offer a sacrifice of a lamb after she had a baby. A poor person could offer two pigeons (or doves) because lambs were expensive (see Leviticus 12).

Simeon's Prophecy

■ What are some things that people usually say to parents with a new baby?

■ How did Simeon describe Jesus in Luke 2:30-32?

■ Read Luke 2:34 to find out what Simeon said about Jesus' future.

■ What do you know about how that prophecy came true?

Even though Mary and Joseph didn't send a messenger to the Temple to tell people they were coming, when they arrived, they met two people who were already expecting them! The first person was a man called Simeon. He truly loved God and was waiting to see the Savior God had promised to send. God had revealed to Simeon that Simeon would not die before he had seen the One God had promised to send to save His people.

When Simeon saw Mary and Joseph with baby Jesus, Simeon went to them and took Jesus in his arms. Simeon KNEW Jesus was the One sent by God!

Simeon described Jesus as a light who would help Gentiles—non-Jewish people—learn about God and who would bring honor to God's people, the Israelites. Jesus was the One who would bring salvation to the world! The name "Jesus" means "the Lord saves."

Simeon said that Jesus would cause many people to fall and many to rise. By using the word "falling," Simeon meant that some people wouldn't believe in Jesus and would reject Him as their Savior. When he used the word "rising," Simeon meant that Jesus would make it possible for many people to rise up and become members of God's family.

The last thing Simon prophesied was that Jesus would meet with lots of opposition. All through His life, there were people who were angry with Jesus. Even the people in Jesus' own hometown became angry while He was teaching. (See Luke 4:28-30.) Jesus encountered so much opposition that He was killed! Today

we know that Jesus' death was part of God's plan—Jesus was to live a perfect life, die to pay the penalty for our sins and come back to life.

Anna's Prayer

■ Read Luke 2:38 to find out what Anna did when she saw Jesus.

As soon as Simeon finished talking with Mary and Joseph, an old woman named Anna came up to them. She loved God and spent all her time in the Temple praying and praising God. She was known as a prophetess—God told her things to tell to other people.

When Anna saw Jesus, she knew that He was someone special. She thanked God and began talking about Jesus to everyone who was looking forward to God's promise of a Savior.

Conclusion

The life that Jesus lived was like a light. Just as lights help us see things clearly, Jesus' life helps us see and understand what God is like and how He showed His love to a sinful world. You have the opportunity to become a part of His family by accepting Jesus and receiving forgiveness for sin. Acts 10:43 tells us that we can receive forgiveness of sin through His name. (Read verse aloud with students.) If you've already become part of God's family, you know that God continues to show His love for you every day. (Pray with students, thanking God for His love and for sending Jesus so that we can be part of God's family. Then talk with interested students about becoming members of God's family, referring to "Leading a Student to Christ" on pp. 10-11.)

Get Going ■ 20-30 minutes

Action: Identify what is true about Jesus and why He is the light of the world, and participate in God's plan of salvation by becoming part of God's family.

Distribute Get Real (p. 24) to students. Invite students to tell or write answers to the questions. End the discussion by completing Get Connected with students. (Optional: Students complete page at home.)

GET REAL

- Why would you say that Jesus is like a light to the world?

- What else do you know about Jesus? What other words would you use to describe Jesus?

- How does Jesus' coming help people learn about God and His plan for them to become part of His family?

- How can a person become a member of God's family?

Get to Know

"Everyone who believes in him receives forgiveness of sins through his name."
Acts 10:43

Get Connected

Think about what you believe is true about Jesus and why He is the light of the world. Tell God what you believe about Jesus.

Get to Know God

Get Started ■ 5-15 minutes

Action: Discover that we show our priorities by our use of time and possessions.

Color Pass

What You Need

Large sheet of paper, one red and one blue marker.

What You Do

1. Show large sheet of paper. **Let's play a game to fill in this paper with important things.** Students sit in a circle. Place large sheet of paper in the center of the circle and give markers to two students. Students pass markers around the circle in different directions until you signal them to stop.

2. Student holding the red marker writes or draws on the large sheet of paper something he or she likes to do (skateboard, hang out with friends, paint, read mystery books, etc.). Student holding the blue marker writes or draws something he or she has to do (chores, homework, go to school, eat vegetables, etc.). Repeat until each student has had a turn to write or draw on the paper or until time is up.

3. Ask these questions.

■ **Which of these things do you think are most important? Why?**

■ **You are starting to make your own choices about different things. What kinds of choices do kids your age get to make?**

■ **How do you think people in Bible times chose to spend their time?**

■ **Do you think their choices would be the same or different from people today? Why?**

■ **What's something you wish you had more time to do? Is there anything you'd like to do less of? Why?**

■ **We all spend a lot of time sleeping and going to school or working. In the time you have free to do whatever you want, what would you do?**

4. Conclude the activity by saying,

■ **The things you spend a lot of time doing show what's important to you—your priorities.**

■ **Today we're going to hear what the priorities were of a man in Bible times.**

Bonus Idea

If you have more than five or six students, pass more than one of each color of marker so that more students may participate in writing or drawing at a time.

The **Message**

Take time to know God.

The **Bible Basis**

Luke 12:13-21

Jesus told a story of a man who foolishly concentrated on storing his wealth, never realizing that all his wealth would be useless in the end.

The **Scripture**

"Store up for yourselves treasures in heaven, where moth and rust do not destroy, and where thieves do not break in and steal." Matthew 6:20

Get It Together ■ 20-30 minutes

Action: Understand that because only our relationship with God lasts forever, getting to know who God is and what He is like is the greatest priority.

Luke 12:13-21

What You Need

Bibles.

What You Do

Lead students to read and discuss the Bible verses listed. Extend the discussion with the questions and comments provided.

Introduction

When have you thought that your brother or sister, or a friend, wasn't treating you fairly? What did you say or do? What happened? How did you feel? A man with these same feelings came to see Jesus one day. Jesus had been talking to people about what is important in life and why people shouldn't worry about certain things. Let's find out what happened.

The Inheritance

■ Read Luke 12:13. What did the man in the crowd want Jesus to do?

■ What do you think was important to the man who talked to Jesus?

■ Read what Jesus warned this man in Luke 12:15. What did Jesus want this man to know about?

In Bible times, a father's money and possessions were divided between his sons, but the oldest son received TWICE as much as the younger son. The Bible doesn't say whether the older brother wasn't giving this man any of the inheritance or if the man just wanted more money than he was legally entitled to.

Jesus knew the real reason behind this man's question. This man was asking for Jesus' help in the situation with his brother because money was the MOST important thing to this man. It was even more important than getting along with his brother!

The Parable

■ Read the beginning of the parable in Luke 12:16-17. What could the man have done with his extra crops?

■ What do you think the man decided to do? Compare your idea with what he did. Read Luke 12:18-19. What did the man decide to do? Why?

Jesus told a parable, or story, as He often did, to help everyone understand what He was talking about. This particular story is sometimes referred to as the parable of the rich fool.

The man could have left some of the crops in the fields for poor people to harvest for food. The man could have taken the extra grain to the market and sold it. The man could have given the extra grain to the poor. The man could even have started a bakery!

The rich man probably thought he wouldn't have to work so hard next year—that now he was set for life. Maybe he dreamed about all the stuff he could buy with the money from the crops—maybe a new coat, more donkeys, more chickens, maybe even a bigger house!

Keeping his crops for himself was all this man thought about. And THAT was the problem. He put all his trust and hope for the future into building bigger barns for his crops.

The Problem

■ Read Luke 12:20 to find out how God described this man and what happened next.

■ Read verse 21 to discover what Jesus told the crowd. What do you think "rich toward God" means?

The man didn't know it, but he was going to die that very night! The rich man had spent all his time thinking about how to keep the crops for himself so that he would have them later, and now there wasn't going to BE a "later"! He was not going to need those crops anymore. No wonder the man was called a fool! He'd paid attention to only one thing all his life and missed the MAIN thing!

A person who is rich toward God is someone who puts God first, someone who spends time getting to know God and shows love and obedience toward Him.

Conclusion

The parable Jesus told makes it clear that money and possessions don't last forever. Matthew 6:20 tells us to store up treasures in heaven and not on Earth. (Read verse aloud.) The only thing the Bible says will last forever is our relationship with God. Getting to know who God is and what He is like is the most important thing we can do in our lives. (Pray with students, thanking God for His love and asking for His help in getting to know Him more.)

Getting to know God begins with becoming a member of His family. God sent Jesus to take the punishment for our sins so that we can be forgiven and enjoy God's love for us. (Talk with interested students about salvation, referring to "Leading a Student to Christ" on pp. 10-11.)

Get Going ■ 20-30 minutes

Action: Plan ways of getting to know God.

Distribute Get Real (p. 28) to students. Invite students to tell or write answers to the questions. End the discussion by completing Get Connected with students. (Optional: Students complete page at home.)

Get Real

- What are some things you do when you want to know a friend better?

- In order to be remembered as a person who knows God, what sort of things would you need to do?

- What are some things you can do to show that getting to know God is important to you?

- What specific thing can you plan to do this week to get to know God more?

- How can getting to know God help us? Why is spending time with God important?

Get to Know

"Store up for yourselves treasures in heaven, where moth and rust do not destroy, and where thieves do not break in and steal."
Matthew 6:20

Get Connected

What will you do to remember to read your Bible or pray this week? Ask God to help you remember to spend time with Him.

Obey All the Way

Get Started ■ 5-15 minutes

Action: Discover the benefits of completely following instructions.

Pudding Mix-Up

What You Need

Paper, tape, box of instant banana or vanilla pudding mix, milk, banana, cooking utensils, pencils, bowl, small serving bowls, spoons.

What You Do

1. Tape over the instructions on the box of pudding.

2. Set out box of instant banana or vanilla pudding mix, milk, banana and cooking utensils. Students form pairs. Provide paper and pencils. Ask students to write instructions for making banana pudding.

3. After students have written instructions, collect them. Have a student randomly choose one paper and read it aloud. Follow the instructions exactly as written. For example, if a student writes "Put pudding mix in bowl," put the box itself into the bowl without opening it. Students will enjoy observing the omissions in their instructions. When it becomes apparent that one set of instructions isn't correct, begin again with another set of instructions or ask students to correct the instructions as you follow them. Guide students to correctly make pudding.

4. Ask these questions as students serve and eat pudding.

■ **What did you learn about the importance of good instructions?**

■ **What are some other things for which you need instructions?**

■ **When are some times you have followed someone else's instructions to learn something?**

5. Conclude the activity by saying,

■ **You learned the importance of following the instructions for something as simple as a pudding recipe.**

■ **When God gives us instructions for life, He wants us to follow them.**

■ **A man in Bible times learned the hard way the difference between wholeheartedly and halfheartedly obeying God. Let's find out what happened.**

Bonus Idea

Students work in pairs or trios to design a board game and write instructions for it.

The
Message

Wholehearted obedience results in a life of integrity.

The
Bible Basis

1 Samuel 15:1-29

Jesus told a story of a man who foolishly concentrated on storing his wealth, never realizing that all his wealth would be useless in the end.

The
Scripture

"I seek you with all my heart; do not let me stray from your commands."
Psalm 119:10

Get It Together ■ 20-30 minutes

Action: Understand the importance of paying attention to all of God's instructions.

1 Samuel 15:1-29

What You Need

Bibles.

What You Do

Lead students to read and discuss the Bible verses listed. Extend the discussion with the questions and comments provided.

Introduction

What happened the last time you tried to build something without reading the instructions first? Our Bible study is about a king who thought he knew what he was doing and didn't need to completely follow God's instructions. Let's see what happened to him.

God's Instructions

■ Read 1 Samuel 15:2 to find out what the Old Testament prophet Samuel said to King Saul.

■ Why do you think God wanted Saul to destroy the Amalekites?

Samuel was a prophet of God. He told God's messages to the people of Israel. Samuel was very careful to follow God's instructions exactly. Saul was Israel's first king. In today's story, Samuel was hurrying on his way to Saul. He had an important message from God—and Saul needed to hear the message right away.

God wanted Saul to know that the Amalekites were to be punished for the wrong actions they had done against His people. God said, "Destroy ALL the Amalekites and EVERYTHING they own!"

Destroying the Amalekites sounds like a terrible thing to do. For many years, the Amalekites had not only rejected God and worshiped other gods, but they had also constantly tried to destroy the people who were following God! In fact, one time the Amalekites purposely attacked and killed the weakest Israelites. (See Deuteronomy 25:17-19.) Because the Amalekites had done such a terrible thing, God said that He would destroy them. God gave the Amalekites a long time to change their ways. But the Amalekites never did.

Saul's Actions

■ What did Saul and his soldiers do? Read 1 Samuel 15:9 to find out.

■ Why do you think Saul and his soldiers might have done this?

Saul set out to obey God's command. And at first, everything went OK. Saul ordered the army to attack the Amalekites; and sure enough, just as God had promised, the Israelites won the battle and destroyed all the Amalekites. Well, ALMOST all of them.

Saul and his soldiers destroyed all the things they wouldn't want anyway, but they kept the BEST things. In Bible times, soldiers were often paid by being allowed to keep some or all of the possessions of those they had defeated in battle. Saul also captured the king of the Amalekites. By having a king as his prisoner, Saul would look very powerful to other kings.

Saul's Excuses

■ How do you think God felt about Saul's actions? Read verses 10 and 11 to find what God told Samuel.

Samuel was very upset by Saul's actions and he talked to God all night! The next morning Samuel went out to greet Saul, who should have been on his

■ Read 1 Samuel 15:13-20 to find out what happened next.

■ What was Saul's excuse for bringing back the best things, instead of destroying everything?

way home. But there was no Saul. Saul had gone to another city and built a monument to himself!

Samuel hastily strode off to the city where Saul had gone next. Saul saw Samuel coming, and Saul could probably tell by the way Samuel was walking that Samuel was not at all happy.

Not only did Saul claim to have obeyed God, but also he implied that it was his soldiers' idea to bring the stuff. THEN he claimed they disobeyed in order to give the things as a gift to God!

A Sad Ending

■ How did Samuel respond to Saul's excuses? Read 1 Samuel 15:22.

■ What would you have done if you were Saul? Read 1 Samuel 15:24-25 to find out what Saul said.

■ Read 1 Samuel 15:27-28 to find the sad result of Saul's disobedient actions.

Samuel made it very clear to Saul that God was much more pleased by obedience than by sacrifices. (A sacrifice was something offered to God. In Old Testament times, in order for people to receive forgiveness for sins, animals were killed, objects were burned or things were given to the priests as a symbolic way of giving them to God.)

Even though Saul said he was sorry, Samuel still refused to go with him to worship God. As far as Samuel was concerned, the discussion was over. Saul wasn't really sorry about what he'd done—Saul was only sorry Samuel was angry with him. Saul knew how much the Israelites liked Samuel and followed what he said. If Samuel was obviously angry with Saul, then the people might not follow Saul anymore. Saul was really only thinking of himself.

This story ended in a sad way. As Samuel turned to leave, Saul reached out to grab Samuel to stop him. But all Saul grabbed was a part of Samuel's coat, which ripped off in Saul's hand. Samuel turned and saw Saul standing there, holding that piece of cloth. Samuel sadly explained that Saul's kingdom would be torn away from him because he did not obey God.

Conclusion

Even when Samuel came to Saul and tried to tell Saul how he'd disobeyed God, Saul didn't listen. He didn't want to accept responsibility for his actions. Saul chose not to pay attention to God's words of instruction. Saul said he wanted to obey God, but he didn't. That's the kind of person who is known as a hypocrite or a phony. The opposite of a hypocrite is someone whose words and actions match—a person with integrity.

People today have choices about whether or not to completely obey God's Word, too. Sometimes it seems easier to pick and choose when we'll obey what God has said to do. Sometimes we put off obeying God by thinking, *When I'm older I'll obey*, or, *Because this is a small lie, God probably doesn't care about it.* But someone who is really being honest with God and others know it's important to completely obey God's Word and follow its instructions all of the time. We can do as the writer of Psalm 119:10 says. (Read verse aloud with students. Pray with students, asking for His help in obeying God.)

Get Going ■ 20-30 minutes

Action: Plan ways to obey God's instructions completely, even in difficult circumstances.

Distribute Get Real (p. 32) to students. Invite students to tell or write answers to the questions. End the discussion by completing Get Connected with students. (Optional: Students complete page at home.)

Get Real

■ What are some excuses kids your age might make about why they're not completely obeying God's Word?

■ When might a kid your age miss out on something good because he or she disobeyed?

■ What good things happen when you obey God?

■ What might happen if a kid only obeys God's instructions some of the time? When it's easy? Only when a parent is watching?

■ Because none of us is perfect, there will be times when we disobey. What can we do?

Get to Know

"I seek you with all my heart; do not let me stray from your commands."
Psalm 119:10

Get Connected

We all need help obeying God completely. Think of one way you need to obey God more fully. Ask God for help in obeying Him every day.

Depend on God's Wisdom

Get Started ▪ 5-15 minutes

Action: Identify ways in which people make choices.

Choices

What You Need

Several catalogs and/or newspaper advertising inserts, scissors.

What You Do

1. Students look at advertisements in the catalogs or inserts. Ask these questions to guide students in thinking about the advertisements they find.

▪ **What kinds of products are being advertised?**

▪ **What kinds of choices are you being asked to make?**

▪ **How do ads get you to want to buy a product?**

▪ **Based on what the advertisement says, would you be able to make a good or bad choice?**

▪ **What other information might you need?**

▪ **How do kids your age make choices about how to spend money? Time?**

▪ **Who helps you make choices?**

2. Each student cuts out one or two ads of the things he or she would like to buy. After several minutes, guide students to discuss their choices by inviting volunteers to show ads for items they would buy and tell reasons why they would buy the items.

3. Conclude the activity by saying,

▪ **Some choices we make are easy—like what we'll eat for breakfast. Other times it's hard to know what to choose.**

▪ **Today in our Bible study, see if you can find out who made a really wise choice and what happened as a result of this choice.**

Bonus Idea

If student cannot find items he or she is looking for, provide paper and markers for students to use in drawing pictures.

The Message

God's wisdom will help me discern right from wrong.

The Bible Basis

1 Kings 3:4-28; 4:29-34

Solomon asked God for wisdom, and God made him wiser than anyone else.

The Scripture

"Trust in the Lord with all your heart and lean not on your own understanding; in all your ways acknowledge him, and he will make your paths straight."
Proverbs 3:5-6

Get It Together ■ 20-30 minutes

Action: Realize that God's wisdom helps us choose between right and wrong.

1 Kings 3:4-28; 4:29-34

What You Need

Bibles.

What You Do

Lead students to read and discuss the Bible verses listed. Extend the discussion with the questions and comments provided.

Introduction

If you could ask for anything, what would you ask for? Today we are going to talk about someone who really was given a chance to ask for anything he wanted.

Solomon was about 20 years old when his father, King David, died. Solomon's older brothers might have been expected to take David's place as king. After all, they had much more experience and knowledge than a young man of 20! But God had told David that Solomon was to be the next king of Israel.

Shortly after he was proclaimed king, Solomon went to a city called Gibeon to worship God. Solomon probably went there to thank God for making him king. While he was there, something happened that changed Solomon's life forever. Let's find out what it was.

Solomon's Request

■ Read 1 Kings 3:5 to find out what God told Solomon.

■ What would you have asked God for if you had been Solomon?

■ Read 1 Kings 3:7-9 to find out what Solomon asked for. Why did Solomon ask for wisdom?

■ How do you think Solomon's request showed he wanted to trust God?

■ Read 1 Kings 3:12-14. How did God respond to Solomon's request?

Solomon could have asked for immense wealth so that he could live in luxury. Or he could have asked for great power to keep himself safe from his enemies. He could have asked to be very popular or to have a long life.

But instead Solomon asked for wisdom. (Wisdom is the ability to know what is best and the willingness to do it.) Solomon wanted to do a good job of leading God's people.

God gave Solomon wisdom (and more!), and God described how this wisdom would help Solomon to become the world's most successful king!

Solomon's Decision

■ Read 1 Kings 3:16-23 to find out what Solomon was asked to decide.

■ How would you determine whose baby it was?

■ Read 1 Kings 3:24-25 to find what Solomon did.

■ If you were in the courtroom, what might you have thought of Solomon's solution?

One day, while Solomon was hearing complaints and deciding cases, two women came to see him. They lived together in the same house and each had recently given birth to a baby. Sadly, one of the babies died during the night.

Both women claimed the living baby as her own! Unfortunately, they were the only ones who could identify the babies because no one else had seen them. This was a tough case. Without modern DNA testing and lie-detector tests, it would have been an impossible task to decide which woman was lying. Probably no one in the courtroom expected Solomon to have an answer.

Because of God's gift of wisdom, Solomon was able to discover which woman was lying.

The woman who lied said the baby was hers, not because she wished to have a baby to love and raise, but because she wished to have what the other woman had. (In Bible times, women without children were thought to be cursed.)

So Solomon devised a test that would reveal the true mother. God's gift of wisdom had helped Solomon make the best decision.

Solomon's Wisdom

■ What did the people of Israel think of Solomon in 1 Kings 3:28?

■ Read 1 Kings 4:29-34. Besides being able to solve tough cases, what were some of the other things Solomon was able to do with his wisdom?

Solomon's wisdom made him very famous! Solomon had such a good name that kings from other countries sent men from their courts to learn from Solomon!

One result of King Solomon's wisdom is the book of Proverbs. God helped King Solomon write many of the wise sayings in the book of Proverbs. King Solomon's wise sayings help us know how to be successful and popular in God's eyes.

Conclusion

God offered Solomon anything he wanted. And what did Solomon want? He wanted wisdom. Solomon understood the big responsibility he had, and he wanted to be able to do his job well. He knew he needed God's wisdom and help. Because Solomon's desire was to show faithfulness to God, God honored Solomon's request. As a result, even when Solomon had to decide who the true mother was, Solomon made the right choice. As long as Solomon remembered to obey God and trust in God's wisdom, he was truly successful. That's what the Bible explains to us in Proverbs 3:5-6. (Read verses aloud with students.)

As we grow older and do new things, we're going to be faced with lots of choices to do right or wrong. Sometimes the choices will be really clear—we all know that God doesn't want us to lie or purposely hurt someone. But sometimes the choices won't be easy. We might wonder whether it is right or wrong to watch a particular movie, or do what a friend wants us to do. In situations like that, we really need to remember to ask God for His help and for His wisdom; He promises to help all those who are members of His family and who love and trust in His Son, Jesus (see James 1:5). Then we'll be successful in God's eyes! (Lead students in prayer, asking God to help them make wise choices.)

Get Going ■ 20-30 minutes

Action: Identify situations in which it is difficult to make right choices, and plan to follow God's wisdom.

Distribute Get Real (p. 36) to students. Invite students to tell or write answers to the questions. End the discussion by completing Get Connected with students. (Optional: Students complete page at home.)

Get Real

- What would a person making a hard decision do to show he or she trusted only in God?

- How might you show at school that you want to depend on God's wisdom?

- What's one way to show you are depending on God while playing a game? Taking a test? Choosing a movie to see?

- When is it easy for you to remember to talk to God, asking Him for wisdom in making right choices? When is it hard?

- What are some choices kids your age have to make? How would you describe a kid your age who is wise?

Get to Know

"Trust in the Lord with all your heart and lean not on your own understanding; in all your ways acknowledge him, and he will make your paths straight."
Proverbs 3:5-6

Get Connected

Think about one difficult situation in your life in which you need God's wisdom. How will you learn and follow God's wisdom? Ask God to give you His wisdom and help you make right choices.

Faithful Friends

Get Started ■ 5-15 minutes

Action: Discover reasons why people become friends.

Common Ground

What You Need

Paper plates, markers.

What You Do

1. **What are some things you like to do with your best friend?** Distribute paper plates and markers. Students write their names on paper plates. **Let's play a game to think about some other things you like to do.** Students stand in the middle of the room. Ask one of the questions below and give two to four possible answers, pointing to a different location (on the table, under the chalkboard, next to the bookshelf, etc.) for each answer.

- ■ **What is your favorite sport?**
- ■ **What do you like to do for fun?**
- ■ **What is your favorite movie?**
- ■ **Who would you like to spend time with?**
- ■ **What is your favorite ice cream flavor?**
- ■ **Where would you like to go for vacation?**

2. For each question, students toss paper plates like frisbees, attempting to have plates land in designated areas to show their answers to each question. Students quickly retrieve their plates. Repeat with additional questions.

3. Conclude the activity by saying,

- ■ **Often, we become friends with people who like the same kinds of things we do.**
- ■ **What are some other reasons people might become friends?**
- ■ **What do you think it is important for a friend of yours to do?**
- ■ **In our Bible study today, we'll find out about two people who became friends, even though they really didn't have much in common with each other.**

Bonus Idea

Pairs of students take turns acting out situations that show what kids who are friends like to do together. Videotape students acting out situations and then play back video for students to enjoy.

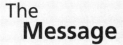

The Message

Be a true friend!

The Bible Basis

1 Samuel 18:1-16; 19; 20; 2 Samuel 1; 9

David and Jonathan remained faithful friends, even though others thought they should have been enemies.

The Scripture

"Each of you should look not only to your own interests, but also to the interests of others." Philippians 2:4

Get It Together ■ 20-30 minutes

Action: Understand that God wants true friends to care for and protect each other just as they care for themselves.

1 Samuel 18:1-16; 19; 20; 2 Samuel 1; 9

What You Need

Bibles.

What You Do

Lead students to read and discuss the Bible verses listed. Extend the discussion with the questions and comments provided.

Introduction

Think about some of your friends. Did you become friends right away, or did it take time? The friendship of David and Jonathan, two faithful friends we read about in the Old Testament, began soon after they met.

Unlikely Friendship

■ What do you know about David and Jonathan?

■ Read 1 Samuel 18:3. What do you think it means to make a covenant with someone?

■ Why did Jonathan make this promise of friendship?

■ What might kids today give each other to show that they really wanted to be friends?

Saul was King of Israel, and Jonathan was his son, a prince. David was just a young shepherd who lived way out in the country. But after David defeated Goliath, Israel's enemy, Saul brought David to the palace to live with him. David and Jonathan quickly became very good friends.

The people who knew David and Jonathan probably would NEVER have predicted they would be friends—especially not BEST friends. But they were! And the Bible gives us some good clues about how they showed their friendship in spite of great pressures that could have made them into enemies.

The word "covenant" means an agreement or promise between two or more people. David and Jonathan promised to be trustworthy friends to each other.

Jonathan cared about what happened to David as much as he cared about what happened to himself! To prove his friendship, he gave to David several of his prized possessions—his robe, sword, bow and belt.

A Jealous King

■ What happened in Samuel 18:5 that sounded good but caused trouble for David?

■ Read 1 Samuel 18:8-11 to see how Jonathan's dad began to feel about David and what he did to show his feelings.

■ How do you think Jonathan might have felt about his father's actions?

King Saul continued to send David out as a warrior for Israel. And David did a fantastic job! The Israelites were so proud of David's skill in protecting Israel that they made up this song: "Saul has killed his thousands, and David his tens of thousands!"

Hearing the words of that song did something to King Saul! He became jealous of David's popularity—so jealous that he threw a spear at David. One day Saul even commanded his servants and Jonathan to kill David!

A Loyal Friend

■ Read 1 Samuel 19:1-2 to find out what Jonathan chose to do after hearing his father's plot to kill David.

■ What happened in 1 Samuel 19:11-12 when Saul became angry at David again?

■ One of the last times David and Jonathan saw each other is described in 1 Samuel 20. Read verse 42 to see what they said to each other.

To show his friendship, Jonathan chose to warn David about King Saul's death threat. Jonathan also planned a way to make peace between the two men. And for a while, Jonathan's plan worked. David was once again accepted in the palace—but not for long!

Once again, Saul grew horribly jealous and hateful toward David. David had gone to battle again for Israel and defeated the Philistines. Eventually, Saul's anger grew so strong that David had to run for his life! Jonathan knew that David was God's choice to be the next king. So he helped David escape unharmed. Even though he knew that helping David meant he himself would never be king, he was glad to help his friend.

Because David and Jonathan's friendship was so strong, they promised they would always show kindness to each other and to each other's children.

David kept his promise of friendship, too. Later in his life, David learned that King Saul and Jonathan had been killed in battle. David grieved terribly over the death of his friend. He wrote a song honoring Saul as a mighty king and describing what a loving friend Jonathan had been to him.

A Promise Kept

■ Read 2 Samuel 9:1 to find out another way David kept his promise of friendship after he became king.

■ Read 2 Samuel 9:7 to learn how David showed kindness to Mephibosheth for his friend Jonathan's sake.

In those days, a new king usually killed everyone related to the old king. One of King Saul's servants knew that Jonathan's son Mephibosheth was alive. Mephibosheth's legs had been broken when he was young and he became crippled.

David gave Mephibosheth everything he needed. Mephibosheth ate his meals in the palace as part of the royal family.

Conclusion

God gave us a great example of true friendship in the record of David and Jonathan. David and Jonathan cared for each other, and Jonathan protected David, even when it was difficult to do so. They stood up for each other and kept their promise of friendship throughout their lives. David and Jonathan truly obeyed the words of Philippians 2:4. (Read verse aloud with students.)

Jesus calls people who love and obey Him His friends (see John 15:15). When we become Christians, Jesus cares for us as "best friends." (Pray with students and then talk with interested students about salvation, referring to "Leading a Student to Christ" on pp. 10-11.)

Get Going ■ 20-30 minutes

Action: Identify and plan ways to be true friends.

Distribute Get Real (p. 40) to students. Invite students to tell or write answers to the questions. End the discussion by completing Get Connected with students. (Optional: Students complete page at home.)

Get Real

■ What characteristics of true friendship did David and Jonathan show?

■ Think about someone God has given you as a friend. What has this person done to show friendship to you?

■ When might you need to stand up for a friend?

■ What are some ways you can show that you care for a friend the same way as you care for yourself?

■ Which characteristics of a friend are most important to you? Why?

GET TO KNOW

"Each of you should look not only to your own interests, but also to the interests of others."
Philippians 2:4

Get Connected

Take a moment to think about one of your friends. Plan one or two specific things you will do to be a true friend to that person. Ask God's help in showing true friendship to others.

Live Honestly

Get Started ■ 5-15 minutes

Action: Discuss situations when dishonest communication and actions cause problems.

Trust Toss

What You Need

Drop cloth, hard-boiled eggs (one for every two students, plus extras); optional—raw eggs.

What You Do

1. Spread drop cloth on the floor.

2. **How good are you at telling the difference between a truth and a lie? Let's play a game to find out.** (Optional: Play game outside using raw eggs.) Students form pairs. Give each pair of students an egg.

3. Pairs stand close together facing one another. First student in each pair says a statement that is either a truth or a lie. (For example, "I am 20 years old.") Partner identifies statement as either a truth or a lie. When a truth is told, the student's partner stays in place. When a lie is told, the students take a step away from each other. If a student says a lie and his or her partner doesn't identify it as a lie, the student who lied takes a step back. Then first student tosses egg to partner. Pairs continue playing game until the egg breaks.

4. Ask the questions below.

■ **How is our game like what happens in a relationship when a lie is told?**

■ **When someone lies to you, how do you feel about that person?**

■ **What does "trusting someone" mean?**

■ **What happens to trust when a lie is told?**

■ **When is a time you have felt hurt or angry by someone else's dishonest talk?**

5. Conclude the activity by saying,

■ **Telling a lie can separate people, or break up a relationship.**

■ **Today we are going to hear about what happened to a family because of a lie.**

Bonus Idea

Assign pairs or trios a key phrase from 1 Corinthians 13:4-5. On a small paper strip, each group writes their phrase in their own words. Each group puts their paper strip into a balloon and blows up and ties balloons. Students bat balloons around room for 10 seconds and then at your signal, quickly pop balloons and put paper strips in verse order.

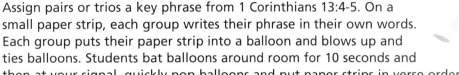

The Message

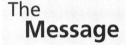

Honest communication and actions in a family show God's love.

The Bible Basis

Genesis 27:1-45

Jacob and Rebekah's dishonest actions and words caused serious problems in their family.

The Scripture

"Love is patient, love is kind. It does not envy, it does not boast, it is not proud. It is not rude, it is not self-seeking, it is not easily angered, it keeps no record of wrongs."
1 Corinthians 13:4-5

Get It Together ■ 20-30 minutes

Action: Realize that truthful words and attitudes are ways of showing God's love.

Genesis 27:1-45

What You Need

Bibles.

What You Do

Lead students to read and discuss the Bible verses listed. Extend the discussion with the questions and comments provided.

Introduction

We've been talking about situations in which dishonesty causes problems. The same sort of thing happened to a family in Bible times. A man named Isaac and his wife, Rebekah, had twin sons. This family didn't do a very good job of communicating honestly with each other. Let's find out what happened.

The Family

■ Isaac and Rebekah's sons' names were Esau and Jacob. What do you remember about Esau and Jacob?

■ Read Genesis 27:1-5 to find out what Isaac wanted Esau to do.

■ Read Genesis 27:8-10 to find out what Rebekah did when she overheard what Isaac said. Why do you think Rebekah acted this way?

■ Read verses 11 and 12 to find out what Jacob was worried about.

■ Why do you think Jacob agreed to trick his father?

The oldest son, Esau, loved to hunt. He was big and hairy, and he was Isaac's favorite. Jacob, the younger son, was not much like his brother. Jacob liked to stay at home, and he had very smooth skin. Rebekah considered Jacob HER favorite son. Esau and Jacob didn't always get along very well. And Esau even gave away his birthright inheritance to Jacob for just a bowl of good stew!

When Isaac said he wanted to give Esau the blessing, it was a big event. The blessing was an important prayer for good things that a father usually gave to his oldest son as a proof of his approval. The things the father said in this prayer were held to be true and legally binding—which meant they couldn't be changed.

Rebekah didn't like what she heard! She wanted her favorite son, Jacob, to receive this blessing. Jacob wasn't sure it would be so easy to trick his father.

It's interesting that Jacob wasn't worried about tricking his father because it was dishonest; Jacob was worried that he would get caught and get in trouble!

The Lies

■ How did Rebekah and Jacob get ready to lie to Isaac in Genesis 27:14-17?

■ What was the first lie Jacob told? Read verses 18-19.

■ Read Genesis 27:20 to find out one reason why Isaac doubted Jacob and what Jacob said to convince his father.

■ Two more times Jacob deceived his father. Read what he did in verses 22-23 and 26-27.

Rebekah fixed Isaac's favorite food. She got out Esau's best clothes and gave them to Jacob to wear. Then Rebekah covered his hands with hairy goatskin, and she cut another piece of goatskin to tie around Jacob's neck. Now Jacob would feel as hairy as Esau if his father, Isaac, touched him. Because Isaac was so old, his eyesight was very poor.

When Jacob claimed to be Esau, Isaac wasn't convinced. It usually took a LONG time to hunt wild animals and cook them. Jacob brought food that had been made from some animals in the flock they kept at home. When Jacob talked to his father, not only did he tell a lie about having to hunt for the animals, Jacob told a lie about God!

Isaac still wasn't convinced, so he asked Jacob to come close so that he could touch Jacob. When Isaac felt Jacob's hairy hands, he said something interesting.

Isaac knew it was Jacob's voice, but he also knew that Jacob did not feel hairy. So Isaac asked again, "Are you really my son Esau?" Jacob lied AGAIN and said he was Esau.

Then Isaac ate the food Jacob brought him. But Isaac still wasn't sure it was Esau he was talking to. There was one more test. After Isaac ate, he asked Jacob to come close and kiss him. When Isaac smelled Esau's clothes, he finally believed that he was really talking to his son Esau. So Isaac pronounced the blessing.

The Trouble

- What do you think a blessing is?

- Isaac gave the blessing to Jacob, but trouble happened right away. Read Genesis 27:30-33 to find out what happened.

- How do you think Esau felt about Jacob? How would you have felt? Read Genesis 27:38 and 41 to find out what Esau said.

- What were the results of the lies?

When you bless someone, you ask God to give them good things. When Isaac blessed Jacob, Isaac asked God to give Jacob and his descendants plenty of water and food. He asked that Jacob's family would become a powerful nation. Isaac knew that as he said these things before God, he was passing on the spiritual blessing he had received from his father, Abraham, to be the leader of God's chosen people.

After Isaac finished speaking, Jacob left. At the SAME time, Esau came back with the animal he had caught and prepared. Esau went into his father's tent and told him to get up and eat. Right away Isaac realized that his suspicions had been correct all along! Jacob had TRICKED him!

Esau begged for a word of blessing from his father, but the blessing had already been given.

When Rebekah heard that Esau planned to kill Jacob as soon as Isaac died, she made a new plan. Rebekah told Jacob to run away and live with his uncle, far away in another country. Bible scholars say that Rebekah probably never saw her favorite son, Jacob, again. Jacob and Rebekah's dishonest actions and words ended up separating their family and causing great pain!

Conclusion

It is easy to see that Rebekah and Jacob did not show what love really is like. Compare their actions with what the Bible says in 1 Corinthians 13:4-5. (Read verse aloud with students.)

Showing God's love by being truthful with others, particularly the people we live with, is about more than just being honest in the things we say. There are lots of ways to be truthful in the ways we communicate with others. When our words and actions reflect how we really feel, we are being truthful. When we tell the truth instead of lying, we're showing God's love. (Pray with students, asking God to help them tell the truth.)

Get Going ■ 20-30 minutes

Action: List examples of actions and ways of communicating that will show God's love in families.

Distribute Get Real (p. 44) to students. Invite students to tell or write answers to the questions. End the discussion by completing Get Connected with students. (Optional: Students complete page at home.)

Get Real

- When are some times that people who live together might be tempted to tell lies?

- When are some other times that family members might find it difficult to choose to act honestly instead of dishonestly?

- What do you think might be some of the results of honest communication in a family?

- Why do people sometimes not want to tell others their true feelings or thoughts? What are some possible results of not talking about true thoughts or feelings?

- How might being honest and loving in communicating how you think and feel help family members to get along?

GET TO KNOW

"Love is patient, love is kind. It does not envy, it does not boast, it is not proud. It is not rude, it is not self-seeking, it is not easily angered, it keeps no record of wrongs."
1 Corinthians 13:4-5

Get Connected

Think about the way you talk to people in your family. What is one thing you could change in order to show more of God's love to people at home? Ask God to help you make those changes this week.

Who's Your Neighbor?

Get Started ▪ 5-15 minutes

Action: Discover some consequences of treating others unfairly.

Label Game

What You Need

Pens, small adhesive labels.

What You Do

1. Write each of these words on a separate label: "mean," "popular," "sad," "funny," "forgetful," "dumb," "smart," "silly," "friendly," "shy," "liar," "greedy" and "selfish." Make one label for each student and yourself, repeating words if needed. Cut apart labels. Place all labels facedown on a table.

2. Ask a student to choose one of the labels and without letting you see what the label says, place the label on your back. **The word on this label describes what some people might be like.** Students silently read the label. Then ask questions of students, trying to guess what the label says. For example, **Is my label something good or bad? What might I do or say if I acted according to my label?** After you have identified the word, invite students to attach labels to their backs without seeing what the label says. Students ask questions of each other, trying to guess what their labels say. Be available to help students identify labels, prompting them with additional questions or clues as needed.

3. After several minutes, students remove their labels and gather together. Ask the following questions:

▪ **Was it hard or easy for you to guess your label?**

▪ **How might you feel if people always treated you as if you were a liar? Smart? Popular? Selfish?**

▪ **What are some unkind labels kids sometimes give each other? Why are those labels unfair?**

▪ **Some people may also believe stereotypes about certain groups of people. What are stereotypes some kids in your school or neighborhood believe?**

4. Conclude the activity by saying,

▪ **Even in Jesus' day, people often treated others unkindly by using unfair labels or believing stereotypes.**

▪ **Even worse, they believed God did the same. In today's study, we'll find out what Jesus thought about that!**

Bonus Idea

To introduce the idea of stereotypes and labels, invite volunteers to pantomime well-known descriptions of animals for others to guess (quiet as a mouse, hungry as a hippo, busy as a bee, mad as a hornet, etc.).

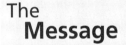

The Message

Obeying the intent of God's law helps us break down barriers between people.

The Bible Basis

Luke 10:25-37

Jesus told the story of the Good Samaritan to illustrate that God's love was not restricted to Jewish people.

The Scripture

"Love your neighbor as yourself." Luke 10:27

Get It Together ■ 20-30 minutes

Action: Discover that obeying the intent of God's law breaks down unfair barriers between people.

Luke 10:25-37

What You Need

Bibles.

What You Do

Lead students to read and discuss the Bible verses listed. Extend the discussion with the questions and comments provided.

Introduction

Think of two of your friends who don't get along very well. Jesus once told a story about two groups of people who weren't friends. Let's find out what Jesus wanted people to learn from the story He told.

A Man's Question

■ A religious expert wanted to test Jesus. Read Luke 10:25 to learn how he did this.

■ Why do you think he asked Jesus this question?

■ Read Luke 10:26-28. How did the man answer Jesus?

■ Read Luke 10:29 to find out what the man then said and why he said it.

The man who was talking to Jesus knew the law backward and forward. He probably knew the more than 600 finer points of the law. But the man didn't just want to have a question-and-answer period with Jesus. This expert in the law wanted to debate Jesus and test His knowledge.

Then instead of giving an answer, Jesus asked a question. The expert gave a very good answer, and Jesus commended him. But the expert was not satisfied with Jesus' response to his answer.

The man wanted to make himself look good! Perhaps he was hoping that Jesus wouldn't be able to answer the question correctly.

Jesus' Story

■ Jesus told a story about the relationship between two different groups of people: Jews and Samaritans. What do you know about Samaritans?

■ Tell what you remember about the story of the good Samaritan, or read it in Luke 10:30-35.

■ Who would you have expected to help the injured man? Why do you think they didn't?

■ What reasons might the Samaritan have had for helping someone he didn't even know?

The Samaritans were people who lived in an area called Samaria. They were only partly Jewish. Jewish people looked down on the Samaritans because the Samaritans were a different race and had different religious beliefs and practices. The Jews disliked the Samaritans so much, they wouldn't even travel through Samaria. For hundreds of years the Jews and Samaritans had been enemies!

Priests and Levites were religious teachers and leaders. The Old Testament law said that anyone who touched a dead body would be considered unclean, or displeasing, to God and would not be allowed to worship in the Temple (see Numbers 19:11). The priest and Levite might have been afraid that the man was already dead. They might have thought that obeying this law was more important than doing good. Or they may have been afraid of being attacked themselves!

Jesus told this story to make a point. If a Samaritan would choose to help someone he didn't even know, then it's clear Jesus wants all of us to help people in need.

Jesus' Question

■ Read Luke 10:36-37 to find out what the question was that Jesus asked and how the expert answered.

When He'd finished telling the story, Jesus asked the expert a question. The man had no choice but to recognize how the Samaritan in the story showed mercy to the hurt Jewish man.

Conclusion

The people listening to Jesus' story might have thought that God's love was intended for Jews alone. Jesus wanted them to realize that God's love was for everyone—even people they considered to be enemies!

By telling a story in which a Samaritan was the good example, Jesus showed His listeners that their stereotype of Samaritans was not true. Jesus taught them to obey the intent of God's law: Love and care for the needs of all people.

Because they don't know any better or they feel afraid, people sometimes think that certain kinds of people are bad or always do wrong things. When people believe stereotypes like these, they often end up treating others unfairly. But because we know that God loves everyone the same, we can ask God's help in obeying His command to love our neighbors as ourselves. (Read Luke 10:27 aloud.) We can realize that our neighbor includes everyone, particularly anyone who is in need. (Lead students in prayer, asking God to help them love all the other people around them.)

Get Going ■ 20-30 minutes

Action: Identify situations in which we may follow the intent of God's law and treat people fairly.

Distribute Get Real (p. 48) to students. Invite students to tell or write answers to the questions. End the discussion by completing Get Connected with students. (Optional: Students complete page at home.)

Get Real

■ How might Jesus' story about the Good Samaritan be told differently today?

■ What does being called a Good Samaritan mean?

■ When have you had the opportunity to be a Good Samaritan to your neighbor—someone who was different from you in some way?

■ In what situations might kids your age believe stereotypes about others? How do those kids act? What are the results of their actions?

■ What can you do or say when a friend says something unkind about a person who is different from both of you? How can we help others learn to treat people fairly?

GET TO KNOW

"Love your neighbor as yourself."
Luke 10:27

Get Connected

Who is a neighbor you can show love to this week? How can you do this? Ask God to help you to show love to your neighbor and to those who are different from you.

Tongue Control

The Message

My choice of words can help or hurt others.

The Bible Basis

James 3:2-12

Although the tongue is small, it has power to cause great damage.

The Scripture

"Everyone should be quick to listen, slow to speak and slow to become angry."
James 1:19

Get Started ■ 5-15 minutes

Action: Discover the power of words to help or hurt others.

No Words Allowed!

What You Need

Nothing; optional—index cards, marker.

What You Do

1. Select two volunteers. Whisper one of these tasks to first volunteer: sharpen a pencil, get a Bible, turn the lights off and on, jump three times, write name on white board, clap ten times, sing a song, etc. (Adjust tasks according to your classroom equipment.) (Optional: Write each task on a single index card. Volunteers choose cards.)

2. Without using spoken or written words and without actually doing the task him- or herself, first volunteer attempts to get the second volunteer to do the task. Repeat with other volunteers and tasks as time permits. Ask the questions below.

■ **Since you couldn't use words, how did you communicate your ideas?**

■ **How would being able to use words have make your job easier?**

■ **What are some things that are easy to communicate with words? What kinds of things are hard to communicate? Why?**

3. Conclude the activity by saying,

■ **Words are an important part of communicating.**

■ **How we choose to use words can make a powerful difference in whether we help other people or hurt them. Let's find out what the Bible says about the way we use our words.**

Bonus Idea

Divide groups into two teams. Volunteers on one team use pantomime to identify the actions on the cards. The other team draws pictures on large sheets of paper, as in Pictionary, to identify the actions. After several rounds, teams switch methods. Lead students in discussing the different methods.

Get It Together ■ 20-30 minutes

Action: Identify how the Bible says we should communicate with each other.

James 3:2-12

What You Need

Bibles.

What You Do

Lead students to read and discuss the Bible verses listed. Extend the discussion with the questions and comments provided.

Introduction

What do you think is the most important word in the English language? Why is this word so important? Today we're talking about why the words that we say are so important. The verses we're going to study are from the book of James.

James, the writer of this book, was probably the half brother of Jesus. He was also one of the first church leaders. He wrote this book as a letter to Jews who believed that Jesus was the Messiah sent by God. These people lived in many different places and were persecuted by people who did not love Jesus. They needed lots of help in knowing how to live the Christian life. James's letter helps us know how God wants us to live, too.

A Perfect Person

■ If you were going to describe a perfect person, what would you say he or she is like?

■ What does James say in James 3:2 about a perfect person?

James tells his readers that a perfect person is anyone who does not sin by what he or she says. Now that may seem very simple: Just say only good things and then you are perfect! But that's not what James meant. James meant that if you could control your tongue and never sin in what you say, then you would have enough control to keep yourself from sinning in other ways, too.

Two Comparisons

■ Read James 3:3. What does James compare the tongue to?

■ Read James 3:4 to find what else James says a tongue is like.

■ How is a person's tongue like a bit and a rudder?

■ If James were writing today, what small but powerful things might he compare with a tongue?

Because James wanted to help the readers of his letter understand how important it is to control the tongue, he talked about some things the people knew about.

A bit is a small piece of metal about the thickness of two pencils. The bit is put into a horse's mouth and attached to the horse's reins. The direction a strong horse travels is controlled by the way the rider moves the reins and that very small bit.

A ship slices through the water like a knife. The front part of the boat pushes the water away as it glides through. The rudder is at the back of the boat. When the rudder is held straight, the boat slices through in a straight line. But when the rudder is turned at an angle, the boat also turns in the rudder's direction. A very small rudder controls the direction of a boat much larger than its rudder.

The bit and rudder are very small, but what they do makes a BIG difference! The tongue is just a small part of our bodies, but the way in which it is used can make a big difference, too.

The Tongue's Power

■ Read James 3:5. What does James compare the tongue's power to?

■ How does a tiny spark start a forest fire? How might one unkind or hurtful word start a lot of trouble?

■ What are some examples in history of how one person's words have begun something good? Have begun a lot of trouble?

The tongue has so much power that how it's used affects the whole body. Just as a little spark can cause a huge, uncontrollable fire, so just a few words can cause a lot of trouble! Words can be used to persuade others to do good or bad things. The sermons and speeches of Martin Luther King, Jr., encouraged people to treat others fairly, without regard to race. Adolph Hitler's speeches stirred up hatred of Jewish people.

There have been times when people have done some extremely bad things because someone else convinced them it was the right thing to do. What people have said has led to anger, unfairness, prejudice and war.

Taming Your Tongue

■ Read James 3:7-8 to see what James says about taming the tongue's power.

■ In verse 9 what are two opposite things people use their tongues to do?

James tells us that all kinds of animals and birds can be tamed by people. But often we can't control our own tongues.

In fact, James says that sometimes we even use the same mouth to praise God and to say unwholesome things. James says that we shouldn't allow that to happen. James explains that fresh water and salt water don't come from the same source, and that a fig tree can't produce olives—only figs. Our tongues should only be used for good.

Conclusion

James was using his words to help others. After reading James's instructions, it might seem like it's better not to talk at all! James's point, though, is that with God's help our words can do a lot of good.

Communicating with others is something we all do a lot. And our words have the power to help or to hurt others. The Bible tells us to use our words wisely. (Read James 1:19 aloud.) Learning to communicate in good ways is an important skill for all of us. As we learn ways to tame our tongues, we will be more able to use helpful words. James wanted us to realize that we need a source for goodness. God's power and love is the source we need. (Pray with students, asking God to help them use their tongues to say kind and helpful words.)

Get Going ■ 20-30 minutes

Action: Identify and practice using words that help others.

Distribute Get Real (p. 52) to students. Invite students to tell or write answers to the questions. End the discussion by completing Get Connected with students. (Optional: Students complete page at home.)

Get Real

- How does it help to talk to others the way you would like to be spoken to?

- How does your tone of voice affect the meaning of your words?

- When is it hard for kids your age to control what they say?

- When have you seen the results of someone using their words in a harmful way? What happened? What could the person have said instead?

- What should we do when we make a mistake and say something that hurts another person?

- When at your school might someone need to speak in a way that shows goodness? At your house? In our class?

GET TO KNOW

"Everyone should be quick to listen, slow to speak and slow to become angry."
James 1:19

Get Connected

Think about a situation in which it might be hard to use helpful words. Now think of a sentence to use in this situation. Practice saying your sentence. Ask God for help in using encouraging words.

Be Angry, But Sin Not

The Message

I can choose to express anger in constructive ways.

The Bible Basis

Matthew 18:1-4,15-16; Mark 9:33-37; Luke 9:46-48

Jesus gave guidelines for resolving conflicts.

The Scripture

"A fool gives full vent to his anger, but a wise man keeps himself under control." Proverbs 29:11

Get Started ■ 5-15 minutes

Action: Discuss helpful and unhelpful ways of handling anger.

Build Up/Tear Down

What You Need

Grocery bags, a variety of construction materials (paper, newspapers, cardboard tubes, chenille wires, aluminum foil, glue, tape, masking tape, etc.).

What You Do

1. Put a variety of construction materials in each grocery bag. Prepare one bag for each group of three to four students.

2. Students form groups of three or four. Give each group one of the bags you prepared. Tell groups to quickly make a display using the materials in their bags in a constructive way—to build something.

3. After students have had time to build, lead students to guess what each group has constructed.

4. Students create new displays illustrating the word "destructive"—to tear something down. Encourage students to think creatively and not simply destroy their first display. Ask the questions below.

■ **What is different about the constructive and destructive displays you created?**

■ **When you're angry, do you think it's easier to do something constructive or destructive? Why?**

■ **What are some destructive things kids your age do when they are angry? Constructive things?**

■ **When you are in an angry situation, how do you control your anger?**

5. Conclude the activity by saying,

■ **God knows that we all get angry sometimes. But we can learn how to handle the anger and deal with conflict in constructive ways.**

■ **God can help us learn helpful ways of dealing with arguments.**

■ **Let's find out what Jesus told His friends to do when they had an argument.**

Bonus Idea

If you are short of time, half of the groups makes a display illustrating the word "constructive," while the other half makes a display illustrating the word "destructive." After time is called, students compare the displays and discuss the questions.

Get It Together ■ 20-30 minutes

Action: Discover God's guidelines for resolving conflicts.

Matthew 18:1-4,15-16; Mark 9:33-37; Luke 9:46-48

What You Need

Bibles.

What You Do

Lead students to read and discuss the Bible verses listed. Extend the discussion with the questions and comments provided.

Introduction

When have you or someone you know done something that led to an argument or conflict? Conflicts or arguments can be caused in many different ways. Let's find out what Jesus' friends argued about.

A Big Argument

■ Read Mark 9:33-34. Where were Jesus and His disciples and what were the disciples arguing about?

■ Have you ever had a big argument with a brother or sister, and when your parents asked you what the problem was, you suddenly realized how silly your argument was and didn't want to talk about it?

■ When might kids your age argue about who is the greatest or best?

Jesus and His disciples spent a lot of their time traveling from city to city, helping others learn about God. On this particular day, they were walking on the road to Capernaum, a city near the Sea of Galilee.

Jesus could hear muttering going on behind Him. And even though the disciples tried to be quiet, Jesus must have heard the angry words that shot back and forth.

They were arguing over who would be the greatest in the kingdom of God. They were certain they would all have the top places because, after all, they were Jesus' disciples. But who would be the GREATEST of all? Each disciple probably had a reason why he should be above the others and many reasons why the other disciples should not!

Jesus' Response

■ Read Mark 9:35 to find what Jesus said when He heard what they had been arguing about.

■ How would you explain Jesus' words to a friend? What was Jesus telling His disciples about being the greatest?

Since Jesus already knew what their argument was about, He told them how to REALLY be a great person.

Jesus' words must have surprised the disciples, because what Jesus said was the opposite of what most people thought. Jesus was saying that a great person acts like a servant!

A Child's Example

■ What did Jesus say and do to make sure His disciples understood what He meant? Read Matthew 18:2-4 to find out.

■ What does "humble" mean? How did Jesus say the disciples should act toward each other?

■ Why did Jesus say that small children are humble?

Jesus explained that in order for His followers to even make it into the kingdom of God, they must become humble before each other, just like a young child.

Small children know they need other people's help. Someone who is humble doesn't think that he or she knows the answer to everything and doesn't brag about him- or herself. Jesus knew that having a humble attitude would help people avoid a lot of arguments and conflicts.

Jesus' Command

■ Later in His teaching, what did Jesus say to do about problems with friends or neighbors? Read Matthew 18:15.

■ If our friends won't listen, then what should we do? Read Matthew 18:16. How will that help?

Jesus realized that people have problems getting along, so He taught His disciples another important lesson about how to handle conflicts.

Often, someone who was not part of the situation can help make peace between people who are upset. Jesus wanted His disciples to know how to help each other solve conflicts.

Conclusion

Because none of us is perfect, we WILL sometimes have conflicts with others. Having a humble attitude in the way we treat others and talking directly to the people we're having a problem with are two ways we can handle our conflicts.

Just like in Bible times, people today need to know how to handle conflicts and arguments. Some of the things we are likely to do when we're having a conflict aren't very helpful. Our actions sometimes just make the problem worse! (Read Proverbs 29:11 aloud.) But remembering Jesus' words can help us learn what to do to resolve the conflict in helpful ways. Even in the middle of an argument, we can ask God's help in knowing what to do. (Pray with students, asking God's help in handling conflicts and communicating with others.)

Get Going ■ 20-30 minutes

Action: Identify helpful ways to handle conflicts.

Distribute Get Real (p. 56) to students. Invite students to tell or write answers to the questions. End the discussion by completing Get Connected with students. (Optional: Students complete page at home.)

Get Real

- When are some times kids your age might have conflicts, or arguments, with friends?

- What can you do if you have a problem, or conflict, with a friend? What might you say to begin your conversation? To end your conversation?

- What might happen if you don't talk to your friend but tell someone else about the problem?

- What are some guidelines to remember when talking to a friend about a problem?

- Why does it help to talk to God about our angry feelings?

GET TO KNOW

"A fool gives full vent to his anger, but a wise man keeps himself under control."
Proverbs 29:11

Get Connected

Think about a time you need God's help to resolve a conflict or an argument. Pray about this situation, and ask God's help acting in helpful ways to resolve problems.

The Gift of Forgiveness

Get Started ■ 5-15 minutes

Action: Discover times kids feel like getting even instead of forgiving others.

Balloon Catch

What You Need

Bibles, balloons of various shapes and sizes, permanent markers, children's music CD and player.

What You Do

1. Give each student a balloon to blow up and tie. Assign each student a section (a phrase or a sentence) of Colossians 3:13 to write on his or her balloon.

2. As you play music, students bat all the balloons around the room, trying to keep balloons from touching the ground. When you stop the music, each student catches a balloon. Students arrange themselves in verse order and read the words aloud.

3. Repeat activity as time permits. After several rounds, ask the questions below.

■ **When are some times someone your age might want to get even with someone?**

■ **How might someone your age try to get even, or get revenge?**

■ **What usually happens when someone tries to get even, or get revenge?**

4. Conclude the activity by saying,

■ **The words of this Bible verse tell us that there is something else we can do when we feel like getting even.**

■ **In our study today, see if you can find out what Jesus had to say about getting even.**

Bonus Idea

One student stands in the middle of the room. Give rolls of toilet paper to other students. Student in the middle holds the end of each roll of paper while other students walk around the room unrolling toilet paper and tangling paper together. After 5 to 10 seconds, signal students to stop. **When might a kid your age want to get revenge instead of forgiving someone? When we choose not to forgive each other, it's kind of like getting into a tangled mess.** Students work together to carefully untangle the toilet paper.

The **Message**

I can choose to show compassion by forgiving others, as God has forgiven me.

The **Bible Basis**

Matthew 18:21-35

Jesus told about the unforgiving servant to teach us to forgive grievances.

The **Scripture**

"Bear with each other and forgive whatever grievances you may have against one another. Forgive as the Lord forgave you." Colossians 3:13

Get It Together ■ 20-30 minutes

Action: Realize that communicating forgiveness through words and actions is a way to show God's love to others.

Matthew 18:21-35

What You Need

Bibles.

What You Do

Lead students to read and discuss the Bible verses listed. Extend the discussion with the questions and comments provided.

Introduction

What are some things kids your age argue about? When we argue with others, we may end up feeling like all we want to do is get even! When we feel that way, it's easy to say things that make the situation worse and cause more problems. Today we'll talk about what God wants us to say and do to make the situation better.

Peter's Question

■ Read what Peter asked Jesus one day in Matthew 18:21.

■ Read Matthew 18:22. How did Jesus answer Peter?

■ Why did Jesus use this big number? Did Jesus really want Peter to keep track of that many times Peter forgave someone?

Peter had just heard Jesus tell the disciples how to resolve their conflicts with their friends and neighbors. Now Peter wondered, *When my friend does something against me, I go to my friend and work it out, and then I forgive him. But if my friend keeps on offending me, how many times do I have to forgive him?*

Some religious teachers of Peter's time had decided that a person should forgive his friend three times. But after that, never again! Peter probably suspected Jesus wouldn't agree with this low number. So that may be why he asked Jesus this question. And when Peter said "seven times," he probably thought that was a generous number of times.

Jesus used this big number as a way of emphasizing the fact that we should ALWAYS forgive others, no matter how many times they have done something wrong.

Jesus' Story

■ To help Peter understand the real meaning of forgiveness, Jesus told a parable in Matthew 18:23-35. A servant owed a rich king some money. How much did the servant owe? Read verse 24.

■ Read verse 25 to find what the king said. If you were the servant, what would you have said to the king?

■ But then the king forgave the servant. If you were the servant, how would you have felt then? What would you have said?

A parable is a story that teaches a truth. Jesus' story was about a king and his servants.

The servant owed lots and lots of money! His debt would be like MANY millions of dollars today!

In Bible times, if a person could not pay a debt, he and his family would have to be sold as slaves.

Jesus said that the king took pity on his servant. "You don't have to pay me back—ever!" the king said. The king cancelled the debt of the servant.

Even though the second servant could have worked hard and paid back the money he owed, the first servant didn't give the man more time to pay his debt! He didn't tell the man, "That's OK. The king just said I didn't have to pay back my debt of MILLIONS of dollars, so I won't make you pay back the money you

■ Compare the king's actions with how the forgiven servant acted. Read Matthew 18:28-30. Since the first servant had been forgiven so much, what do you think he might have done when he saw someone who owed him much less money?

■ How would you describe the first servant's actions?

God's Forgiveness

■ Read Matthew 18:31 to find what the people who watched the first servant's actions did.

■ The king was upset at the first servant's actions. Read what he asked the servant in Matthew 18:33.

■ Read Matthew 18:35 to find out what Jesus wanted us to know about this story.

owe me." Instead, the first servant had the second servant thrown into jail. "You'll have to stay there until you pay me back," the first servant said.

Some people who watched what happened were upset by the first servant's actions. "How can he be so mean?" they probably asked each other.

When the king heard what had happened, he was very angry with the first servant. He had the servant brought to him immediately. Because of the servant's unforgiving actions, the angry king turned to his helpers and said, "Throw him in jail."

That was the end of Jesus' story. But it wasn't the end of what Jesus wanted Peter—and us—to know. The king's forgiveness should have resulted in the first servant forgiving the second servant. The king in this parable is like God who, when we ask Him, forgives us all our wrong actions so generously.

Conclusion

Forgiveness is so important to God that He sent Jesus to take the punishment for our sins. Because God loves and forgives us, He wants us to pass on His love and forgiveness to others—no matter how many times we feel angry because of what someone has done or said to us. (Read Colossians 3:13 aloud.)

There will be times when we will need to choose between getting even or forgiving. When God forgives us, He forgets our wrong actions (see Psalm 103:11-12). Even though we may not forget the wrong actions of a person, we can still forgive and show God's love by treating the person kindly. We can speak to the person in a way that helps—instead of hurts. And we might need to ask an adult for help in knowing what to do when someone keeps doing wrong things that hurt us. (Pray with students, thanking God for His forgiveness and asking for His help in showing forgiveness to others.)

Get Going ■ 20-30 minutes

Action: Plan ways to show God's love and forgiveness.

Distribute Get Real (p. 60) to students. Invite students to tell or write answers to the questions. End the discussion by completing Get Connected with students. (Optional: Students complete page at home.)

Get Real

- What words might a kid your age say to forgive others? What actions might the kid do?

- When has someone forgiven you? How did you know you were forgiven?

- When is a time you need to show forgiveness to others? What can you do to remember to show God's love and forgiveness in these times?

- What's the best part about being forgiven by someone? Forgiving someone else?

- What might happen if two people never forgive each other?

GET TO KNOW

"Bear with each other and forgive whatever grievances you may have against one another. Forgive as the Lord forgave you."
Colossians 3:13

Get Connected

What can you do to remind yourself to show God's forgiveness this week? Thank God for His love and forgiveness, and ask His help in passing His forgiveness on to others.

Living Water

Get Started ■ 5-15 minutes

Action: Discover characteristics and benefits of water.

Can't Live Without It!

What You Need

Several empty milk jugs (or other containers), food coloring, Post-it Notes, marker, measuring cups, funnel, water, pens.

What You Do

1. Add food coloring to each of the empty milk jugs.

2. Brainstorm with students a list of ways people use water. Print each way on a separate Post-it Note and then attach each Post-it Note to a different milk jug.

3. Each student uses a measuring cup and a funnel to add water to jugs to show how important each of the ways is to him or her: one cup of water to jug with way that is most important, ½ cup of water to jugs with ways that are needed in general, ¼ cup of water to jugs with ways that he or she could do without, and no water to jugs with ways that he or she does not use. Ask the questions below.

■ **How many different ways does your family use water?**

■ **What would you do differently each day if you only had a little bit of water to use?**

■ **What would you change if you could use all the water you wanted to?**

4. Conclude the activity by saying,

■ **In our study today, we will find out what happened when Jesus compared Himself to water.**

Bonus Idea

Find more water experiments by searching online for children's science activities.

The **Message**

Jesus gives living water.

The **Bible Basis**

John 4:4-42

Jesus told the woman at the well in Samaria that He could give her the living water of eternal life.

The **Scripture**

"Jesus said, 'Whoever drinks the water I give him will never thirst. Indeed, the water I give him will become in him a spring of water welling up to eternal life.'" John 4:14

Get It Together ■ 20-30 minutes

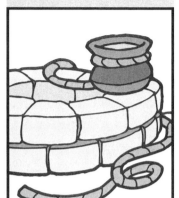

Action: Realize that because Jesus is the Messiah, He is the only One who can give us the living water of eternal life.

John 4:4-42

What You Need

Bibles.

What You Do

Lead students to read and discuss the Bible verses listed. Extend the discussion with the questions and comments provided.

Introduction

What are some things that last a really long time? (Mountains. Certain kinds of trees.) Let's talk about something that lasts forever!

A Surprising Question

■ Read John 4:7-9 to find out what Jesus asked a Samaritan woman and what the woman asked Jesus.

■ Why was she surprised?

Jesus and His disciples walked a lot! A short time after Jesus had begun teaching people how to know and obey God, He and His disciples were traveling through an area called Samaria.

A Samaritan woman came to the well to get some water. When this woman saw a Jewish man sitting by the well, she was probably surprised; but since men and women usually didn't speak to each other, she probably ignored Him. Then Jesus REALLY surprised the woman! He asked her for a drink of water.

A Surprising Answer

■ Read John 4:10 to find out what Jesus said He could give the woman.

■ Read what Jesus said about this water in John 4:13-14. What do you think Jesus meant? What made the water He was offering unique?

■ Read John 4:15. What was the woman's response to Jesus?

Jesus not only talked to this woman, asking for water, but He also answered her question by offering her something special in return. Jesus' answer confused her. She could see He didn't have anything to put water in. The woman didn't understand that Jesus was talking about a different kind of water.

Jesus said that the living water He could give was eternal life—life as a member of God's family now and forever! Jesus' gift of living water could satisfy a person's spiritual thirst—their desire to know and love God and experience His love for them.

Even though the woman didn't understand exactly what Jesus meant, she knew that this living water sounded amazing—almost too good to be true. She wanted her thirst for water to be quenched forever!

Jesus realized the woman didn't understand what He was talking about. She was still thinking about her physical thirst for water. But Jesus knew the woman desperately needed the kind of living water He was talking about. Because Jesus is God's Son, He also knew that the woman's sins were keeping her from accepting His gift of living water. The woman had been married five times. And she was now living with a man who wasn't her husband. When Jesus told her that He knew about her past marriages, the woman was surprised again!

Another Question

■ Read John 4:19-20 to find what the woman said about Jesus and the way in which Jews worshiped God.

■ Read what Jesus said about worshiping God in John 4:23.

The woman must have wanted to avoid talking about her sins. So she brought up an old argument between Samaritans and Jews about where people were supposed to worship God. The Samaritans claimed to believe in the same God as the Jewish people, but they didn't worship God in the Temple. They said that a mountain in their country was the place to worship God.

Jesus told her that a new time was coming when it wouldn't matter WHERE a person worshiped God.

Now the woman was really confused! "Look, I don't know much about all this," she said. "When the Messiah gets here, He'll explain everything." The Samaritans and Jews were both waiting for God to send the Messiah, the One God had promised to send.

The Savior of the World

■ Read John 4:26 to find out what Jesus said about Himself.

■ Read John 4:28-29 to find how the Bible describes what the woman did.

■ In John 4:42, what happened as a result of Jesus' teachings?

Jesus wanted the woman to know that He was the Messiah she had been waiting for! He was the Messiah sent by God who would be not only a great teacher or prophet but also the Savior of the world—the only One who could offer the living water of eternal life.

The woman's amazement at Jesus' words was too great to keep to herself.

When the Samaritans heard her words, many of them rushed to see Jesus. They eagerly invited Him to teach them.

Conclusion

Jesus' gift of living water can be ours, too. Jesus explains why we never have to thirst again in John 4:14. (Read verse aloud with students.) Jesus offered the woman the gift of living water—life as a member of God's family both now and forever, even after her physical body had died. Only the Messiah could give this gift that was more precious than any water from a well.

If you're hearing for the first time about living water, you can accept God's love for you and become a member of His family. If you've already become a Christian, it's good to realize again what good things God gives you. (Pray with students, thanking God for His good gifts. Continue your discussion about becoming a Christian with interested students. Follow the guidelines in the "Leading a Student to Christ" article on pp. 10-11.)

Get Going ■ 20-30 minutes

Action: Identify the benefits of receiving Jesus' living water, and accept Jesus as God's Son.

Distribute Get Real (p. 64) to students. Invite students to tell or write answers to the questions. End the discussion by completing Get Connected with students. (Optional: Students complete page at home.)

GET REAL

■ How would you say the words of John 4:14 in your own words?

■ How would you define "living water"?

■ Why is the living water Jesus gives better than the kind of water we drink?

■ How would you describe to a kid younger than you what it's like to be a member of God's family? Why do you think it is good for people to become members of God's family?

■ If someone asked you how to become a member of God's family, what would you tell him or her?

get to know

"Jesus said, 'Whoever drinks the water I give him will never thirst. Indeed, the water I give him will become in him a spring of water welling up to eternal life.'"
John 4:14

GET CONNECTED

What are some of the things you receive when you accept Jesus' gift of living water? Ask God to help you understand what it means to have living water. Thank Him for His love that never ends.

Bread of Life

The Message

Jesus is the bread of life.

The Bible Basis

John 6:1-15,25-51

After Jesus fed a large crowd from just a small lunch, He described Himself as the bread of life—the source for what we need to live as Christians.

The Scripture

"Jesus declared, 'I am the bread of life. He who comes to me will never go hungry, and he who believes in me will never be thirsty.'" John 6:35

Get Started ■ 5-15 minutes

Action: Discover why bread is called the "staff of life."

Bread Toss

What You Need

Empty bread bag, newspaper.

What You Do

1. Stuff bread bag with newspaper. Knot securely to close bag.

2. Stand with students in a circle. Toss stuffed bread bag across the circle. Student who catches bag then quickly tosses it to someone he or she is not standing directly next to, as in a Hot Potato game. Signal "Stop" after most students have tossed the bag.

3. Students quickly call out names of items they have in their rooms at home. Then begin tossing game again. Each time a student catches the bread bag, he or she names something in his or her room before tossing the bag to another student.

4. Ask the questions below.

■ **What are some things you have that you could really live without?**

■ **What do you think people really need to live?**

5. Repeat activity, naming things people really need in order to live. Conclude the activity by saying,

■ **Sometimes bread is called the "staff of life." Why do you think people describe bread in this way?**

■ **Jesus called Himself "the bread of life" in order to teach some important things** (John 6:35,48). **In today's study, see if you can find out what Jesus wanted His followers to learn about Himself.**

Bonus Idea

Bring in ingredients and utensils to make a quick bread (bread made without yeast) recipe of your choice with students. Suggested breads include cornbread, tortillas, fry bread, pancakes, zucchini bread and muffins.

Get It Together ■ 20-30 minutes

Action: Understand that only Jesus can give us what we need to live every day as a Christian.

John 6:1-15,25-51

What You Need

Bibles.

What You Do

Lead students to read and discuss the Bible verses listed. Extend the discussion with the questions and comments provided.

Introduction

Jesus' teaching about bread came as part of a miracle—something only God could do. This miracle was considered so important that all four writers of the Gospels wrote about it.

Feeding the Five Thousand

■ Let's read John 6:1-13 to find out about this miracle.

■ What are some things we learn about Jesus from this story?

Jesus showed that He cared about the needs of the crowd. They were hungry! And Jesus wanted to feed them. Jesus also demonstrated His great power. To feed over 5,000 people from two small fish and five small loaves of bread was an awesome miracle!

A Miraculous Sign

■ Read John 6:14-15 to find what the people in the crowd thought about Jesus and what they wanted to do.

■ If you had been in the crowd that was fed from one small lunch, how do you think you might have felt about Jesus?

■ Read John 6:26 to find why Jesus said they were looking for Him.

After this miracle, the people went looking for Jesus. Jesus would have been happy if the people had been looking for Him to listen to more of His teaching or because they wanted to become His followers. But Jesus knew what these people REALLY wanted.

Jesus knew they were only looking for Him because He gave them food. But He told them not to make getting food for their bodies the most important thing in their lives. Jesus told them to look for the food that will give them eternal life.

The people might have thought He must be talking about those good things they're supposed to do to get into heaven. But when they asked, Jesus told them that ALL they needed to do to get into heaven was to believe in Him.

Now the people wondered if Jesus was trying to tell them He's the Messiah. The people in Bible times had many ideas about who the Messiah, God's Son, would be and what He would do. Some of the things they believed were right. Others were just rumors and superstitions.

Bread from Heaven

■ Read John 6:30-31. What did the people ask Jesus to do to prove He was the Messiah?

■ Read John 6:32-33 to find who Jesus said had really sent the manna.

Because the people were still thinking only about their physical lives, they wanted Jesus to give them manna just like in the time of Moses. Manna was the food God gave the Israelites after they escaped from Egypt and were on their way to the Promised Land. Maybe the people were thinking how great it would be to have more free food!

Jesus then explained that just as God had sent manna to the Israelites many years ago, now God had a different kind of bread for them—bread that would

give them life forever. Now the people were thinking how great it would be if they never died!

"Give us some of that bread!" the people said eagerly.

Never Hungry or Thirsty

■ Read John 6:35,51 to find out what Jesus said about that bread.

■ What does it mean to believe in Jesus?

■ Read John 6:41-42 to find out what the people thought about Jesus' claim to be the bread of life.

To believe in Jesus means to love Him as God's Son and to depend on Him to give us eternal life and to supply us with everything we need. Jesus went on to explain that He was the bread of life. His Father in heaven had sent Him so that everyone who believed in Him could have eternal life.

Jesus knew what the people were saying and that they still didn't understand what He meant. He said one more time, "I am the bread of life. God sent your ancestors manna to feed their physical needs. God sent Me to supply your spiritual needs. If you will believe in Me and listen to Me, you will be part of God's family—now and forever! I will even give up My life so that your sins will be forgiven!"

Conclusion

Jesus wanted His listeners—and us—to know that He is the only One who can give people what they need to live as members of God's family—now and forever! John 6:35 tells us why Jesus is all we need. (Read verse aloud with students.) Just as we all need to eat food every day in order to have healthy bodies, we need to depend on Jesus every day in order to live as healthy and growing Christians. We can depend on Jesus for many things: to forgive our sins, to remind us of what is right, to protect us and to help us know what to do. All we need to do is to ask for His help and believe that He will do what He has promised. (Pray with students, thanking God for Jesus.)

Get Going ■ 20-30 minutes

Action: Identify ways in which Jesus gives us what we need to live as Christians.

Distribute Get Real (p. 68) to students. Invite students to tell or write answers to the questions. End the discussion by completing Get Connected with students. (Optional: Students complete page at home.)

GET REAL

- What are some of the things we can depend on Jesus to do for us to help us live as Christians?

- In what ways do kids your age need help to live as Christians by loving and obeying Jesus? How can Jesus help them?

- When have you seen someone depend on Jesus? What did the person do? How did Jesus help this person?

- What are some things that might be hard for a Christian to do? What could you do if you were having a hard time obeying Jesus?

get to know

"Jesus declared, 'I am the bread of life. He who comes to me will never go hungry, and he who believes in me will never be thirsty.'"
John 6:35

GET CONNECTED

One of the best things to do to remember to depend on Jesus is to talk to Him! Tell Jesus about a way you need His help to love and obey Him. What will you do to remember to talk to Jesus and depend on Him this week?

The Good Shepherd

Get Started ▪ 5-15 minutes

Action: Discover the importance of distinguishing between good and bad guides.

Who's True?

What You Need

Snack, two paper bags, blindfold.

What You Do

1. Place snack in one of the bags. Blindfold a volunteer. Place each bag in a different location in the room. Silently select one student to be the Good Guide and another student to be the Bad Guide.

2. Good Guide calls out directions to lead the blindfolded student to the bag with the snack in it. At the same time, Bad Guide calls out directions to the empty bag. Blindfolded student must choose a guide to follow in order to find a bag. Still blindfolded, student opens bag to find out if he or she followed the best guide. Ask one or more of the questions below.

▪ **Who did you think was a good guide? Why did you choose that person?**

▪ **What were some things that helped you choose which guide to follow?**

▪ **When have you listened to and followed someone who ended up being a bad guide? A good guide? What happened?**

3. Repeat activity with other students, changing the location of the bags each time. After several students have had a turn, students eat the snack.

4. Conclude the activity by saying,

▪ **It's hard to know whom to listen to when you don't know if the person is giving you good directions or not.**

▪ **In our study, listen to find out to what Jesus compared good and bad guides.**

Bonus Idea

Students arrange and tape down lengths of yarn on the floor to create a path. Place snack at end of path. Good Guide and Bad Guide give directions to blindfolded volunteer to lead him or her through the path.

The Message

Jesus is the Good Shepherd.

The Bible Basis

John 10:1-30

Jesus described Himself as the Good Shepherd who lovingly leads and protects His sheep.

The Scripture

"I am the good shepherd. The good shepherd lays down his life for the sheep." John 10:11

Get It Together ■ 20-30 minutes

Action: Realize that because Jesus is God's Son, He offers us love and protection in all the circumstances of our lives.

John 10:1-30

What You Need

Bibles.

What You Do

Lead students to read and discuss the Bible verses listed. Extend the discussion with the questions and comments provided.

Introduction

What do you know about shepherds? Sheep and shepherds were very common in Bible times. Raising sheep was essential to the survival of many Bible-times families. The wool of the sheep was used to make wicks for lamps and to make clothing and rugs. The milk of the sheep was used in daily cooking. Occasionally, a sheep or lamb was killed to make food for a special dinner.

Families with larger flocks of sheep usually had their own shepherds—often the sons of the families. But those families who only had a few sheep joined with other families to hire a shepherd from their village. The village shepherd would collect the sheep together in the morning and take them out to pasture. Then in the evening, he would return the sheep to the village.

A Shepherd's Actions

■ How would you describe a good shepherd? Read John 10:1-2 to find the first thing Jesus said about what a good shepherd does.

■ Read John 10:7-9 to find out which part of the sheep pen Jesus said He is like.

■ Who do you think the thieves and robbers were?

When Jesus announced that He was the Good Shepherd, the people had a pretty good idea of what Jesus was talking about. But Jesus didn't take any chances they might miss the point. He described HOW He was the Good Shepherd.

When Jesus said He is the gate, He means that He is the only way in which we can come into God's family and know God.

Jesus used the words "thieves" and "robbers" to describe people who claimed to be sent by God but were not.

When shepherds had been traveling a long distance to find water and food for their sheep and couldn't get home before nightfall, they would either find a cave to use as a sheep pen, or they would build a sheep pen from rocks. The shepherd would then sleep in the opening of the pen so that no sheep could leave and any predators would have to step over him to get to the sheep.

Sometimes we think of sheep as being soft and cuddly, or we think that taking care of them is easy work. But in reality, while a shepherd was very loving, he had to be very strong and sometimes very fierce. The sheep were so important that to lose one sheep might mean his family would not have enough milk or wool to survive. So if a wolf, lion or even a robber came and attacked the sheep, the shepherd sprang into action to protect his sheep. If necessary, the shepherd was even willing to die to keep his sheep safe.

Lesson Three
Depending on Jesus

Jesus' Actions

■ In John 10:11, what did Jesus say He will do because He is the Good Shepherd? When did Jesus do this?

■ Read John 10:14. What else did Jesus say about Himself?

■ How does Jesus lead us in the best ways?

■ Read John 10:19-21 to learn what the people said about Jesus.

■ What did the people ask Jesus in John 10:24?

Because of His incredible love for us, Jesus was willing to die in order to save us from the punishment our sins deserved.

Realizing that His listeners were still not really understanding what He was talking about, Jesus offered more proof that He is the Good Shepherd sent by God. Jesus said that those who knew Him would follow Him, just like sheep follow their shepherd. Sheep know the voice of their shepherd.

When several shepherds brought their sheep to the same watering hole, all a shepherd had to do was call to his own sheep and they would come running to him and only to him. In unfamiliar territory, shepherds always went first, so the sheep would follow them. A shepherd could then pick the best and safest path for the sheep.

After hearing Jesus' claims to be the Good Shepherd sent by God, the people listening to Him weren't sure what to believe. They even argued about Him! Soon after this, some people questioned Jesus about who He really is.

Jesus told them that His words and miracles were proof that He was the Good Shepherd sent by God. The people who believed and followed Him would be given eternal life as members of God's family. Just like people today, some people believed Jesus' words and some did not.

Conclusion

Jesus wanted His listeners in Bible times and His followers today to realize that if we follow Him—the One sent by God to be the Messiah and Savior—He will care for us even better than a good shepherd cares for his sheep.

Just as a shepherd knows and understands his sheep, Jesus knows and understands what we are like. He knows what we are good at doing, what things are hard for us to do and what things we wish we could do or have. Jesus values us more than a shepherd values his sheep. John 10:11 tells us that He is even willing to die for His sheep! (Read verse aloud.) Because He loves us and knows us, Jesus knows how to care for us and help us in the best way possible! Jesus doesn't promise to make our lives perfect or easy. But in any circumstance, good or bad, we can depend on Him to lead us, care for us and help us—even better than the best shepherd! (Lead children in prayer, thanking Jesus for His love and care. Then talk with interested students about becoming members of God's family, referring to "Leading a Student to Christ" on pp. 10-11.)

Get Going ■ 20-30 minutes

Action: List ways in which Jesus is like a shepherd to us.

Distribute Get Real (p. 72) to students. Invite students to tell or write answers to the questions. End the discussion by completing Get Connected with students. (Optional: Students complete page at home.)

© 2007 Gospel Light. Permission to photocopy granted to original purchaser only. *The Big Book of Discipleship Basics*

71

GET REAL

■ What are some ways that shepherds take care of their sheep? What are some of the things Jesus does for us that are like a shepherd's care for his sheep?

■ Tell about a time when it might help a kid your age to remember that Jesus is his or her shepherd. How do you think Jesus might care for a person in that situation?

■ How has Jesus cared for you or someone you know?

■ Why do you think it's important to know that Jesus cares for us like a shepherd cares for his sheep?

get to know

"I am the good shepherd. The good shepherd lays down his life for the sheep." John 10:11

GET CONNECTED

Think about times you need the Good Shepherd to help, protect or provide for you. Thank Jesus for caring for you as a shepherd cares for his sheep.

The Way

Get Started ■ 5-15 minutes

Action: Discover that the word "grace" means undeserved love.

Is That Fair?

What You Need

Nothing.

What You Do

1. Students stand in the center of the room. Designate one side of the room "fair" and the other side "foul." Read one of the situations listed. Students move to the fair side of the room if they think the person got what was deserved or to the foul side of the room if they don't think the person got what was deserved. Situation 1: Your younger brother gets the same allowance as you, but your parents say it's because he does extra chores. Situation 2: A kid was put in the starting lineup even though she didn't come to practice one day last week (her mom's car broke down on the way to practice). Situation 3: You got an A on a test even though you didn't study. Situation 4: You are invited to a birthday party at a water park, but you have to pay your own way. A kid from school who lives in a homeless shelter gets to go for free.

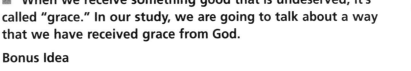

2. Invite volunteers to tell other situations. Students show their responses to each situation mentioned.

3. Ask these questions:

■ **When has someone you know gotten something good he or she didn't deserve? What makes you think the person didn't deserve it?**

■ **What do kids usually say when someone gets something good that's undeserved?**

■ **When have you been treated better than you really deserved?**

4. Conclude the activity by saying,

■ **We think it's fair when someone gets what we think they deserved. But sometimes people get good things that we think they don't deserve.**

■ **When we receive something good that is undeserved, it's called "grace." In our study, we are going to talk about a way that we have received grace from God.**

Bonus Idea

Students find the word "grace" in a concordance and locate verses in Romans that describe God's grace.

The Message

Jesus is the way, the truth and the life.

The Bible Basis

John 12:12-15; 14:1-14

After Jesus was welcomed to Jerusalem as the One sent by God, He taught His disciples how they could know God.

The Scripture

"Jesus answered, 'I am the way and the truth and the life. No one comes to the Father except through me.'"
John 14:6

Get It Together ■ 20-30 minutes

Action: Understand that the only way to know God is by having faith in Jesus to provide God's gift of salvation.

John 12:12-15; 14:1-14

What You Need

Bibles.

What You Do

Lead students to read and discuss the Bible verses listed. Extend the discussion with the questions and comments provided.

Introduction

If you had lived in Bible times and met Jesus for the first time, what would you have wanted to know about Him?

It may seem to us that when Jesus, God's Son, lived on Earth, people should have easily recognized who He is and understood what He was teaching about how to know God. But it wasn't that easy. The people wondered about who Jesus is, and they had lots of questions about what He was teaching. Let's look at what these people thought and some of the questions they asked.

The Triumphal Entry

■ Read John 12:12-15. What did crowds of people do and say on the famous day when Jesus arrived in Jerusalem?

■ Why do you think the people were so excited and glad to see Jesus?

At the beginning of Jesus' last week on Earth, something happened that made it seem as though most everyone recognized who Jesus is.

After the events of this exciting day, the disciples, Jesus' friends and followers, probably expected great things to happen! Maybe they were hoping that Jesus would lead the crowds in a revolt against the Roman rulers. Because they hated the Romans so much, they hoped that Jesus would be their new ruler. But Jesus knew that God had a different plan in mind, and Jesus wanted the disciples to know all about it.

A Special Message

■ What did Jesus say in John 14:2 that might have worried the disciples?

The disciples gathered together with Jesus to celebrate the Passover feast. This celebration was one of the Jews' most important feasts because it reminded the Jews how God had freed their people from slavery in Egypt. During this Passover celebration, Jesus talked to His disciples about who He is and what was going to happen to Him. Jesus knew that soon He would be arrested and killed. And even though His death and resurrection were part of God's great plan to bring forgiveness for sins, the disciples were worried about what would happen to Jesus.

Jesus was trying to prepare His disciples for some big changes. The events that would soon take place would completely overwhelm the disciples if they weren't ready.

A Special Promise

■ Read John 14:5 to find out what Thomas asked.

■ How did Jesus answer Thomas in verse 6?

■ Read what another disciple, Philip, said to Jesus in John 14:8.

■ How did Jesus respond to Philip in verse 9?

The disciples were upset by this news that Jesus would be leaving them. One of the disciples, Thomas—never one to keep his doubts to himself—asked a question.

Certainly the disciples were familiar with the fact that Jesus had been teaching them the right way to live. But Jesus was saying more than that. Jesus was explaining that believing in Him was the only way for people to come to know God. In fact, Jesus went on to say, "If you really knew who I am, you'd know that I have shown you what God is like."

Jesus wanted Philip and the other disciples—and all His followers from then until now—to know that He and God are one. Because Jesus is God's Son, He is the only person who can show us what God is like and make it possible for us to know God. When we believe, or have faith, in Jesus, we can become members of God's family.

Conclusion

John 14:6 tells us that Jesus is the way and the truth and the life. (Read verse aloud.) Jesus called Himself "the way" because He makes it possible for us to become part of God's family. Jesus called Himself "the truth" because His teachings about God are true and dependable. Jesus called Himself "the life" because He gives us life forever as members of God's family.

You might have questions, just as the people in Bible times did, about who Jesus is. As you read and think about God's Word, however, God promises to help you understand more about Jesus. One important thing we can all know and understand about Jesus is that His life and death did all that was necessary for us to receive a place in God's family. Today we can praise God and thank Him, not only for sending Jesus to Earth, but also for His gift of grace that makes our salvation possible. (Talk with interested students about becoming members of God's family, referring to "Leading a Student to Christ" on pp. 10-11. Pray with students, thanking God for His grace.)

Get Going ■ 20-30 minutes

Action: Recognize ways God has shown grace—undeserved love and forgiveness—and thank God for His grace.

Distribute Get Real (p. 76) to students. Invite students to tell or write answers to the questions. End the discussion by completing Get Connected with students. (Optional: Students complete page at home.)

GET REAL

■ When you hear the word "grace," what do you think about? When has someone shown grace to you? When have you shown grace to someone else?

■ How did Jesus' death on the cross show God's grace to us?

■ Why do people need God's grace and forgiveness?

■ What actions of Jesus do you want to thank Him for?

■ What birthday or Christmas gift have you been glad to receive? How did the giver know you liked the gift? In what ways can you thank God for His grace?

get to know

"Jesus answered, 'I am the way and the truth and the life. No one comes to the Father except through me.'"
John 14:6

GET CONNECTED

Why did God make it possible for us to be members of His family? How is your life different because you know of God's grace? What might you say to express your thanks to God? Thank Him for His gifts of grace and salvation.

The Vine

Get Started ■ 5-15 minutes

Action: Tell about things that plants and people depend on to live.

Water Race

What You Need

Large paper cups, food coloring, water, paper in a variety of weights and finishes (paper towels, napkins, stationery, tissue, etc.), scissors.

What You Do

1. Students form pairs. In one or two cups, mix water with food coloring. Partners work together to complete a water race. Students cut strips from several kinds of paper. Each team places its strips in an empty cup and folds the edges of the strips over top of cup.

2. Invite students to predict on which kind of paper the water will travel the quickest. Then, while one partner holds strips in place, the other partner pours a small amount of colored water into the cup, being careful not to pour the water on the strips. Students watch to see the water crawl up the strips to the top of the cup.

■ **On which kind of paper did the water travel the quickest? Why?** (Paper that has larger pores attracts water faster.) **This process is called "capillary attraction." It is the same action that allows water and nutrients to move from the roots of a plant through tiny tubes, called capillaries, to its leaves. Plants depend on this process to survive.**

■ **What are some things that people depend on to live? Why do you think these things are necessary?**

■ **What are some things that you think are very dependable? Only slightly dependable?**

3. Conclude the activity by saying,

■ **When a plant receives all the nutrients it needs, it can produce good fruit. Jesus used an illustration of a plant and its branches to teach His listeners.**

■ **See if you can find out what Jesus wanted them to learn.**

Bonus Idea

Invite students to read more information about capillary attraction and other plant processes from online sources. Search for and download information from appropriate websites ahead of time.

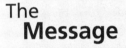

The Message

Jesus is the living vine.

The Bible Basis

John 15:1-17; 18:1—20:31

Jesus compared Himself to a vine and His followers to branches, showing how we need to depend on Him completely.

The Scripture

"I am the vine; you are the branches. If a man remains in me and I in him, he will bear much fruit; apart from me you can do nothing."
John 15:5

Get It Together ■ 20-30 minutes

Action: Realize that because Jesus is alive, we can depend on Him as we learn to know God and help others know God.

John 15:1-7; 18:1—20:31

What You Need

Bibles.

What You Do

Lead students to read and discuss the Bible verses listed. Extend the discussion with the questions and comments provided.

Introduction

When have you been to an important, or special, dinner? Who was there? Why was it important? One night, near the end of His life on Earth, Jesus and His disciples had a special dinner together.

After the dinner, Jesus was teaching the disciples some important things He wanted them to know. Jesus used the word picture of a vine and its branches and fruit to help His disciples—and us—understand some very important things.

Produce Good Fruit

■ In John 15:1, what did Jesus say He was?

■ How can you tell if a plant or vine is healthy?

■ What are other vines that produce fruit? What kind of fruit do you think Jesus was talking about?

Grapevines were a common sight in Bible times. By describing Himself as the true vine, Jesus was saying that He is the only One who can give us everything we need to grow as believers in Him and produce good fruit. We know that a healthy vine produces good fruit we can eat.

What Jesus meant when He used the word "fruit" was our actions that grow out of our love and obedience to God. The ways in which we show our love for God and the ways in which we help others to know and love God are like fruit.

Depend on Jesus

■ Read John 15:4. What do the branches need to do to produce fruit?

■ Read John 15:7 to find what Jesus says His followers can do.

■ What are some other ways to depend on Jesus? Read John 15:9 for a clue.

For three years, Jesus had been teaching the disciples about this fruit they should produce—show love to God and others. But producing this fruit wasn't going to be an easy task, especially if the disciples had to do it alone. In fact, it would be impossible!

Just like branches depend on the vine to get the nutrients they need to grow, Jesus' followers need to depend on Him to grow and produce fruit.

Jesus described one very important way to depend on him. Jesus' followers can pray, talking to God about what they need. As we get to know Jesus and follow His teachings, we become more like Him and we begin to know what will please Him. Whenever we ask for Jesus' help to love and obey Him, He will give it to us! This promise was for ALL the people who follow Jesus!

It's amazing to think that Jesus loves us as much as His heavenly Father loves Him! Jesus came to Earth to show God's love for us. But God's love isn't something we get and just hold on to for ourselves. It is meant to be shared. Jesus shared God's love with us. And when we depend on Jesus, He gives us the ability to share His love with others.

Show Love to Others

■ In John 15:12, how did Jesus describe the way we should love others?

■ What does Jesus say in verse 13? How did Jesus demonstrate this kind of love?

■ Why was Jesus arrested?

■ Why was Jesus willing to die on the cross?

Just as Jesus always showed His love for His disciples, His disciples should always show love for others.

Right after this last dinner with His disciples, Jesus was arrested. The religious rulers in Jerusalem were afraid Jesus would gain the support of large numbers of people, which might lead to problems with the Roman rulers and diminish their power and authority. So they made up a false charge against Him and took Him to the Romans to be crucified on a cross. Even though Jesus had the power to stop them, He didn't. He let them kill Him.

Jesus died on the cross to take the punishment for our sins. This was Jesus' greatest demonstration of love—that He was willing to suffer and die so that we might be able to be forgiven for our sins and become members of God's family! That's how much He loves us!

Jesus Is Alive

■ Read John 20:10-16. How did Jesus show His friendship and love for Mary?

Jesus was dead. He'd been buried three days. Very early Sunday morning, one of Jesus' best friends, Mary, went to His tomb. She was going to put spices on His dead body. This was a way of showing respect and caring for someone who died. When she got to Jesus' tomb and found it empty, Mary stood in the garden near the tomb and wept bitterly. She barely noticed a man approaching her.

Jesus knew how upset Mary was, so He came to comfort her. He showed her that He was alive! Mary didn't have to be sad anymore! When Mary learned that Jesus is alive, she didn't keep this good news to herself. She ran to tell the other disciples.

Conclusion

Jesus is alive! Just as a dead vine cannot produce living branches and fruit, Jesus could not have saved us from the punishment for our sins and helped us unless He is alive. He is the true vine like John 15:5 says. (Read verse aloud with students.) He conquered death. So we can depend on the living Jesus.

Sometimes people think being a Christian means that there's a list of things we aren't supposed to do. But when Jesus taught about the importance of depending on Him, He said following Him would give us joy (see John 15:11). As we experience His love and show His love to others, we discover the true joy God gives. (Pray with students, thanking God for His love and asking His help in depending on Jesus.)

Get Going ■ 20-30 minutes

Action: Describe ways to depend on Jesus so that we can have joy and show God's love to others.

Distribute Get Real (p. 80) to students. Invite students to tell or write answers to the questions. End the discussion by completing Get Connected with students. (Optional: Students complete page at home.)

GET REAL

■ What do you know about Jesus and His love for you that makes you feel joyful, or glad?

■ Describe someone you know who depends on Jesus and shows His love to others. What is that person like?

■ What are some good reasons for depending on Jesus?

■ What do you think Jesus might say to kids your age about ways to depend on Him?

■ What are some ways kids your age depend on Jesus?

get to know

"I am the vine; you are the branches. If a man remains in me and I in him, he will bear much fruit; apart from me you can do nothing."
John 15:5

GET CONNECTED

Now that you know about God's awesome love for you, what is one thing you will do to show His love to someone else this week? Ask God's help.

Doers of the Word

The Message

Learning about God's Word leads me to know Him and teaches me how to obey Him.

The Bible Basis

2 Kings 22—23:30

After the scrolls of God's Word were found, King Josiah led the people in renewing and obeying the covenant and celebrating the Passover.

The Scripture

"I love your commands more than gold, more than pure gold." Psalm 119:127

Get Started ■ 5-15 minutes

Action: Discover ways in which a mirror gives knowledge.

Mirror Me

What You Need

Several handheld mirrors and a variety of items that give a reflection (spoon, shiny bowl, piece of aluminum foil, etc.).

What You Do

1. Place items that give a reflection on table. Students view and compare their reflections as seen in the different items. **What do mirrors do?** (Reflect an image, or picture.) **How can we mirror something?**

2. Group students in pairs. Partners face each other. One person begins a slow movement, such as pretending to play a sport in slow motion, which his or her partner tries to imitate to make a mirror image. Partners switch roles and speed up the movement with each switch.

3. Discuss the activity by asking the questions below.

■ **How many different ways and places are mirrors used?**

■ **What kinds of information do we learn from mirrors?**

■ **What might be different if we didn't have any mirrors?**

4. Conclude the activity by saying,

■ **The Bible says that what we do with God's Word is similar to the way we use mirrors.**

■ **Today we'll find out how God's Word is like a mirror.**

Bonus Ideas

1. Students have a contest to see who can hold a pose the longest.

2. Videotape students' actions during this activity. Show the images before discussing the activity.

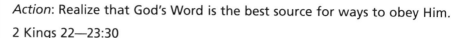

Get It Together ■ 20-30 minutes

Action: Realize that God's Word is the best source for ways to obey Him.

2 Kings 22—23:30

What You Need

Bibles.

What You Do

Lead students to read and discuss the Bible verses listed. Extend the discussion with the questions and comments provided.

Introduction

When have you needed to make an important decision? We are fortunate to have Bibles that we can read. Knowing God's truth for our lives can help us make good choices.

Just like a mirror shows us we have dirt on our faces that needs to be washed off, God's Word helps us see what we need to do to make good choices. Seeing the dirt in the mirror and then forgetting about it, and leaving it on your face, is like hearing an instruction from God's Word and then not doing anything to obey it, or doing the same wrong thing over and over again. Today, we'll talk about what a king in Bible times did when he looked into the mirror of God's Word.

The Young King

■ Read 2 Kings 22:1-2 to find out about this king. What was his name? How old was Josiah when he became king?

■ What do you think an eight-year-old would do if he became king?

■ What do you learn about Josiah in verse 2?

■ What does "walked in all the ways of his father David" mean?

■ What do you think Josiah's father, Amon, and his grandfather Manasseh were like? Read 2 Kings 21:19-22 to find out.

When Josiah became king, it was more difficult to learn about God than it is for you and me. Josiah had no Bible to read to tell him what God's commands were. Josiah must have learned about God's commands from some people who still loved and obeyed God.

Josiah was a descendant of David and he obeyed God as David had done.

Josiah's father and grandfather disobeyed God by leading the kingdom to worship false gods and to reject the commands of the one true God. Amon and Manasseh had even built idols and temples to use in worshiping the false gods.

When Josiah was 26 years old, he decided to clean up the Temple. The Temple was in bad condition because it was unused. Josiah wanted people to be able to worship God in the Temple.

A Hidden Book

■ Read 2 Kings 22:8. What did the priest find when he was cleaning up the Temple?

■ Read 2 Kings 22:11 to find out what Josiah did when he heard the words on the scroll.

■ Why do you think Josiah was so upset? What did he say in verse 13?

The Book of the Law usually refers to the first five books of the Bible. The books were written by Moses. The Book of the Law tells rules God wanted the people to obey. Moses had also described what would happen if God's people did not obey His Word and what would happen if they did obey God's Word.

When Hilkiah found the book, he KNEW that it was important! He gave the book to Shaphan (SHA-fahn), who read it. Shaphan knew how much Josiah wanted to know about God, and Shaphan understood that this book would help Josiah and the people in his kingdom. Shaphan took the book to Josiah right away!

The Bible tells us that Josiah was sad and cried because of the way God's people had ignored God and done all kinds of evil things that God had forbidden them to do.

A Promise to God

■ Find out what message God gave to Josiah by reading 2 Kings 22:15-16,19.

■ Read 2 Kings 23:3 to find what the king and the people promised to do.

■ What words would you use to describe Josiah? Read 2 Kings 23:25 to find out how the Bible describes him.

There was a woman named Huldah, who was a prophetess of God. (A prophetess hears messages from God and tells them to God's people.) Josiah sent a messenger to Huldah to find out what God would do to him and the people. Huldah sent a message back to Josiah: "Because you have chosen to serve God, the punishment the people deserve for their wickedness will not come during your lifetime."

Josiah was relieved, but now he wanted to show his love for God by serving Him. Here's what he did. First, he called together all the elders in his kingdom and all the people in Jerusalem, where Josiah lived. Second, he read the Book of the Law to the people, from the very beginning to the very end. When he'd finished, Josiah made an important announcement to the people. Josiah promised to change his ways and to follow the commandments of the one true God!

Josiah knew that in order to follow God's commands, he must rid his kingdom of the false gods the people had been worshiping. So Josiah and his men rode all over the country, destroying the statues and temples of the false gods. The priests of the false gods were gotten rid of as well, so they would not try to get people to worship the false gods again. Then Josiah held a great feast to honor God. It was the feast of the Passover—a feast that celebrated God's freeing of Israel from Egypt.

Josiah did all these things to show how much he loved God.

Conclusion

Reading God's Word made a big difference in the lives of King Josiah and the people of his country. Psalms 119:127 describes how King Josiah felt about God's Word. (Read verse aloud.) Without God's Word, the king or his people didn't know how to show their love for God by obeying Him.

God's Word, the Bible, helps us know what God is like and how to obey Him. Just like we look into a mirror to see what we really look like, when we look into, or read, the Bible, we see what God wants us to be like as His followers. The instructions we read in the Bible are like God's gift to us, helping us know the best way to live and how to love and follow Christ. (Pray with students, asking God to help them learn and follow His Word.)

Get Going ■ 20-30 minutes

Action: Identify actions that reflect the instructions in God's Word.

Distribute Get Real (p. 84) to students. Invite students to tell or write answers to the questions. End the discussion by completing Get Connected with students. (Optional: Students complete page at home.)

GET REAL

■ What are some things the Bible shows us about ourselves?

■ What does the Bible show us about God?

■ What can you do to learn more about the instructions in the Bible? To remember what you've learned?

■ What are some things the Bible shows us about what He wants us to be like?

■ What are some situations in which Bible commands can help kids your age know how to obey God?

Get to Know

"I love your commands more than gold, more than pure gold."
Psalm 119:127

GET CONNECTED

Think about an instruction or command you've read about in the Bible. Now, ask God for help to obey what you've read.

The Great Temptation

Get Started ■ 5-15 minutes

Action: Identify the guides people use to solve problems and make right choices.

Quick Draw

What You Need

Large sheets of paper, markers; optional—index cards.

What You Do

1. Whisper one of the following words or phrases to a volunteer: "leaky faucet," "toothache," "fight," "illness," "broken glasses," "car accident," "fire" or "hunger." (Optional: Write words or phrases on index cards from which volunteer may choose.)

2. Without speaking and without drawing letters or words, the volunteer quickly draws a picture of the problem you whispered (or wrote). Other students guess the problem pictured. After each word or phrase is guessed, ask,

■ **If you had this problem, where would you go for help?**

3. Repeat with other volunteers using different words or phrases. After completing the activity, ask the questions below.

■ **What are some other problems kids your age might face?**

■ **Who would you go to if you had one of these problems? What is a book you might look at for help?**

■ **What might happen if you didn't have anyone to ask about a problem? If you ask a person who doesn't have good ideas?**

4. Conclude the activity by saying,

■ **We all face problems in life, but knowing where to go for help in solving problems makes all the difference.**

■ **Let's discover what Jesus did when He faced some big problems.**

Bonus Idea

Divide the class into two teams. Give both teams the same word or phrase for each round of the game. Teams compete to see who can guess the word or phrase fastest.

The Message

God's laws will guide me when it's hard to decide what's right.

The Bible Basis

Matthew 4:1-11

Jesus relied on God's Word as a guide when He was tempted.

The Scripture

"I have hidden your word in my heart that I might not sin against you." Psalm 119:11

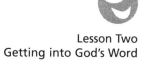
Get It Together ■ 20-30 minutes

Action: Discover that relying on God's laws results in right decisions.

Matthew 4:1-11

What You Need

Bibles.

What You Do

Lead students to read and discuss the Bible verses listed. Extend the discussion with the questions and comments provided.

Introduction

What's the longest you've gone without food? How did you feel? When it was time for Jesus to begin the special job God had planned for Him to do, God's Spirit led Jesus out into the desert. Jesus was alone in the desert for 40 days, not eating a thing.

Jesus was alone and hungry. Then Satan came to tempt Jesus. Satan, sometimes called the tempter or the devil, knew just how hungry Jesus was after not eating for 40 days. Even though there's a lot about Satan we don't know or understand, the Bible tells us that God's enemy does exist and wants to tempt us! Let's find out from Jesus' actions what we can do when we are tempted.

Jesus' Temptation

■ Read Matthew 4:3 to find out what Satan said to Jesus.

■ Why do you think this was a temptation for Jesus?

At first glance, it probably doesn't seem like it would have been so wrong for Jesus to turn the stone into bread. After all, didn't He later turn five loaves of bread into enough food for 5,000 people?

But that wasn't what the devil was REALLY asking Jesus to do. Because Jesus was God's Son, He had the power to do many miraculous things. And Jesus had a choice to use His power to do what God wanted Him to do, or to use it to follow the devil's orders.

Jesus' Answer

■ What did Jesus tell the devil? Read Matthew 4:4.

■ What did Jesus mean when He said that people should live "on every word that comes from the mouth of God"?

Jesus meant that even though having food is important, obeying God's Word is MORE important.

A Second Temptation

■ Read Matthew 4:6 to find what Satan said in his next temptation. How did the devil use the Scriptures?

■ If Jesus jumped off the Temple and angels rescued Him, do you think anyone seeing this happen would have trouble believing Jesus was the Son of God?

Next, the devil took Jesus up to the top of the 15-story Temple. Anyone throwing himself off it would surely die, but the devil told Jesus to jump off anyway.

Satan quoted a psalm that basically said that the angels would catch Jesus (see Psalm 91:11-12). The devil wanted Jesus to prove God's love for Him. But Satan misused Scripture when he talked to Jesus.

The devil might have been asking Jesus to do something else as well. The devil may have been offering Jesus an easy way to prove He was the Son of God.

■ What did Jesus tell the devil? How did Jesus use the Scriptures? Read Matthew 4:7 to find out.

■ How was Jesus' use of the Scripture different from how the devil used the Scriptures? What does this tell you about Satan?

A Third Temptation

■ Read Matthew 4:8-9 to find the third way in which Satan tempted Jesus. Why do you think Satan's offer might have been especially tempting to Jesus?

■ What did Jesus tell the devil? Read Matthew 4:10. Why did Jesus turn down the devil's offer?

■ Was it easy for Jesus to obey God's commands? Why or why not?

■ Why is it important for us to know that even Jesus was tempted? What did Jesus depend on for help?

• Then the devil took Jesus to a place where He could see all the nations of the world. "I will give You ALL of this if You will bow down and worship me," said the devil.

• Again, the devil might have been offering Jesus an easy way out of dying on the cross to save people and to be our King. All Jesus had to do was what the devil wanted.

• Jesus knew God's plan and its importance. Jesus chose to follow God's way. Because Jesus was tempted, He is able to help us when we are tempted.

• Satan left in defeat. No matter how hard Satan had tried to tempt Jesus to do wrong, he hadn't succeeded. Each time Satan tried to trick Jesus into disobeying God, Jesus answered by quoting a law from God's Word.

Conclusion

Even though Jesus was God's Son and had all the power in the world, Jesus did as Psalm 119:11 says. He knew and used the Scriptures as His guide when Satan tempted Him to disobey God. (Read verse aloud.)

When we are tempted to disobey God, we can remember that Jesus understands what we are going through (see Hebrews 2:18 and 4:15). Sometimes we need to make a decision and we don't know the best thing to do. That's when we need to remember God's gift of His commands. All of the Bible was given by God to help us know, love and obey Him. When we become members of God's family, God's Spirit lives in us, helping us love and obey God. No matter what we're tempted to do, God promises to help us (see 1 Corinthians 10:13). (Pray with students, thanking God for His help and forgiveness.)

Get Going ■ 20-30 minutes

Action: Name ways God's Word helps us make decisions in tempting situations.

Distribute Get Real (p. 88) to students. Invite students to tell or write answers to the questions. End the discussion by completing Get Connected with students. (Optional: Students complete page at home.)

GET REAL

■ When are some times kids your age are tempted to do wrong?

■ Even though we know God's rules are good, why is it so hard sometimes to obey God's rules?

■ What are some difficult choices kids have to make at school? While playing sports? At home?

■ Often we know what the right action is, but we choose not to do it. What can we do when we need help to obey? What and who can you depend on for help when you feel tempted?

■ What can you do to avoid being in a situation where you will be tempted?

Get to Know

"I have hidden your word in my heart that I might not sin against you."
Psalm 119:11

GET CONNECTED

When is a time you are often tempted? Think of the ways God has promised to help you resist temptation and ask His help in making right decisions.

The Fruit of God's Word

Get Started ■ 5-15 minutes

Action: Describe the value of God's Word.

People Scramble

What You Need

Markers, 31 5-inch (12.5-cm) squares of paper, large paper bag; optional—stopwatch or watch with a second hand.

What You Do

1. Write each letter of the alphabet on a separate square of paper. Make two squares for these letters: *e, i, s, m, t*. Place letter squares in bag.

2. Students choose letter squares from bag until all squares have been chosen. (It's OK for students to have an unequal number of squares.)

3. Call out the word "wisdom." Students with the appropriate letter squares see how fast they can arrange themselves in order to spell the word. (If a student has two of the necessary letters, he or she quickly gives one to another student who doesn't have any of the letters in the word.) (Optional: Time students as they arrange themselves.) Ask the questions below.

■ **If you want to get wisdom, or be wise, what can you do?**

■ **Reading God's Word is one way to become wise. Let's find out some other benefits of reading the Bible.**

4. Repeat the above procedure with the words "advice," "help," "promises," "hope," "insight," "knowledge," "joy," "commands," "peace," "direction" and "strength," allowing students to choose new letter squares (or trade squares) after each word. Invite volunteers to tell an example of how the Bible gives us each of these things.

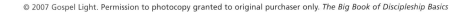

5. Conclude the activity by saying,

■ **Today we're going to find out what Jesus said about paying attention to the good things we find in the Bible.**

Bonus Idea

For an added challenge, students spell words backwards by lining up in reverse letter order.

The **Message**

Valuing God's Word leads to a life of integrity.

The **Bible Basis**

Mark 4:1-20

Our lives can either be barren or fruitful, depending on our responses to God's Word.

The **Scripture**

"Do not merely listen to the word, and so deceive yourselves. Do what it says." James 1:22

Get It Together ■ 20-30 minutes

Action: Realize that people are like good soil when they pay attention to and obey God's Word.

Mark 4:1-20

What You Need

Bibles.

What You Do

Lead students to read and discuss the Bible verses listed. Extend the discussion with the questions and comments provided.

Introduction

What do you think would be the best thing about living on a farm? The worst thing? Farmers know a lot about soil. They know which soil to plant in and which soil to avoid. They know what the soil needs to help plants grow. They can tell just by looking at a plant what needs to be added to the soil to help the plant grow. Some farmers even hire scientists to test their soil to make sure it has everything in it that plants need to grow.

How do you think people in Bible times might have farmed different from today's farmers? They didn't have machines, so they had to do everything by hand. The farmer scattered the seed across his field, letting it fly from his hand as he swept his arm back and forth. Finally the farmer plowed his field so that the seed would be covered up. Sometimes, if there was someone to help the farmer, one person plowed the field while another person followed behind, scattering the seed over the recently plowed field. Then the oxen that had pulled the plow would be led across the field again to help trample the seed into the ground.

A Command to Listen

■ Read Mark 4:1-2. Where was Jesus when He told a parable about seeds? Who was Jesus speaking to?

■ What's the definition of a parable?

■ When Jesus got ready to tell this parable, what was the first word He said to the people? Read Mark 4:3 to find out.

In Bible times, most people grew their own food on their own farms. Why do you think that was true? There were no refrigerators or plastic wrap or other ways to keep food for a long time. So, when Jesus started telling a story about the different soils, He was talking to people who knew all about farming.

A parable is a story that teaches an important lesson or truth.

It was an important point Jesus was about to make. The people needed to pay close attention.

The Parable

■ What was the parable Jesus told the people in Mark 4:3-8?

■ What did Jesus' disciples do at the end of the parable?

Jesus talked about four different kinds of soils and what happened to seeds that were planted in these soils.

Apparently, Jesus' disciples weren't quite sure why Jesus had told this parable. So they asked their teacher, Jesus, to explain what they didn't understand. Jesus answered by saying that His parables would be understood only by those who were ready to love and obey God. Other people, who didn't want to love God, would hear the parables but would never bother to even try to understand them.

The Explanation

■ Read Mark 4:15 to find what kind of people are like the hard path.

■ What kind of people are like the rocky soil? Read Mark 4:16-17 to find Jesus' explanation.

■ Read Mark 4:18-19 to find what kind of people are like the soil with thorns or weeds in it.

■ Read Mark 4:20 to find what kind of people are like the good soil.

■ What kind of crop did these people produce?

Jesus explained what this parable about the seed and soils meant. Jesus said that the seed is like God's Word and the four soils are like people who respond in four different ways to God's Word.

Jesus knew that some of the people listening to His messages really didn't want to change. These people are like the hard path. When they heard God's Word, their hard-heartedness would keep them from remembering what Jesus had said.

Some of the people who listened to Jesus were very happy to hear what Jesus said and they wanted to live as followers of Jesus. But when other people made fun of them or put them down for trying to follow Jesus, they gave up and did things the way they had done before. These people are like the rocky soil.

There would be some people who at first decided to obey God's Word. But then they became so worried about taking care of themselves that they no longer followed God's Word. These people are like soil with thorns in it.

There were some people who heard God's Word and obeyed it. They were able to show others how to live by God's Word as well, so many other people were able to learn about God. These people are like the good soil.

Conclusion

Jesus told this parable so that people would want to pay attention to God's Word and desire to obey it as James 1:22 says. (Read verse aloud.) Just like in Bible times, we can choose whether or not to pay attention to God's Word. Some people might listen to God's Word when they're at church but then don't think about it all the rest of the week. Other people might say they want to obey God's Word, but they never read it or try to understand what it says.

People who are like good soil know the value of God's Word, and it helps them live with integrity. They want to spend time reading and thinking about God's Word and asking His help in understanding and obeying it. The first step in paying attention to God's Word is to believe in Jesus, God's Son, and accept Jesus' death to take away our sin. (Lead students in prayer, asking God to help them be like good soil as they hear God's Word. Then talk with interested students about becoming members of God's family, referring to "Leading a Student to Christ" on pp. 10-11.)

Get Going ■ 20-30 minutes

Action: Plan ways to be like good soil in responding to God's Word.

Distribute Get Real (p. 92) to students. Invite students to tell or write answers to the questions. End the discussion by completing Get Connected with students. (Optional: Students complete page at home.)

- What are some things a person could do in order not to be like the hard path?

- How can a person avoid being like rocky soil?

- What excuses do people use as reasons for not knowing and following God's Word?

- What are some things you have already done to be like the good soil? What are some other things you can do?

- What is the result of being like the good soil Jesus was talking about?

Get to Know

"Do not merely listen to the word, and so deceive yourselves. Do what it says."
James 1:22

GET CONNECTED

Jesus talked about hearing the Word. Reading your Bible is the best way to hear God's Word. Choose an amount of time that you will plan to read your Bible each day (such as five minutes). Ask God to help you with your plans to read His Word.

Hungry for Goodness

Get Started ■ 5-15 minutes

Action: Experience searching for something and being satisfied.

Hidden Treasure

What You Need

Red and blue construction paper, scissors, marker, small prizes (sticks of gum, fish crackers, stickers, wrapped candies, etc.).

What You Do

1. Cut paper into an equal number of small red and blue slips, five of one color for each student. Print Psalm 119:10, one word on each slip, making a set of blue slips and a set of red slips. Hide slips of paper around the room.

2. Divide group into two teams and assign each group a color (red or blue). Show prizes. **To get one of these prizes, search for the slips of paper in your team's color and arrange them so that you can read Psalm 119:10 from the slips. When your team has finished, you may give clues to help the other team finish.**

3. Students search around the room, find papers and arrange them in verse order. Students then help others find papers. Call time after several minutes or when all papers have been found. Read Psalm 119:10 aloud together and then distribute prizes.

4. Ask the questions below.

■ **Are these prizes, or rewards, very satisfying? Why or why not?**

■ **Although it was fun to look for the papers and get the prizes, these aren't very valuable or important prizes. What are some rewards, or prizes, in life that most people think are valuable?**

■ **What are some things a lot of people search for or try to get?**

5. Conclude the activity by saying,

■ **In our study, we'll meet a man who was searching for an important prize. But it wasn't money or a car.**

■ **See if you can discover what he was searching for and what he found.**

Bonus Idea

Bring in a variety of *I Spy* books from preschool classrooms. (Or bring in books with small complex pictures and hidden objects, such as *Where's Waldo.*) Invite students to search books to find the hidden objects. Students count the number of objects they find. Give a prize to students who find 20 or more hidden objects. Encourage students who quickly find objects to **help others** find them as well.

The Message

Search for what is right in God's eyes.

The Bible Basis

John 3:1-21

Nicodemus wanted to know the truth about God so much that he risked his reputation by talking with Jesus.

The Scripture

"I seek you with all my heart; do not let me stray from your commands."
Psalm 119:10

Get It Together ■ 20-30 minutes

Action: Realize that when we search to know God and then do what is right, we will find true satisfaction.

John 3:1-21

What You Need

Bibles.

What You Do

Lead students to read and discuss the Bible verses listed. Extend the discussion with the questions and comments provided.

Introduction

When have you been really hungry? Thirsty? Today we'll find out about something that is worth being really hungry and thirsty for.

A Nighttime Visit

■ Read John 3:1-2 to find out who came to visit Jesus and what he might have been hungry for.

■ What do you learn about Nicodemus from these verses?

■ When did he come to visit Jesus? Why do you think someone might come to see Jesus when it was nighttime?

■ What do you think Nicodemus thought about Jesus?

The man who walked quietly through the night to see Jesus was Nicodemus. Nicodemus, a Pharisee and a highly respected leader. Most of the Pharisees were angry about Jesus. To them, He was an uneducated upstart who was teaching dangerous ideas. But the ordinary people loved Jesus. He had taught and healed great numbers of them. Some of them even said He was the Messiah! The Pharisees didn't think so. And they didn't like Jesus.

When Nicodemus came to see Jesus, he probably didn't want to be noticed—and his walk was a secret. Because Nicodemus was such a well-known Pharisee, talking with Jesus might get him into a LOT of trouble.

Nicodemus was searching for what was true and right—it was like a hunger inside him! He had carefully obeyed the Torah (the first five books of the Old Testament) and all the other laws of Judaism. But all of his good deeds left a hunger inside him. Something was missing from his life. As Jesus taught and healed in Jerusalem, Nicodemus must have heard Jesus' words and seen Jesus heal sick people. Jesus was different from any priest or rabbi Nicodemus had ever met. If anyone could truly satisfy his search for goodness and righteousness, Nicodemus hoped it would be Jesus.

A Surprising Conversation

■ Read John 3:3 to find out what Jesus said to Nicodemus about being born again.

■ What do you think Jesus meant by saying a person needs to be born again to be part of God's kingdom?

■ In verse 4, read what Nicodemus said because he was so confused by Jesus' words.

Jesus knew that Nicodemus had tried hard to obey God's laws. Jesus wanted Nicodemus to understand that performing miracles, being good or even obeying laws would not satisfy his hunger for goodness. Jesus told Nicodemus that there must be a change inside of himself—in his thoughts and attitudes and feelings. Jesus called this change being "born again."

Jesus explained that He was talking about a person's spirit, the part that controls our attitudes and actions. He was talking about being born into God's family, not being born physically as a baby.

A Word Picture

■ To help Nicodemus understand what Jesus was talking about, read John 3:8. What did Jesus compare the Holy Spirit to?

■ Jesus talked about the Son of Man in John 3:13-15. Read these verses. Who do you think the Son of Man is? What did Jesus say would happen to the Son of Man?

■ Then Jesus said some words that people all over the world have heard and read. What did He say? Read John 3:16.

Jesus used a word picture to explain that what God does inside a person is like the wind. Just as we can't see the wind, only what it does, so we can't see God changing a person on the inside, but we can see what it does by the changes in a person's life.

Jesus' explanation was new to Nicodemus. But Nicodemus probably knew just about everything there was to know about the Old Testament, so Jesus used another word picture. He reminded Nicodemus of the time when Moses was leading the Israelites to the land God had promised, when they were bitten by snakes. God told Moses to make a snake from bronze and to tell the people to look at it, so they could be healed from their snakebites. (See Numbers 21:4-9.)

Jesus said He would have to be lifted up just like Moses lifted up the bronze snake. "Just as the sick people who looked at the bronze serpent were healed and didn't die, so anyone who believes in Me will have eternal life," Jesus said. He was talking about the time when He would be put on a cross to die for all our sins.

The words Jesus said helped Nicodemus, and everyone in the world, learn of God's gift of His Son, Jesus.

We don't know whether or not Nicodemus believed in Jesus that night. But we do know that he is mentioned later in the book of John (see John 7:50-53; 19:38-42) as a follower of Jesus.

Conclusion

Nicodemus realized that even though he tried to do the right things, he still had a hunger for goodness that had not been satisfied. We can learn to seek God like Nicodemus did. (Read Psalm 119:10 aloud.) Jesus taught Nicodemus that only God can truly answer our search for righteousness because only Jesus' death and resurrection make it possible for our sins to be forgiven.

To search for goodness, or righteousness, doesn't mean we are going to be perfect and never do anything wrong. But it does mean that we can become members of God's family and then continually ask His help in loving and obeying Him.

Sometimes it's hard to know what's right to do. The first step is to pray—ask for God's help. Then think about what action would show God's love the most—which action leads to goodness. God promises to help us make the right choice. And when we make wrong choices, we have His promise to forgive us when we ask. (Lead students in prayer, asking God to help them choose to love and obey Him.)

Get Going ■ 20-30 minutes

Action: Describe situations in which we want to know what is right, and ask God's help in loving and obeying Him.

Distribute Get Real (p. 96) to students. Invite students to tell or write answers to the questions. End the discussion by completing Get Connected with students. (Optional: Students complete page at home.)

Get Real

■ When are some times it's easy to know the right thing to do? When are some times a kid your age might have trouble knowing what is right?

■ Who are some people you know who seek righteousness? How do they act?

■ What are some ways you can find out what God wants you to do in a difficult situation?

■ What should you do if you've made the wrong choice in a situation? How can you keep seeking goodness?

■ How can we get better at knowing what is right in God's eyes?

■ What are some ways that kids your age can seek to know the right thing to do? When are some times it would be important to know the right thing to do?

Get to Know

"I seek you with all my heart; do not let me stray from your commands."
Psalm 119:10

Get Connected

Think about a time that you need God's help in knowing the right way to act. Silently ask God to help you in times like this. Ask God to help you be hungry for goodness and to love and obey Him in all situations.

Love Is God's Law

Get Started ■ 5-15 minutes

Action: Discover how important a missing item can be.

Missing Parts

What You Need

A variety of household items missing a crucial element (hand mixer without beaters, pencil without eraser, pen without ink, game instructions without a game, padlock without key, shoe without laces, flashlight without batteries, matchbox without matches, etc.), large cloth or sheet, paper, pencils.

What You Do

1. Place objects on table or floor.

2. Students examine each item. **What do all these items have in common? In a few minutes, I'll be asking you questions about these items.** After several minutes, cover the items. Distribute paper and pencils. Give students several minutes to list what the items were and what important part was missing from each item.

3. Uncover items. As you briefly discuss each item and how the missing part of the item is useful, students compare lists they created with items. Ask the questions below.

■ **What are some other things that make a really big difference if they're missing?**

■ **What are the results if they're missing?**

■ **What might happen if you tried to ride a bike without pedals? To play soccer without a ball?**

4. Conclude the activity by saying,

■ **Just as these objects were missing important parts, it is possible to miss the important part or point of God's rules.**

■ **Some leaders in Bible times thought they totally understood something, but because they were missing something very important, they really didn't understand at all! In our study today, see if you can figure out what they were missing.**

Bonus Idea

Provide large sheets of paper and markers. Challenge students to draw a place or an object with important things missing (ferris wheel without seats, Christmas tree without ornaments, zoo without animals, etc.).

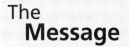

The Message

Following God's laws is a matter of love, not just obedience.

The Bible Basis

Exodus 20:8-20;
Matthew 12:9-14;
Mark 3:1-6; Luke 6:6-11

Jesus healed a man on the Sabbath because He understood the loving intent of God's law.

The Scripture

"Love the Lord your God with all your heart and with all your soul and with all your strength and with all your mind."
Luke 10:27

Get It Together ■ 20-30 minutes

Action: Realize that following God's laws requires love, not just obedience.

Exodus 20:8-10; Matthew 12:9-14; Mark 3:1-6; Luke 6:6-11

What You Need

Bibles.

What You Do

Lead students to read and discuss the Bible verses listed. Extend the discussion with the questions and comments provided.

Introduction

Who is someone famous that lots of people like? Why might some people not like that person? Today we're going to learn about some people who did not like Jesus—many of the religious leaders in Jesus' time. A large number of people were beginning to believe and follow Jesus. And that made many of the religious leaders angry and jealous!

The Pharisees were a group of those religious leaders, and some of them began to look for ways to get Jesus into trouble. They thought if they could trap Jesus into breaking a law or doing something against His own preaching, the people would think of Him as a phony and would stop following Him. Let's find out what happened when Jesus acted in a way the Pharisees did not like.

A Day of Rest

■ What do you remember about the Sabbath?

■ What was God's law for the Sabbath? Read Exodus 20:8-10.

The Sabbath is the weekly day of rest and worship that God planned for all people. In the Old Testament it is the seventh day of the week (Saturday). Because Jesus rose from the dead on a Sunday, most Christians set aside Sunday as the day of rest and worship.

The Pharisees had made this law of resting on the Sabbath very complicated. They had hundreds of OTHER rules telling all the kinds of work no one could do on the Sabbath.

According to the rules the Pharisees taught, if you were thirsty and needed a drink of water, you couldn't go to the town well and get some water. You were supposed to have gotten enough water from the well the day before! Or if you were hungry and wanted some bread to eat, you couldn't bake a loaf of bread. You were supposed to have made enough bread on the day before the Sabbath. The Pharisees made sure that everyone knew ALL these rules and obeyed each one!

A Man in Need

■ One day when Jesus went into the synagogue, who did He see? Read Matthew 12:9-10.

■ What did the Pharisees ask Jesus? Why did they ask this question?

■ What did Jesus often do when He saw someone who needed help?

On this particular Sabbath day when Jesus came to the synagogue, He saw a man who had a withered, crippled hand. The Bible doesn't tell us exactly what was wrong with this man's hand, but he probably could not use his fingers. Imagine how hard life would be if you couldn't use your fingers!

Because the Pharisees knew that Jesus often healed people in need, the Pharisees thought they had found the perfect opportunity to get Jesus into trouble! The Pharisees had decided that healing was work, and they had a rule preventing people from healing on the Sabbath! According to their rules, no one, not even Jesus, was supposed to HEAL someone on the Sabbath, unless the person was in danger of dying.

A Surprising Question and Answer

■ When Jesus had to decide what to do, what do you think He thought about?

■ Read Matthew 12:11 to find what Jesus asked. How would you have answered this question?

■ How do you think the Pharisees would have answered this question?

■ What did Jesus want the Pharisees to learn from this question?

■ Read Matthew 12:12. What point did Jesus make with His answer?

Jesus had to choose! Would He break the Pharisees' rules and heal the man's crippled hand? Or would He ignore the man's need and refuse to heal him? Everyone watched very closely to see what Jesus would do.

Jesus could have tried to get out of the Pharisees' trap by leaving the synagogue or telling the man to meet Him later in a more private place. The man's hand had been crippled for a long time. Waiting one more day to heal the man's hand would not hurt! But Jesus did something else instead.

The Pharisees would have recognized that saving the life of an animal, even on the Sabbath, was permissible.

In His answer to the Pharisees, Jesus wanted to show how the Pharisees had missed the point of the law. Jesus wanted the Pharisees to see that doing good was more important than obeying a rule. God's laws were made to help people, not to harm people.

A Choice to Heal

■ Now read Matthew 12:13. What happened?

■ How were Jesus' actions an example of God's laws helping us do good?

■ What do you think the Pharisees would want everyone to know about God's laws?

■ What advice would they give about obeying God?

■ Do you think these Pharisees learned this lesson about the importance of God's love? Read Matthew 12:14 to find out.

Jesus showed love and did good. He healed the man. Jesus had said it is good to help people in need, and His actions backed up what He had said.

These Pharisees didn't get the idea of showing love at all! Instead, they were angry (see Luke 6:11). The Pharisees loved the law! In fact, they loved it so much, it seems like they loved the law even more than they loved God!

Conclusion

Jesus knew that it is possible to obey the laws and still not show love to others. But Jesus' words and actions help us remember that the main intent or reason for all God's laws is to show love for God and for others. God didn't give us the law because He wanted to be like a police officer or judge, or keep us from having fun. He gave the laws to us so we would know the best ways to show His love to others. (Read Luke 10:27 aloud. Pray with students, asking God to help them obey Him with a loving attitude.)

Get Going ■ 20-30 minutes

Action: Discuss situations in which we need to obey God's laws in loving ways.

Distribute Get Real (p. 100) to students. Invite students to tell or write answers to the questions. End the discussion by completing Get Connected with students. (Optional: Students complete page at home.)

Get Real

■ What are some specific ways to treat others to show them God's love?

■ Sometimes you might be in a situation where there isn't a law or rule to tell you what to do. How can Luke 10:27 help you then?

■ When might it be possible for someone to obey one of God's commandments and not act in a loving way? When have you been in a situation like that? What happened? What could a person do in that situation to obey God's commandment in a loving way?

■ How can you obey the Bible command to do your best work (see Colossians 3:17) in a loving way? How can you obey the Bible command to tell the truth (see Zechariah 8:16) in a loving way?

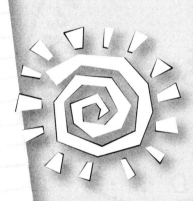

Get to Know

"Love the Lord your God with all your heart and with all your soul and with all your strength and with all your mind."
Luke 10:27

Get Connected

Think about one Bible command you want to obey this week. Ask God to help you obey Him in loving ways and thank Him for His commands that help us know the best way to live.

Faithful Habits

Get Started ■ 5-15 minutes

Action: Discover the results of practicing.

Obstacle Challenge

What You Need

Items for obstacle course (chairs, balls, boxes or baskets, hula hoops, ropes, paper, etc.), stopwatch or watch with second hand.

What You Do

1. Create an obstacle course that is appropriate for your classroom. In the obstacle course, include two or more skill challenges (tossing ball into a box or basket, jumping rope five times, making and flying a paper airplane, etc.).

2. Time how long it takes each pair of students to move through the obstacle course.

3. After everyone has had a chance to go through the obstacle course, allow students to look at the course and plan the fastest way to complete it. Then invite students to go through the course another time to see if they can complete it faster. Ask the questions below.

■ **Was the course easier the second time? Why or why not?**

■ **What can you do to get better at doing something?**

■ **What do you like to practice doing? What don't you like to practice? Why?**

■ **When has practicing something really helped you?**

4. Conclude the activity by saying,

■ **In our study today, we are going to learn about someone who did something regularly and often—in other words, he practiced.**

■ **See if you can discover how this good habit helped him.**

Bonus Idea

Instead of an obstacle course, find and bring in appropriate tongue twisters. (Use the keywords "tongue twisters" to find websites that provide tongue twisters.) Students see how many times it takes them to say tongue twisters correctly.

The Message

In risky situations, the faithful habits of God's followers give courage to obey God.

The Bible Basis

Daniel 6

Even when his life was in danger, Daniel did what was right by continuing to pray to God.

The Scripture

"Be careful to do what the Lord your God has commanded you; do not turn aside to the right or to the left."
Deuteronomy 5:32

Get It Together ■ 20-30 minutes

Action: Recognize that developing a pattern of loving and following God helps us obey Him, even when it's hard.

Daniel 6

What You Need

Bibles.

What You Do

Lead students to read and discuss the Bible verses listed. Extend the discussion with the questions and comments provided.

Introduction

When have you wished that you could live somewhere else? Why did you wish that? Today we're going to hear about a young man who left his home to live in a new country—and it wasn't because he wanted to!

Daniel's Love for God

■ What do you remember about Daniel—a man who lived in Old Testament times?

■ How do you think Daniel became known as someone who loved and followed God?

Daniel had learned to worship God as a young boy in the country of Judah. When he was captured and taken to Babylon as a slave, he continued to love and follow God.

Daniel even helped three of his friends obey God by refusing to eat King Nebuchadnezzar's food, which had been offered to false gods. Daniel's choices gave him quite a reputation! Everyone knew that he loved and followed God.

Daniel's New Job

■ When a new king became the leader of Babylon, what job was Daniel given? Read Daniel 6:3 to find out.

■ How do you think the other satraps felt about Daniel's new job?

■ What did the governors try to do? Read Daniel 6:4 to find out.

■ Read Daniel 6:5 to find out the governor's next idea.

Toward the end of Daniel's life, Babylon was captured by the Persians, and Darius became the new king in Babylon. But Daniel didn't retire!

Because Daniel did such an excellent job as a governor, King Darius decided to put Daniel in charge of the country! That meant he was going to be the leader of all the satraps. Satraps were governors over different parts of Persia.

Some of the other governors, or satraps, however, were pretty upset when they heard Daniel had been appointed over them.

Daniel's reputation was flawless! The governors couldn't find anything bad about Daniel. So the governors decided that they would make a law against something Daniel always did to show His love and worship for God.

Daniel's Choice

■ Read Daniel 6:7 to find out the new law and the punishment for breaking this law.

■ What do you remember about Daniel's actions and what happened next?

It was no secret that Daniel was devoted to God. The governors knew that Daniel prayed by his window three times every day. The governors might have thought, *If we make it against the law to pray to anyone except the king, Daniel might break that law.*

For Daniel, the choice was clear. He believed he must continue to do what he did every day—pray to God. Daniel probably could have gone to pray somewhere in hiding. But instead, Daniel did what he always did. Daniel went upstairs to his

■ If you had been Daniel, what would you have said to God when you prayed to Him? Read Daniel 6:10 to find out what he prayed. What do you think he thanked God for?

Daniel's Rescue

■ What did Darius say to Daniel as Daniel was taken to the lions' den? Read Daniel 6:16 to find out.

■ Read Daniel 6:19-22 to find out what Darius did the next morning. How did Darius refer to Daniel's God? What was the result of Daniel's faithful obedience?

■ Read Daniel 6:26-27. What did the new law created by Darius tell everyone to do?

■ Why did Darius want everyone to respect Daniel's God?

room, knelt down by the open window that faced Jerusalem and prayed. And, of course, the governors saw him and reported his actions to King Darius.

Darius was horrified at what had happened! Daniel was the most trusted and honest man in his country! And Darius was going to have to punish Daniel for breaking a foolish law—which Darius now realized he'd been tricked into signing.

Darius spent the whole day trying to figure out a way to save Daniel. But those governors were insistent. They reminded Darius that in their country, the king couldn't undo a law once it was made, no matter how absurd it turned out to be!

But even as Darius ordered Daniel to be thrown into the lions' den, he must have remembered the faith Daniel had in his God. Darius knew that if anyone could save Daniel, it would be Daniel's God.

When Darius realized that God had sent an angel to rescue Daniel from death, Darius recognized God's greatness!

Conclusion

Daniel's habit of loving and following God helped him choose to obey God in this difficult situation. All his life, Daniel had shown others what it meant to follow and obey God as the Bible says in Deuteronomy 5:32. (Read verse aloud.) In tough times, Daniel stood up for what he believed. When it came time to choose whether to pray to God and face a terrible death, Daniel's habit of always obeying God helped him make the right choice.

Usually when we think of habits, we think of little things like always eating peanut butter and jelly sandwiches for lunch, or always sitting in a certain chair at the dinner table. But important things can become habits, too.

Showing our love for God by our words and actions can get to be a habit! For example, making a habit of telling the truth, even in situations where it seems like the truth doesn't matter, will help us tell the truth in important situations. As you grow older and begin to make more and more choices yourself, think about the habits in your life that will help you love and follow God. (Lead students in prayer, asking God to help them develop habits of loving God.)

Get Going ■ 20-30 minutes

Action: Discuss habits that help us love and follow God.

Distribute Get Real (p. 104) to students. Invite students to tell or write answers to the questions. End the discussion by completing Get Connected with students. (Optional: Students complete page at home.)

Get Real

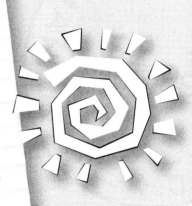

■ How can people show they want to love and follow God? What are some things that kids your age could do regularly to help them obey God?

■ What habits could you develop that would help you obey God, even when it is hard?

■ What do you have to do to make something a habit? What can you do when you need help in starting or developing a habit of loving and following God?

■ What good habits have you already developed in your life? Which habit would you like to increase? How do you think you could do this?

Get to Know

"Be careful to do what the Lord your God has commanded you; do not turn aside to the right or to the left."
Deuteronomy 5:32

Get Connected

What is a new habit you want to start this week? Talk to God about developing habits to love and follow Him. Thank God for His love and forgiveness, even when you forget to obey Him.

Faith That Leads to Obedience

Get Started ■ 5-15 minutes

Action: Discover that having faith means putting trust in something.

How Much Faith?

What You Need

Index cards, marker, masking tape, measuring stick.

What You Do

1. Print the numbers 1 through 5 on separate index cards. Tape cards to the floor in a line at 2-foot (.6-m) intervals.

2. **Let's see how much faith you have that certain events will happen. How much faith do you have that you will get to school on time tomorrow?** Students line up behind the number indicating how much faith they have in that event occurring—1 being no faith at all and 5 being very certain.

3. Repeat with the events below. **How much faith do you have that:**

■ **When you flip the light switch, the light will go on?**

■ **Your parents will give you a car when you graduate from high school?**

■ **Your best friend will invite you to his or her party?**

■ **Your best friend won't tell your secret?**

■ **You will be the first person to walk on Mars?**

■ **You will get the award for best-dressed person at your school?**

4. Ask the questions below.

■ **Which of the events did most of us have faith would happen?**

■ **Which event did most of us have the least faith would happen?**

■ **How would you define the word "faith"?**

5. Conclude the activity by saying,

■ **Today we are going to investigate the most important thing in life for us to have faith in. You can compare your definition of faith to what the Bible says faith is.**

Bonus Idea

Students think of a variety of ways to complete the sentence "Faith is . . ." Videotape students saying the sentences. Play back the video at the end of the session.

The Message

Faith in Jesus gives us hope and courage.

The Bible Basis

Hebrews 11—12:3

Heroes of faith showed their belief in God through their actions.

The Scripture

"I will hasten and not delay to obey your commands." Psalm 119:60

Get It Together ■ 20-30 minutes

Action: Understand that our faith in Jesus enables us to be forgiven and live as part of God's plan.

Hebrews 11—12:3

What You Need

Bibles.

What You Do

Lead students to read and discuss the Bible verses listed. Extend the discussion with the questions and comments provided.

Introduction

What are some things that help you decide if you are going to have faith in someone or something? It helps us to have faith in an object, like a car, if we've seen it work. We have faith in people who have kept their promises to us. But in the Bible, there's a whole chapter written about people, heroes, who had faith in someone whom they had never seen.

A Definition of Faith

■ Read Hebrews 11:1-2. These verses describe the faith of these people. How is faith defined in verse 1?

■ Who did these people have faith in?

The word "ancients" refers to Bible-times people who lived long before Jesus. These people believed in God and His plan for salvation, even though they had never seen Him. They believed that God exists and that He does what He promises to do.

The rest of Hebrews 11 tells how these people showed their faith in God.

Noah's Faith

■ What does Hebrews 11:7 say that Noah did because of his faith in God?

■ What was the unseen thing that Noah believed would happen?

■ What was the result of Noah's faith?

One of the first heroes mentioned is Noah. Even though Noah lived in a place where no one could imagine a flood, he believed and obeyed God. And God's Word was shown to be true: There was a great flood. Noah's faith in God and his decision to follow God's instructions led to his salvation.

Abraham's Faith

■ Read Hebrews 11:8-9 to find what Abraham did because of his faith in God.

■ Why might it have been hard for Abraham to leave the land where his family had always lived?

■ What did God promise Abraham would happen if Abraham obeyed Him?

■ Why do you think Abraham had faith in God?

Abraham had a big decision to make. Even though Abraham didn't know where he was going, and even though he would have to live like a stranger in a foreign country, Abraham obeyed God's command to leave his home and travel to the new land God had promised him.

Moses' Faith

■ What event is described in Hebrews 11:29? What else do you remember about the story of Moses?

■ What were the results of Moses' faith?

The list of heroes continues with Abraham's children and grandchildren, eventually including Moses. The writer of Hebrews must have had a hard time telling only a few of the ways in which Moses led the Israelites in demonstrating their faith in God. The dramatic event in verse 29 showed the awesome power of the God in whom Moses had faith.

God protected Moses and the Israelites from the Egyptians, making it possible for them to return to the land which God had given them.

Heroes of Faith

■ Read Hebrews 11:34 for just a few examples of the ways in which God helped His faithful people. What kinds of events are described?

Hebrews 11 could have filled up page after page telling about the many heroes of the faith. Even the writer admits to not having enough time to tell about the many ways believers in God showed their faith.

All of these heroes of the faith lived and died without seeing the fulfillment of God's plan: Jesus' coming to Earth to pay the penalty for sin. These people, and many more whose names were not listed in Hebrews 11, were sure of God's promise to send a Savior.

Faith in Jesus

■ What difference does it make to us to know about these heroes of the faith?

■ What word picture does the writer of Hebrews use to describe our life in Christ? Read Hebrews 12:1 to find out.

The heroes of the faith in Hebrews 11 are like an audience in the stands of a sports stadium. The Bible compares our lives as Christians to a race. Disobeying God slows us down and can make us trip and fall. To keep on running in the race, however, we need to keep our faith in Jesus and receive the forgiveness He offers for sins. The heroes of the faith in Hebrews 11 are good examples to us of what faith in God accomplishes.

Conclusion

The situations in which we show our faith in Jesus might not be as dramatic as the events described in Hebrews 11. But our faith can be just as strong as the faith of these Bible-times heroes. God's promise to forgive and help His faithful people is the same today as it was in Bible times. We can follow the instructions in the Bible in Psalm 119:60. (Read Psalm 119:60 aloud. Pray with students, thanking God for His promises and asking God to help students have faith in Him and receive His forgiveness. Talk with interested students about showing faith in God by becoming members of His family, referring to "Leading a Student to Christ" on pp.10-11.)

Get Going ■ 20-30 minutes

Action: List and discuss ways to show faith in Jesus.

Distribute Get Real (p.108) to students. Invite students to tell or write answers to the questions. End the discussion by completing Get Connected with students. (Optional: Students complete page at home.)

Get Real

■ Who is someone you know who has faith in Jesus? How do you know this person has faith in Jesus?

■ What are some situations in which kids your age can show faith in Jesus?

■ What might make it hard to show faith in Jesus?

■ When it's difficult to show faith in Jesus, what can you do?

■ What is something you could do to help others and show your faith in Jesus?

Get to Know

"I will hasten and not delay to obey your commands."
Psalm 119:60

Get Connected

Think about someone you know who has a lot of faith in Jesus, or think of someone you learned about in your Bible study today. What can you do to follow the example of that person? Ask God to help you show faith in Jesus during the coming week.

Love and Pray for God's Family

Get Started ■ 5-15 minutes

Action: Discover why people come to church.

Activity Search

What You Need

Large sheet of paper, tape, markers, a variety of old church bulletins and newsletters.

What You Do

1. Tape large sheet of paper to wall. Place several markers on the floor near the paper. Place old church bulletins and newsletters on a table across the room from large sheet of paper.

2. Students gather near table. **Let's find out some of the reasons people come together at our church.** Students quickly look through old church bulletins and newsletters to find announcements of different activities (meetings, prayer groups, English classes, feeding the poor, parties, choir practices, dinners, etc.).

3. When a student finds an activity, he or she runs to the paper on the wall and writes the activity on the paper. Encourage students to find as many activities as possible. After a few minutes, call time.

4. Students take turns choosing an activity. Ask the questions below.

■ **How does this activity help people?**

■ **What might people like about this activity?**

■ **Why do you think our church has this activity?**

■ **What is another activity you would like to see added? Why?**

■ **Why do you think visitors come to our church?**

5. Conclude the activity by saying,

■ **People come to church to do many different things.**

■ **Let's compare what the people in our church family do together with what people in Bible times did when they met together.**

Bonus Idea

Print out information about church activities from your church website.

The Message

Come together in God's love.

The Bible Basis

Matthew 21:12-16

After Jesus drove out the money changers in the Temple, He healed the blind and the lame.

The Scripture

"Jesus said, 'My house will be called a house of prayer,' but you are making it a 'den of robbers.'"
Matthew 21:13

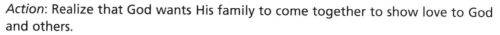

Get It Together ■ 20-30 minutes

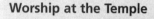

Action: Realize that God wants His family to come together to show love to God and others.

Matthew 21:12-16

What You Need

Bibles.

What You Do

Lead students to read and discuss the Bible verses listed. Extend the discussion with the questions and comments provided.

Introduction

What is your favorite place at our church? What are some other areas in our church where different activities take place?

Worship at the Temple

■ Where do people meet for worship in our church? For prayer? Who usually leads the people in our church in these activities?

■ What do people give as offerings to God in our church? Why do they give to God?

■ In Bible times, why do you think people came to the Temple? How might worship at the Temple have been different from what we do at our church?

The Temple had different areas for different activities. One courtyard of the Temple was available for anyone to come in and pray to God. In other Temple courtyards, priests would lead groups in prayer or special worship services. Teachers of the Law and other men would gather in groups to discuss what the Scriptures meant. Other Temple areas could be entered only by men or by healthy Israelites or by priests.

To the Bible-times Israelites, an important part of worshiping God was bringing special gifts and offerings to give to God. The animals that people brought as gifts were always healthy, perfect animals from their flocks. People who traveled from a long distance away or who were too poor to own their own flocks usually bought animals in Jerusalem to give as offerings.

Trouble at the Temple

■ What do you remember about the day that we call Palm Sunday?

■ But when Jesus arrived in Jerusalem and went to the Temple, what did He see? What did He do? Read Matthew 21:12 to find out.

■ How would you describe Jesus' feelings?

■ Read Matthew 21:13 to find out what Jesus said about what was happening.

On Palm Sunday, Jesus rode a donkey into Jerusalem and went to the Temple with a parade of happy, shouting and singing people. We celebrate this day every year.

When Jesus arrived at the Temple, He saw that some of the things going on in the Temple were NOT good!

First, there were money changers. In addition to giving gifts, the Israelites paid a Temple tax of one half-shekel—the amount of money most people would make for two to three days' work. This money helped pay to keep the Temple in good repair. But the problem was that only certain coins made of pure metal were considered good enough for the Temple tax. If a person arrived with the wrong coins, he or she had to exchange his or her coins for the right kind of coins. To make this exchange, the money changers charged one fee to exchange the money and an ADDITIONAL fee just for giving change!

THEN there were animal sellers. Historians believe inspectors inside the Temple decided whether or not an animal was good enough to be a gift to God. Frequently, if the animal hadn't been purchased inside the Temple, the inspectors wouldn't OK the animal. And animals for sale inside the Temple were often EXTRA expensive. There was a whole lot of cheating going on, right in God's Temple!

All this greedy money changing and animal selling caused a lot of arguing and shouting to be going on in the only place where Gentiles and sick people could come to worship God and pray!

When Jesus saw the money changers and animal sellers in God's Temple making money for themselves by taking advantage of others, He was ANGRY! His anger showed by His actions of knocking over the money changers' and sellers' tables and benches! Those people must have been very shocked!

Jesus said that the money changers and animal sellers had made God's house a place where people were cheated—a "den of robbers"—instead of a "house of prayer." Jesus was actually quoting an Old Testament verse—Isaiah 56:7—that talked about God's house as a place of prayer.

God's People at the Temple

■ After He'd cleared away the money changers and animal sellers, what did Jesus do that showed how people SHOULD treat each other in God's Temple? Read Matthew 21:14 to find out.

■ Many people and children had followed Jesus into Jerusalem. How do you think they felt about what Jesus had done? What did the children do? What did the Pharisees think of all this? Read Matthew 21:15 for some clues.

■ How did Jesus respond to the Pharisees? Read Matthew 21:16 to find out.

Jesus showed God's love by healing the lame and the blind. The lame and blind were people who really needed help! They had probably been ignored by the money changers and animal sellers.

The children were singing songs of praise to Jesus, but the Pharisees weren't pleased with what Jesus had done or with how the children were responding!

The children seemed to be the only ones who understood Jesus' actions. By His actions, Jesus was telling everyone that HE is the Son of God, the Messiah, the one to whom the Temple really belonged. It was right for the children to sing HIS praises in His Temple! Praising Jesus was something God's people should do!

Conclusion

Jesus wanted people to know that when they gathered in God's house, they were to love and care for each other. They were not there to cheat each other! Instead they should help each other, pray for each other and worship God. (Read Matthew 21:13 aloud.)

Each of you may be here today for a different reason. You may like to see your friends, you may want to learn more about God and His love for you, you might like to play games and have snacks, or you come because your parents make you come. Whatever your reason, though, God is glad you are here. He wants all of His family to feel loved and cared for when they meet together. Whether we meet in a classroom, outdoors or in a house, we can worship God in ways that show love for Him and others. We can pray for each other and help each other in many ways. (Lead students in praying, and asking God to help them show His love to their church family.)

Get Going ■ 20-30 minutes

Action: Plan ways to show love for God and others when we come together as God's family.

Distribute Get Real (p. 112) to students. Invite students to tell or write answers to the questions. End the discussion by completing Get Connected with students. (Optional: Students complete page at home.)

GET REAL

- Why do you think we have a church? How does coming to our church show love to God? How does it show love to others?

- What can you do to show love to God when you meet with God's family? What can you do to show love to other people?

- How can you help to welcome someone to our church family?

- Which activities of our church help people show love to God? To others?

- Who are some of the people at our church for whom you can pray?

Get to Know

"Jesus said, 'My house will be called a house of prayer,' but you are making it a 'den of robbers.'"
Matthew 21:13

Get Connected

What is a way in which you already show love for God and others at church? What is a new way in which you can start showing love for God? Ask God for help in completing your plans to show love.

One Spirit

Get Started ■ 5-15 minutes

Action: Discover ways to accomplish tasks as a team.

Together Feats

What You Need

Rope, measuring stick.

What You Do

1. Students work together to accomplish one or both of the feats described below.

■ Long, Long Jump: Students line up facing the same direction. First student in line jumps as far as he or she can. Next student in line moves to the spot where first student landed and then jumps. Continue until all students have added to the long jump. Measure the total distance. Repeat activity to see if students can extend the distance.

■ Tug-of-Peace: Students sit in a circle. Tie a strong rope into one loop, allowing approximately 1 foot (30 cm) of rope length for each student. Students grab the rope at the same time and raise themselves to a standing position by pulling back on the rope. (If everyone works together, the group should be able to stand up simultaneously.)

2. Ask the questions below.

■ **What kinds of tasks are easier to do with someone else than by yourself?**

■ **How can we help each other to make difficult tasks easier?**

3. Conclude the activity by saying,

■ **In our Bible study today, we are going to find out what happened when many people worked together to accomplish something.**

Bonus Idea

Have students experiment with having one student not try very hard to accomplish the task. Compare the results with times when everyone worked together.

The Message

As God's family, be united in love for God and others.

The Bible Basis

Acts 1:4-5; 2

The believers in the first church showed their love for God and each other, and as a result many people believed in Jesus.

The Scripture

"Now you are the body of Christ, and each one of you is a part of it."
1 Corinthians 12:27

Get It Together ■ 20-30 minutes

Action: Understand that God wants Christians to worship Him and treat each other in ways that demonstrate His love.

Acts 1:4-5; 2

What You Need

Bibles.

What You Do

Lead students to read and discuss the Bible verses listed. Extend the discussion with the questions and comments provided.

Introduction

What are some big events you have been to? How many people were there? In our Bible story today, a big event had brought many people from all over the Roman Empire to Jerusalem.

The Day of Pentecost

■ Read Acts 2:1 to find out the name of this special event.

■ Read Acts 1:4-5 to find out why Jesus' disciples were together in Jerusalem.

■ What happened that made this day so important? Read Acts 2:2-3 to find out.

Pentecost is a Greek word that means "fiftieth." It was a holiday that celebrated the fiftieth day after Passover (the time when the Jews remembered how God helped them escape from slavery in Egypt). At Pentecost the people gave thanks to God for helping their crops to grow. Pentecost was one of the important holidays that every Jewish male over 13 years old tried his best to travel to Jerusalem to be a part of.

Jesus' disciples were there too, gathered together in one house. Every day since Jesus had ascended to heaven, they had met together to pray.

On this special day, the promise of God's gift came true. Suddenly, the sound of a mighty heaven-sent wind filled up the room! (In Bible times, wind was a symbol of God's presence. In fact, the Hebrew and Greek words for wind also mean "spirit.")

The Holy Spirit

■ Read Acts 2:4 to find out what happened after the flames of fire came to rest above each person.

■ Read Acts 2:5-8 to find out why people crowded around and what the people in the crowd were thinking.

■ If you had seen these events, what would have surprised you the most?

■ Find out what some of the people thought in Acts 2:13.

■ In verse 14, who stood up to preach to the crowd and explain what had happened?

While this wind of God poured through the room, what seemed like small flames of fire came to rest above each person! The Holy Spirit had come at last—just as Jesus had promised! Imagine the excitement and noise of Jesus' followers all speaking in different languages! It was a miracle!

Because of all the excitement, a curious crowd gathered, running from many directions to see what was happening! The people were amazed to hear the disciples. "How is it they are speaking in my own language?" each one asked.

Others who didn't understand what was going on laughed and said, "These people have had too much wine! They're drunk! And so early! It's only nine o'clock in the morning!"

The Holy Spirit gave Peter power and boldness to explain what had really happened. Peter told everyone that what had happened was predicted by the prophet Joel hundreds of years ago! (See Joel 2:28-29.) Then Peter quoted familiar passages from the Old Testament to explain that Jesus, who had been crucified and had risen again, was the Messiah—the Savior God had promised to send. He explained that what they were seeing and hearing, from the sound of the mighty wind to the miraculous languages, was evidence of God's promised gift, the Holy Spirit.

The New Believers

■ When the people heard Peter's preaching and asked him what they should do, read Peter's answer in Acts 2:38.

■ Read Acts 2:41 to find out how many people chose to accept Peter's message and be baptized that day.

■ Read Acts 2:42-47. How would you describe the first church? What were they like? What did they do?

The same Holy Spirit caused many people in the crowd to be deeply sorry that Jesus had been killed and that they had not believed in Him. They cried out to Peter, "What shall we do?"

Peter made it clear that anyone—a person listening in the crowd that day or a person like you and me reading these words today in the Bible—who is sorry for his or her sins can be forgiven and receive God's gift of the Holy Spirit.

On that very day, many people did exactly what Peter told them they needed to do! They were baptized to show that they were now followers of Jesus!

This group of Jesus' followers and new believers began meeting together every day. They wanted to show their love for God and for each other. Knowing Jesus as God's Son and receiving God's gift of the Holy Spirit resulted in a BIG group of people who lived and worked together for one purpose: to love God with all they had and to love others as much as they loved themselves.

God had made it possible for people from all over the known world to become just like a family! As a result of their love for God and each other, the Bible says that every day new people heard about Jesus and chose to believe in Him and become a part of the Church, God's family.

Conclusion

This description of the first church family is a good picture of the ways in which God wants His followers to love Him and each other.

We're part of a church family, too. (Read 1 Corinthians 12:27 aloud.) The reason we come together is because we want to show our love for God and learn more about Him. The first step in showing love for God is accepting His love for us and believing that Jesus, His Son, died to take the punishment for our sins. Then when we come together with other believers, we praise and thank God for His love and forgiveness. When we're together, we can pass His love on to others in our church family—and to others who don't know about God yet—by treating them in caring, loving ways. (Pray with students and then allow time for students to talk with you about becoming Christians. Follow the guidelines in the "Leading a Student to Christ" article on pp. 10-11.)

Get Going ■ 20-30 minutes

Action: Identify how we show our love for God in the ways we worship Him and treat others in our church family.

Distribute Get Real (p. 116) to students. Invite students to tell or write answers to the questions. End the discussion by completing Get Connected with students. (Optional: Students complete page at home.)

GET REAL

■ What are some ways our church family shows our love for God?

■ Why do you think it's important for a church family to show love for God in the way we treat each other? What might keep someone from showing God's love to another person?

■ How has someone in our church family shown God's love to you?

■ How could someone your age show God's love to someone younger at church? An elderly person?

■ What are some things that make it hard to show God's love to others at church?

Get to Know

"Now you are the body of Christ, and each one of you is a part of it."
1 Corinthians 12:27

Get Connected

Think about what you can do at church to show love for God and for others. Ask God to help you show love for Him during the week.

Accept Each Other

Get Started ▪ 5-15 minutes

Action: Compare and contrast the ways kids treat each other.

Better or Worse?

What You Need

Large bag containing several items students use (ball, CD, T-shirt, shoe, lunch bag, candy bar, book, skateboard, squirt gun, video game, etc.).

What You Do

1. Students sit in a circle. Volunteer takes an item from the prop bag and uses the selected item in a made-up story about a problem a kid might have. ("Joshua got hit in the face by the ball.")

2. Student passes the item to the person to the left (or a volunteer in the circle) who continues with a reason for the problem. ("Joshua got hit in the face by the ball because Mike accidentally threw the ball too hard.")

3. Student passes the item to the next student, who tells something that might make the problem worse. ("Joshua yelled at Mike and shoved him.")

4. Then invite several students to tell what kids might say or do that would make the situation better. ("Sorry, I didn't mean to hit you.") Ask the questions below.

▪ **What do you think would happen in this situation if both friends spoke and acted kindly? If both spoke and acted unkindly?**

▪ **What do you think you would do in this situation? Why?**

5. Repeat activity, giving each student the opportunity to take an item and begin a story.

6. Conclude the activity by saying,

▪ **There are many different ways we can treat each other.**

▪ **Let's find out how Barnabas, a man in the Bible, chose to treat a man many people did not like.**

Bonus Idea

Students use blank sheets of paper to draw scenes from made-up stories about problems kids might have with items from the prop bag.

The Message

Encourage and build up God's family.

The Bible Basis

Acts 8:3; 9:1-31

Barnabas welcomed Saul to the church in Jerusalem and defended Saul to the church leaders, even though Saul had persecuted the church.

The Scripture

"Accept one another, then, just as Christ accepted you, in order to bring praise to God."
Romans 15:7

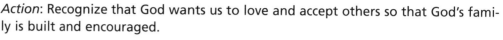

Get It Together ■ 20-30 minutes

Action: Recognize that God wants us to love and accept others so that God's family is built and encouraged.

Acts 8:3; 9:1-31

What You Need

Bibles.

What You Do

Lead students to read and discuss the Bible verses listed. Extend the discussion with the questions and comments provided.

Introduction

What would you think if a friend of yours started saying good things about a person you knew had done a lot of bad stuff? Well, something like that happened in the Early Church in Jerusalem.

Jesus' followers knew some pretty bad stuff about a man named Saul—not the King Saul who lived in Old Testament times. This Saul lived much later, after Jesus had lived on Earth, and Saul had definitely done some wrong things. But suddenly, a man named Barnabas started saying GOOD things about Saul.

Barnabas was a highly respected leader of the Early Church. He had a great reputation and was known for his generosity and helpfulness. His real name was Joseph, but he was such a good person to be around that the other believers named him "Barnabas," which means "The Encourager!"

Saul had a very different reputation from Barnabas! Barnabas must have thought very carefully before he began saying good things about Saul. Let's look at some of the things Barnabas must have considered.

Saul Persecutes the Christians

■ Read Acts 8:3 to discover something Saul was known for doing.

■ But that wasn't all Saul did! Read Acts 9:1-2 to find out Saul's next step.

Saul was a Pharisee who really, REALLY didn't like the followers of Jesus. Saul wanted to make sure that anyone who followed Jesus was severely punished. So Saul persecuted the believers in Jerusalem.

Saul set off for Damascus with letters from the high priest that would authorize him to arrest anyone who followed Jesus in Damascus and take them back to Jerusalem. But something happened on the road to Damascus!

Saul Believes

■ What do you remember about what happened to Saul when he was traveling to Damascus? Read Acts 9:3-9.

■ Read Acts 9:10-18 to see how Saul responded and what God did to help him.

■ What did the believers in Damascus think about Saul's change? Read Acts 9:21 to find out.

Just before he reached Damascus, Saul had a vision that convinced him that Jesus really is God's Son.

Saul was definitely different now! Instead of arresting followers of Jesus, Saul began preaching that people should become Jesus' followers! Saul was away from Jerusalem for three years. The believers in Jerusalem were probably relieved! There must have been rumors during those years about what Saul was doing. But nobody knew if those rumors were true; probably very few people believed them.

Then, one day, the believers in Jerusalem heard that Saul was BACK. Now, however, Saul was claiming that he was one of them—a believer and a follower of Jesus!

- How might the believers in Jerusalem have felt when they discovered Saul was back?

- How would you have acted toward Saul? Read Acts 9:26 to find out how the believers acted toward Saul.

The believers remembered hiding from Saul before, when he was a Pharisee. They thought Saul was just pretending to be one of them so that he could find out who they were. They were afraid he would have them all arrested. So they would have nothing to do with Saul!

It must have been difficult for Saul. He had been preaching that Jesus is God's Son, excited to be a follower of Jesus, and no one would believe him—except one person.

Barnabas Welcomes Saul

- Read Acts 9:27 to find out who was the first person to welcome and accept Saul.

- Why might Barnabas have decided to do this?

- How do Barnabas's actions compare to what most kids your age would probably do?

- Read Acts 9:31 to find out what happened to the Early Church after the events in Saul and Barnabas's lives.

Barnabas listened to Saul's amazing story of how Jesus had changed him. And now Barnabas had to choose: Would he continue to be suspicious of Saul and warn the other believers about him? Or would he use his influence—and his words—to help other believers accept Saul?

Barnabas, this highly respected leader in the Early Church, became the friend of Saul, a man who had been an enemy of the believers!

Barnabas took Saul to meet the other believers. He introduced Saul as his FRIEND! He told others about what had happened to Saul. And Barnabas told them the wonderful things Saul had preached about Jesus. Barnabas knew that even though Saul had done bad things, Jesus loved Saul. Jesus had forgiven Saul. And if Jesus loved and forgave Saul, then Barnabas knew he could, too.

Even if Jesus' followers in Jerusalem didn't trust Saul, they trusted and respected Barnabas a great deal. Because of what Barnabas said and did, they accepted and trusted Saul.

The Bible tells us that after these events, the Church grew and became stronger. Saul, who we also know by his Greek name, Paul, later helped many other people come to believe in Jesus. Paul and Barnabas became close friends and traveled to many cities, spreading the good news about Jesus.

Conclusion

Barnabas could have refused to even SPEAK to Saul. But Barnabas's positive words about Saul and the way he accepted Saul made a big difference in the Early Church. Some of the people at church may be your best friends. Others you might not really like, or you may not know them very well. But the way we treat each other at church can help God's family grow. Since Jesus has loved and accepted us, we can show that same love and acceptance to others. (Read Romans 15:7 aloud.) When people see the good way we treat others, they see how great and wonderful God is. (Pray briefly with students, asking God's help in accepting others in the church.)

Get Going ■ 20-30 minutes

Action: Evaluate the ways in which we show love and acceptance to others at church.

Distribute Get Real (p. 120) to students. Invite students to tell or write answers to the questions. End the discussion by completing Get Connected with students. (Optional: Students complete page at home.)

GET REAL

■ How can you show that you care about the needs and interests of other kids at church?

■ What kinds of things would you say and do if you were trying to obey God and show friendship or acceptance to someone? What kinds of things would you not say or do?

■ Think of someone you know who has a reputation for being kind to others. What does that person say about other people? What does that person do?

■ Do your friends think of you as a person who usually makes fun of others, or as someone who says good things about people? Why?

■ What can you do to remember to treat others in ways that help build them up and encourage them?

Get to Know

"Accept one another, then, just as Christ accepted you, in order to bring praise to God." Romans 15:7

Get Connected

What is one way you can follow Barnabas's example and show that you care for someone in your church family? Thank God for His love and acceptance and ask His help in showing care to others, even when it's not easy.

The Only True God

The Message

Only God gives security.

The Bible Basis

1 Kings 16:29-33; 17:1; 18:7-46

God showed Himself to be the only true God by defeating Baal in a contest.

The Scripture

"I will meditate on all your works and consider all your mighty deeds. Your ways, O God, are holy. What god is so great as our God?"
Psalm 77:12-13

Get Started ■ 5-15 minutes

Action: Discover ways to tell if things are trustworthy.

Mystery Substances

What You Need

Resealable plastic bags, measuring spoons, substances for one or more of the experiment groups you choose.

What You Do

1. Put one or two tablespoons of each substance into separate bags. Seal the bags.

2. Without opening bags, students examine the substances from one or more of the following groups:

■ Group 1—water, white vinegar, flat lemon-lime soda

■ Group 2—vanilla extract, olive juice, soy sauce, coffee, flat cola drink

■ Group 3—cornstarch, salt, baking soda, flour, baking powder

3. For each group, students try to identify each substance. **What would be a trustworthy way to determine what each of these substances is?** (Touching, smelling and tasting each one.)

4. Lead students to experiment to determine what the substances are, inviting them to open the bags and touch, smell and then taste the different substances, telling their guesses after each test. Ask the questions below as students experiment with substances.

■ **Sometimes we can't prove things are true just by seeing them. What's an example of an object that you think is trustworthy? A person? An idea?**

■ **How can we find out if something or someone is true or trustworthy?**

■ **What does "trustworthy" mean?**

5. Conclude the activity by saying,

■ **Compare your ideas about how to tell if something is trustworthy with what a man in Bible times did.**

Bonus Idea

Bring in a variety of items for students to use in constructing bridges or other structures (interlocking blocks, a variety of recyclable items, wood scraps and wood glue, etc.). Students can test the trustworthiness of the structures they create.

Get It Together ■ 20-30 minutes

Action: Understand that because God is the only true God, His power, love and faithfulness are trustworthy.

1 Kings 16:29-33; 17:1; 18:7-46

What You Need

Bibles.

What You Do

Lead students to read and discuss the Bible verses listed. Extend the discussion with the questions and comments provided.

Introduction

What are some things people trust? In our study today we'll discover why God is trustworthy and how one person showed his trust in God.

King Ahab Disobeys God

■ Find out how the Bible describes King Ahab by reading 1 Kings 16:29-30,32-33. How would you describe King Ahab's actions?

■ Read 1 Kings 17:1 to find out what message Elijah had given to King Ahab because of his evil actions. How do you think Elijah felt when he gave this message to Ahab?

King Ahab worshiped Baal, even though he had been told by God's prophets that there was only ONE true God. King Ahab and his wife, Queen Jezebel, did not listen to God's prophets. Instead, they and many of the people in their kingdom worshiped Baal.

Baal was a god who supposedly controlled the sun and the rain so that crops would grow. We know that Baal was a false god. But the people of Israel did many awful things to try to please Baal, hoping he would make their crops grow.

For Bible-times people, the weather was VERY important. If they didn't get just the right amount of rain, their crops would die and there wouldn't be enough food.

God wanted the worship of this false god to end! So He stopped the rain for three years.

Elijah Meets Ahab

■ Read 1 Kings 18:1. What did God tell Elijah to do?

■ Find out how Ahab greeted Elijah in 1 Kings 18:17.

■ In verses 18-19, how did Elijah answer Ahab? What did he tell Ahab to do?

King Ahab blamed Elijah, God's prophet, for the lack of rain. In fact, Ahab was so angry he wanted to kill all of the prophets of God, including Elijah! So Elijah had been hiding from the king and queen. But when God told Elijah to meet Ahab, Elijah arranged with one of Ahab's servants to talk with Ahab.

Ahab wanted to blame his problems on Elijah, but Elijah explained that he hadn't brought these problems to Ahab's kingdom. The trouble had been caused by Ahab and his family.

Elijah challenged the prophets of Baal to a contest. Ahab commanded the prophets of Baal to come to Mount Carmel.

The Contest Begins

■ In 1 Kings 18:21, what did Elijah say to challenge the people? How did they answer?

■ How would Elijah prove which god was true and trustworthy? Read 1 Kings 18:23-24 to find out.

■ Read the Bible's description of the contest in 1 Kings 18:25-26. What was the result of the actions of Baal's prophets?

■ Read verse 27 to see what Elijah said to tease the prophets.

The Final Test

■ Read 1 Kings 18:33-35 to find out what Elijah did to end the contest.

■ Why do you think Elijah soaked the sacrifice?

■ What did Elijah pray and how did God answer his prayer? Read 1 Kings 36-38 to find out.

■ What would you have said and done if you had witnessed this contest? How did the people respond to what they had seen? Read 1 Kings 18:39 to find out.

On the specified day, Elijah met the 450 prophets of Baal. There must have been a great crowd of onlookers who were watching to see which God was the true God.

In Bible times it was the custom to offer an animal as a sacrifice. This animal was killed and then burned so that the smoke would go up into the heavens. Elijah said that he would offer a sacrifice to God and the prophets of Baal would offer a sacrifice to Baal.

Elijah must have had a sense of humor! But Elijah knew that the true God never sleeps and that He is always near. For most of the day, those prophets of Baal tried to get Baal to respond. But, of course, since Baal was a false god, he did not respond.

When it was Elijah's turn. Elijah prepared his sacrifice, and then he did a puzzling thing. It was all part of Elijah's plan to prove who was the one true God.

Elijah's prayer was short and to the point. He simply asked God to prove that He is the only true God who everyone should trust and follow.

The people immediately decided to follow the God Elijah had been talking about! As the first sign of their change of heart, the people got rid of all the prophets of Baal.

Elijah finished off this amazing day by telling King Ahab to hurry home because a big rainstorm was coming. And, sure enough, by the power of the only true and trustworthy God, after three years of drought, it began to rain.

Conclusion

In this contest, God proved that He is the only true God. God wants all people to understand that His power, love and faithfulness are trustworthy. Elijah did as Psalm 77:12-13 said. (Read verses aloud.) He knew that he could trust God completely and he knew that God was able to prove that He was the only true God.

People might depend on having lots of money, being good at sports or getting good grades, but none of these things can ALWAYS be counted on to help us. Only the love, power and faithfulness of God will always be there to give us security and help. We can always trust Him! (Pray with students, thanking God for His love, power and faithfulness.)

Get Going ■ 20-30 minutes

Action: Identify reasons to trust God, and tell ways to express trust in Him.

Distribute Get Real (p. 124) to students. Invite students to tell or write answers to the questions. End the discussion by completing Get Connected with students. (Optional: Students complete page at home.)

Get Real

- What are some things kids might depend on or trust in?

- Why might people think that having lots of money would give them security? Having lots of friends?

- If someone asked you to explain why it's important to trust God, what would you say?

- What are some things that God has done? How do His actions prove that He can be trusted?

- How can you show that you trust in God for your security?

Get to Know

"I will meditate on all your works and consider all your mighty deeds. Your ways, O God, are holy. What god is so great as our God?"
Psalm 77:12-13

Get Connected

How does trusting God make a difference in your actions—how you treat others, how you make decisions and how you spend your time? Talk to God about times you need to trust Him.

God's Faithfulness

Get Started ■ 5-15 minutes

Action: Discover some characteristics of God.

Stuff Toss

What You Need

Bibles, masking tape, index cards, marker, a variety of items to toss (Frisbee, sponge, foil ball, coin, marshmallow, beanbag, etc.).

What You Do

1. Make a large masking-tape grid on the floor as shown in sketch. Print each Bible reference on a separate index card: Genesis 12:2; 15:1; 15:5; 15:7; 17:4; 17:6; 17:7; 17:19; 18:10. Tape cards on grid, one card in each space.

2. Students stand several feet from grid. Place items to toss near students. First student chooses an item and then tosses it onto the grid. Student finds and reads the Bible verse on index card in the space the item landed on or near, identifying what the verse tells about God or the promise God made.

3. Students continue taking turns tossing items and telling promises until all verses have been read. Discuss information with students by asking the questions below.

■ **How would you feel if God made one of these promises to you?**

■ **What do these promises tell you about God?**

■ **What are some other things you know about what God is like?**

■ **Why might people today want to know about God and His promises?**

4. Conclude the activity by saying,

■ **We found some promises God made to a man named Abraham.**

■ **We're going to find out why it's important for us to know about these promises.**

Bonus Idea

If space is limited, make a small grid on a table. Students toss penny onto tabletop grid.

The **Message**

We can depend on God to be faithful and keep His promises.

The **Bible Basis**

Genesis 12:1-5; 15:1-7; 21:1-7

God kept His promises to lead Abraham to a new land and to give Abraham and Sarah a son.

The **Scripture**

"Your love, O Lord, reaches to the heavens, your faithfulness to the skies." Psalm 36:5

Get It Together ■ 20-30 minutes

Action: Recognize that God kept His promises in the past, and we can trust God to be faithful and keep His promises to us.

Genesis 12:1-5; 15:1-7; 21:1-7

What You Need

Bibles.

What You Do

Lead students to read and discuss the Bible verses listed. Extend the discussion with the questions and comments provided.

Introduction

What is the longest story you have read or heard? The Old Testament tells one long story: the story of the Israelites' relationship with God. It tells how they learned about Him and how God demonstrated His love for them. The Israelites were called the Chosen People because God chose them to share their knowledge of Him with the whole world. The Old Testament contains many promises that God made to these people. Let's discover why it is so important to know what God has promised to us and what He is like.

God's Call and Promise

■ Read Genesis 12:1-3 to find out what God told Abram to do.

■ What did God promise Abram?

■ What do you think God meant by saying that Abram would be a blessing?

Abram, later known as Abraham, his wife Sarai (sehr-I), later known as Sarah, their nephew, Lot, and ALL their relatives lived in the city of Ur. Ur was in the southern part of the country we now call Iraq, near the Persian Gulf. Ur was a great city with large two-story homes and harbors for boats that traveled down the nearby Euphrates River. Many people in Ur worshiped false gods.

In the midst of this ancient, busy civilization, the one true God spoke to Abram.

In Bible times, to have a great name meant that the person had many children and was the owner of a great deal of land.

A blessing is actions or words that show God's goodness and presence with people. This was an amazing promise! It meant that through Abram and his descendants, all people—including us today—would have the opportunity to know and love God.

Travel to a New Land

■ If you were told to move to a new home, what would you do? Read Genesis 12:4 to find out what Abraham did.

■ What do you know about traveling in Bible times?

■ How do you think it was different from traveling today?

■ Where did Abram and Sarai end their journey? Read Genesis 12:5.

Even though Abram didn't know where this new land was or exactly how to get to it, he and Sarai and all his family and servants packed up what they had and began to travel to this new land.

Abram and his family probably mostly walked, and they had to bring their herds of animals with them! That meant they had to travel along routes where food and water would be available for the herds.

Eventually, Abram, Sarai, their families, their servants AND their herds arrived in the land God had promised to give them. This land was called Canaan. Today this land is divided among the three countries of Lebanon, Jordan and Israel.

The Promise of a Child

■ Read Genesis 12:7 and 15:2-4. What promise had God made to Abram?

■ In verse 5, what did God tell Abram to look at as a reminder of His promise of a son?

■ If you had been Abram, would you have chosen to believe God's promise? Why or why not?

■ Read Genesis 15:6 to find what Abram chose to believe.

God had kept his promise to bring Abram and his family to a new land. And this land was exactly as God had promised—full of good things—and Abram grew wealthier in his new land. But he and Sarai still had no children. Abram must have wondered how God's promise that he would start a new nation would come true if he had no children—especially since Abram was over 75 years old, and Sarai was over 65 years old.

God explained that he would give Abram a son of his own and told him to look at the stars in the sky. Of course, no one can count how many stars are in the sky, but Abram must have been awestruck, looking up at the endless stretch of bright stars shining in the black night.

Abram must have found it difficult to believe he would have so many heirs. But Abram believed what God said—he trusted God to keep His promise.

The Promised Child

■ Years passed without Abram and Sarai having children. Read Genesis 17:5 and 17:15 to find what God changed their names to.

■ What did Abraham do in Genesis 17:17 when God changed their names and repeated His promise to give them a child?

■ Why would Abraham still believe that they would have the promised child?

■ Read Genesis 21:1-2 to find what God did. How are God and His actions described?

The name "Abraham" meant he would be the father of many people. The name "Sarah" means "princess." Her name showed that she would be the mother of kings and nations. These new names were a strong reminder of God's promises to Abram.

Even though Abraham could not understand how God would keep His promise of a child, God always keeps His promises.

Abraham and Sarah named their long-awaited son Isaac. And in the centuries that followed, just as God had promised, the descendants of Abraham and Sarah grew to be so many that they became the great nation of Israel. And the whole world has been blessed by this nation because God's Son, Jesus, was born in an Israelite family.

Conclusion

Just as God kept His promises to Abraham and Sarah, we can trust Him to keep His promises to us. Psalm 36:5 is a perfect description of God's love and faithfulness. (Read verse aloud.) No one but God is able to be entirely faithful and keep all His promises.

Our way of life and the situations, or circumstances, that we face each day may be very different from the lifestyle and circumstances of Abraham. But God's ability to keep His promises has not changed! Remembering the story of how God was faithful to Abraham can help us depend on God's faithfulness to us. (Lead students in prayer, thanking God for His faithfulness.)

Get Going ■ 20-30 minutes

Action: List and discuss circumstances in which we need to depend on God's faithfulness.

Distribute Get Real (p. 128) to students. Invite students to tell or write answers to the questions. End the discussion by completing Get Connected with students. (Optional: Students complete page at home.)

Get Real

■ If you have a problem and God does not solve it right away, what can you do to remember that God always keeps His promises?

■ How are God's promises different from the promises that other people make to us?

■ How does God show His faithfulness to people today?

■ When are some times kids your age need to depend on God? How do you think God might help a kid your age in these circumstances?

■ How is depending on God different from depending on a friend or a family member?

■ What are some actions that show you are depending on God and His promises?

Get to Know

"Your love, O Lord, reaches to the heavens, your faith- fulness to the skies."
Psalm 36:5

Get Connected

What are some situations you might face this week when you will need to depend on God's faithfulness? Talk to God about these situations and ask His help in depending on Him to keep His promises of love and help to you.

Ever-Present Power

Get Started ▪ 5-15 minutes

Action: Discover ways people act when facing problems.

Foil Toss

What You Need

Aluminum foil, marble.

What You Do

1. Loosely wrap several sheets of foil around a marble to make a foil ball. Make two additional foil balls without marbles to form a set of three.

2. Students stand in a circle. Students toss foil balls to each other in a random pattern. When you call "stop," students holding foil balls open up the balls to find the one with the marble.

3. Student who has the marble describes a problem a kid his or her age might face (not being invited to a friend's birthday party, knowing that someone cheated on a test, parents arguing, family member being sick, not having enough money to do what other kids are doing, having to move to a new school, etc.). Ask the questions below.

▪ **What might a kid do in this situation?**

▪ **What are some positive responses to this problem? Some negative responses?**

▪ **When has someone you know had a problem like this? What happened?**

▪ **What could you do to help a friend with a problem like this?**

▪ **What are some other ways you have seen people respond to problems?**

4. Remake balls and continue game as time allows.

5. Conclude the activity by saying,

▪ **Some people try to solve difficult problems all by themselves, forgetting to ask for help.**

▪ **Compare this way of handling problems by yourself with the actions of the people in our story today when they had a problem.**

Bonus Idea

Bring a children's music CD and player to class. Play music as students toss foil balls to each other. After 10 to 15 seconds, stop the music. Students open foil balls.

The Message

We can depend on God's compassion and power to help us.

The Bible Basis

Exodus 6—12:42

God showed compassion to His people and miraculously rescued them from slavery in Egypt.

The Scripture

"You are the God who performs miracles; you display your power among the peoples."

Psalm 77:14

Get It Together ■ 20-30 minutes

Action: Realize that almighty God helps us when we have problems because of His great love for us.

Exodus 6—12:42

What You Need

Bibles.

What You Do

Lead students to read and discuss the Bible verses listed. Extend the discussion with the questions and comments provided.

Introduction

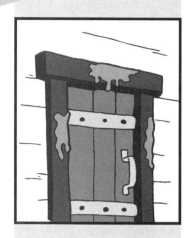

Have you ever seen someone who felt threatened by someone else? Why did that person feel threatened? The book of Exodus tells about a time the people of Israel, then called the Hebrews, were considered a threat.

At this time the Hebrews lived in the land of Egypt—a large and powerful country where the people worshiped false gods. The leader of Egypt, Pharaoh, had decided that the Hebrews were a threat to Egyptian national security because their numbers kept growing! So Pharaoh forced all the Hebrews to work for him as slaves.

For many years, Egyptian slave masters made the Hebrew's lives bitter as they forced the Hebrews to build cities for Pharaoh and work hard in the fields. But God had a plan to rescue the Hebrews. And to do it, He carefully prepared a man named Moses to lead His people.

God's Rescue Plan

■ Read Exodus 3:9-10 to find out what God's plan was. What did God tell Moses to do?

■ When Moses delivered God's message to Pharaoh in Exodus 5:1, what was Pharaoh's response in verse 2? Why did Pharaoh reject the message from God?

■ How did Pharaoh show his anger in Exodus 5:6-9?

■ How do you think the leaders of the Hebrews felt about Moses?

Even though Moses reported God's promise of deliverance to the Israelites, the people were so discouraged about the cruel way the Egyptians were treating them, they didn't even want to listen to Moses! But God still loved them and He didn't change His plan to rescue them from their difficult problem.

In order to teach the Egyptians about Himself and to rescue His people, God said He would send to Egypt disasters that would show He was much more powerful than anything they worshiped.

The first disaster or plague was to change the water in the Nile River to blood. The Nile River was so important to life in Egypt that people worshiped the river. God was showing He was more powerful than the river.

The plagues went on and on—frogs, gnats, flies, death of livestock, boils, hailstorms and locusts! Each time Pharaoh refused to recognize the power of the one true God.

God's Power

■ Read Exodus 6:6-8 to find out how was God promising to demonstrate His power and compassion for the Israelites.

■ What did God say He would do in Exodus 7:3-4 to rescue His people?

Even though Moses reported God's promise of deliverance to the Israelites, the people were so discouraged about the cruel way the Egyptians were treating them, they didn't even want to listen to Moses! But God still loved them and He didn't change His plan to rescue them from their difficult problem.

In order to teach the Egyptians about Himself and to rescue His people, God said He would send to Egypt disasters that would show He was much more powerful than anything they worshiped.

■ Read Exodus 7:20-21 to find out what the first disaster was.

The first disaster or plague was to change the water in the Nile River to blood. The Nile River was so important to life in Egypt that people worshiped the river. God was showing He was more powerful than the river.

The plagues went on and on—frogs, gnats, flies, death of livestock, boils, hail-storms and locusts! Each time Pharaoh refused to recognize the power of the one true God.

The Escape

■ Why do you think God didn't just force Pharaoh to do what He wanted? Read Exodus 9:15-16 to find out what God said.

■ Finally, Moses told the Hebrews what the last terrible disaster would be and he gave the Hebrews God's escape instructions. Read Exodus 12:21-23 to find out what Moses said.

■ Read what the Israelites did in verse 28. Why do you think the Hebrews were willing to follow the instructions of God that Moses spoke?

All through history, God's actions show us what He is like. His actions in the book of Exodus demonstrate how powerful and great God is.

The last and worst of all the plagues was that throughout the land of Egypt, the firstborn male was going to die—even Pharaoh's own child! Only in the Israelites' families would the firstborn males live. But even then Pharaoh would not listen to Moses' warning!

The Hebrews did just as God wanted them to do. They had seen God's power and wanted to worship and obey Him.

This final plague became known as the Passover—because death passed over the homes of the Hebrews—and the Hebrews left that very night for the new home that God had promised them.

Conclusion

At the beginning of this story the Hebrews felt as though their problems were like a big wall. They thought their problems were so big that even God could not help them. By the end of the story, however, the Hebrews not only had experienced God's power in freeing them from slavery, but they also had recognized that God loved them so much that He would help them with their problems.

Each of us faces problems every day. Some problems are easy to deal with, like what to wear or what sport team to sign up for. Other problems are more difficult, like telling your parents you forgot to do something important or admitting you have done something wrong. Still other problems may seem just too hard to face—having to move, or your family not having enough money. As we read the stories of the Old Testament, we learn over and over how God helped people with their problems—whether big or small. And we can know that because God loves us, He will use His power to help us with our problems—big or small just as Psalm 77:14 says. (Read verse aloud.) God may not always help us exactly the way we want, but we can have confidence that God will help us in the very best way. He gives us courage, He helps us know what to do, and He gives us people who care for us. (Pray with students, thanking God for His love and power.)

Get Going ■ 20-30 minutes

Action: Thank God for His compassion, and identify situations in which we need to depend on God's power to help us.

Distribute Get Real (p. 132) to students. Invite students to tell or write answers to the questions. End the discussion by completing **Get Connected** with students. (Optional: Students complete page at home.)

Get Real

- When are some times God has helped someone you know with a problem? What did God do to help?

- How can knowing about God's love and power reassure you when you have a difficult problem to face?

- Who has God provided in your life to help you know what to do in difficult situations?

- What are some problems that might seem overwhelming to a kid your age or might seem too hard to know what to do?

- What do you know about God that can give you confidence in facing difficult problems?

Get to Know

"You are the God who performs miracles; you display your power among the peoples."
Psalm 77:14

Get Connected

When do you need to depend on God's power and help? Talk to God about the times you need His help and thank Him for His love and power.

Everlasting Love

Get Started ■ 5-15 minutes

Action: Compare patience with impatience.

Post it!

What You Need

Construction paper, markers, tape, Post-it Notes.

What You Do

1. On separate sheets of construction paper, print the following sentence starters: "I don't like to wait for . . ."; "It makes me mad when . . ."; "Something I have to wait for every year is . . ."; "Something I don't mind waiting for is . . ." and "When I'm impatient, I . . ." Tape papers to walls around the room.

2. Give each student several Post-it Notes and a marker. Students walk around the room and, on Post-it Notes, write words or phrases to complete the sentence starters. Students attach notes to the appropriate sheets of construction paper.

3. After students have had time to write and attach notes, ask the questions below.

■ **When do you think it is hardest for kids your age to be patient? For adults? For little kids?**

■ **When is it easy to be patient?**

■ **Why do you think it is often hard to wait patiently?**

■ **How does a person act when he or she is waiting for something patiently? How do they act when they are waiting impatiently?**

4. Conclude the activity by saying,

■ **In our Bible study today, we are going to discover how God's patience is different from ours.**

Bonus Idea

Display a large sheet of paper in your classroom. Each student thinks of a time he or she needs to be patient and prints the idea on the paper. If idea is already on the paper, student must think of another idea. After each student has had a turn, read ideas aloud. Students vote on the time that is easiest to be patient and then on the time that is most difficult to be patient.

The  Message

We can depend on God to be slow to anger and rich in love.

The Bible Basis

Jeremiah 31:3,17; 36:1-32

God sent prophets to proclaim His patience and love and to turn His people away from their disobedience.

The Scripture

"The Lord is gracious and compassionate, slow to anger and rich in love."
Psalm 145:8

Get It Together ■ 20-30 minutes

Action: Understand that because of His patience and love for us, God continually offers forgiveness and help to obey Him.

Jeremiah 31:3,17; 36:1-32

What You Need

Bibles.

What You Do

Lead students to read and discuss the Bible verses listed. Extend the discussion with the questions and comments provided.

Introduction

What is something a friend convinced you to do? During Bible times, the Israelites had agreed to worship and love the one true God. Their neighbors worshiped a lot of false, or made-up, gods. God didn't want ANY of HIS people doing such things! But the Israelites were constantly turning away from God and doing things their own way—usually following the ways of their neighbors.

God's Prophets

■ When the Israelites disobeyed God, how do you think God reacted to their actions?

■ Why do you think the people kept going back to their disobedient actions?

■ What are the names of some of the prophets you remember?

Because of His great love, God was VERY patient with His people. God sent messengers called prophets to tell the Israelites to put God first and start obeying Him again. These prophets reminded the people that God had proved He was faithful in the past by leading Abraham to a new home and then later rescuing the people from Egypt. Sometimes after hearing a prophet's message from God, the people changed their ways for a little while, but before long they were back to doing wrong things.

Over hundreds of years, God sent prophets like Elijah, Elisha, Daniel and Isaiah to tell His messages to His people.

One of these prophets was Jeremiah. Jeremiah, like other prophets before him, had been telling the people that doing wrong things would bring BIG trouble. He warned them that God was going to let the Babylonians take them away from their homes. Instead of listening to Jeremiah, the people punished Jeremiah because they didn't like his message! But Jeremiah didn't stop prophesying. He knew God's words were important for the people to hear.

Jeremiah's Job

■ Read Jeremiah 36:1-3 to find out what God asked Jeremiah to do.

■ How do you think Jeremiah responded? Read verse 4 to find out. Why do you think Jeremiah was so willing to obey God?

■ If you were Jeremiah and Baruch, what would you have done with this book of God's warnings? Read Jeremiah 36:10 to find out what they did.

Jeremiah did what God wanted. He called for his secretary, Baruch, and dictated to him everything God had said. (In those days, only a few people knew how to read and write.) Once more Jeremiah told God's message that the people would suffer if they didn't start following God.

Because Jeremiah was no longer allowed to go to the Temple, Jeremiah sent Baruch to read the finished book aloud in front of everyone. So Baruch stood up in front of the Temple and loudly read the message God had sent.

■ Read Jeremiah 36:16-19 to find what the reaction was to the message. Why were Jeremiah and Baruch told to hide?

One man in the crowd understood the seriousness of Jeremiah's message. He ran and found the officials of the country and told them what he'd heard. When Baruch read the message to these officials, they were convinced the king needed to hear the message. But they must have been a little afraid of his reaction!

The King's Anger

■ Read Jeremiah 36:23-24 to find out how the king reacted when he heard God's message. Why do you think the king was so angry?

■ How would you have reacted to the king's actions if you were Jeremiah?

■ How do you think God responded? Read Jeremiah 36:27-28 to find out.

■ Read verse 32. What did Jeremiah do? How do you think he and Baruch felt about repeating their work over again? Why were they so determined to obey God?

■ Despite the people's disobedience, what was God's attitude toward them? Read Jeremiah 31:3,17 to find out.

The king was sitting by a nice warm fire in his palace when he listened to the reading of the scroll so it was easy to just burn up the scroll when he was angry. Even though the officials begged the king not to destroy the scroll, the king did! Then he sent out orders to arrest Jeremiah and Baruch.

It must have taken a lot of patience on Jeremiah's part to rewrite the entire book! But Jeremiah probably thought that if God could be patient, so could he.

Unfortunately, the people didn't listen to Jeremiah. So God kept His Word. God allowed the Babylonians to take the Israelites away from their homeland and force them to live in Babylon. How terrible that must have been for the Israelites! But it wasn't as if God had not warned them. Jeremiah was only one of many prophets to tell the people about what would happen if they did not listen to God and obey His commands.

Conclusion

Over and over, God forgave the Israelites for disobeying Him. Even when their sin resulted in terrible consequences, He never gave up on them. Psalm 145:8 tells us how God is gracious and slow to anger when we sin. (Read verse aloud.) The Old Testament stories about the Israelites help us learn that God is always faithful and ready to forgive us when we change our ways and ask for forgiveness. And we can trust God to always keep His Word!

There will always be times when we sin and disobey God. But even in the Old Testament times, God promised to send a Savior who would make it possible for all people to become God's children. Today, we know that Jesus is the Savior God sent. Jesus' death and resurrection took away the punishment for our sins and made it possible for us to receive God's love. When we sin, we can confess our sins to God and be confident that He will patiently forgive us. (Lead students in prayer, thanking God for His forgiveness. Then talk with interested students about becoming members of God's family, referring to "Leading a Student to Christ" on pp. 10-11.)

Get Going ■ 20-30 minutes

Action: Describe situations in which we have sinned and thank God for His offer of forgiveness.

Distribute Get Real (p. 136) to students. Invite students to tell or write answers to the questions. End the discussion by completing Get Connected with students. (Optional: Students complete page at home.)

Get Real

- Why does everyone need God's forgiveness?

- When is it hard for kids your age to obey God at school? At home? In your neighborhood?

- How does God help us know when we've disobeyed?

- When do kids your age need God's forgiveness?

- What can we do to make things right when we disobey?

- What can you say to God when you have done something wrong? What might you say or do to show that you are thankful for God's forgiveness?

Get to Know

"The Lord is gracious and compassionate, slow to anger and rich in love."
Psalm 145:8

Get Connected

Think about a time that you have not obeyed God. Remember that God promises to love and forgive you, even when you do wrong things. Ask God for His forgiveness and thank Him for His love.

Learn from Your Sin

Get Started ■ 5-15 minutes

Action: Discover ways people learn from mistakes.

Games to Learn By

What You Need

Paper, paper plates, straws.

What You Do

1. **What's something you can do now that at first you failed at or made lots of mistakes the first times you tried it?** Volunteers answer. Be ready to tell a personal example. **We're going to play some fun games today to find out how much we can learn from our mistakes.** Lead students to do one or more of the following activities:

■ Paper Airplane Flight: Fold paper to make paper airplanes, learning from their mistakes to make airplanes that will fly farther. Suggest students adjust the number and type of folds of their airplanes.

■ Paper-Plate Toss: Throw paper plates, trying different methods for throwing their plates the farthest. Suggest students experiment by throwing the plates faceup and facedown.

■ Straw Throw: Throw straws like javelins, trying to throw their straws the farthest. Suggest students adjust their throws by varying the angles at which they throw the straws.

2. As students play games, ask the questions below.

■ **What did you learn about how to make a paper airplane fly the farthest?**

■ **How did you learn the best way to throw the straws?**

■ **What might happen if you just kept throwing your straw or paper airplane in the same way?**

3. Conclude the activity by saying,

■ **Learning to serve and obey God is a lot more important than learning how to make a good paper airplane.**

■ **Just like we learned from our mistakes in these experiments, it's also possible to learn from the sinful mistakes we make in serving and obeying God.**

■ **Learning from our sinful mistakes is what we're talking about today.**

Bonus Idea

For each of the above games, have students compete to see who can fly an airplane the farthest, toss a paper plate the farthest and throw a straw the farthest. Award small prizes to all who compete.

The
Message

It's never too late to learn from your sin and serve God.

The
Bible Basis

Judges 16:4-31

Even after Samson failed as Israel's judge, God answered Samson's request for strength.

The
Scripture

"Have mercy on me, O God, according to your unfailing love; according to your great compassion blot out my transgressions. Wash away all my iniquity and cleanse me from my sin." Psalm 51:1-2

Get It Together ■ 20-30 minutes

Action: Understand that, despite our sin, God's love and help last forever.

Judges 16:4-31

What You Need

Bibles.

What You Do

Lead students to read and discuss the Bible verses listed. Extend the discussion with the questions and comments provided.

Introduction

What famous person do you and your friends talk about a lot? The Bible tells a story about a famous man who made some wrong choices in serving God. He chose to disobey God. The Bible calls that sin. We'll find out if he learned from his sin—and what WE can learn from his sin.

Samson's Secret Strength

■ What are some things you have heard about Samson?

Samson was a very famous man in his time. Samson was supposed to keep some special promises to God. He was not to eat anything made from grapes, he wasn't supposed to touch a dead body, and he was NEVER to cut his hair. This was because God had given Samson a special job to do. God wanted Samson to help the Israelites defeat the Philistines. God had made Samson incredibly strong to help him in this task.

The tales of Samson's strength were probably told far and wide—how he'd killed a lion with his bare hands and how he'd killed 1,000 Philistines with the jawbone of a donkey. The Philistines really, REALLY wanted to get rid of this strong man.

The Plot Against Samson

■ Read Judges 16:4-5 to find out who Samson loved. How did the Philistines want Delilah to help them get rid of Samson?

■ In verse 5, what did the Philistines offer to Delilah to show just how important it was for them to capture Samson?

■ Why do you think Delilah agreed to go along with the plot to capture Samson?

Samson was in love with a Philistine woman named Delilah. He thought she was so wonderful, he'd do just about anything for her. Delilah, on the other hand, was actually much more interested in Delilah than in anyone else. So, when the Philistine leaders came to her to discuss a plan they had, Delilah was willing to listen. They convinced her to help them set a trap for Samson.

Eleven hundred shekels of silver! That was a great deal of money. And if she received it from each of the leaders, Delilah would be a very, very wealthy woman. And all she had to do was help them capture Samson. Delilah agreed.

Delilah's Deception

■ How did Delilah get Samson to tell her his secret? Read Judges 16:8-17.

Once Delilah knew Samson's secret, it was easy for the Philistines to capture him. While Samson slept, they shaved off his seven braids of hair. Samson had disobeyed God one too many times. Samson's long hair was supposed to show his love and obedience to God.

■ Why did Samson finally tell the secret of his strength to someone who obviously wasn't trustworthy?

■ By his actions, who did Samson show he loved the most? Who was Samson supposed to love the most?

■ What was Samson's sinful mistake? Read Judges 16:20 to discover the consequences of his sin.

An Answered Prayer

■ Read Judges 16:22 to find what happened while Samson was in prison. What do you think Samson thought about while he was in prison?

■ At a great Philistine feast, read Judges 16:28 to find what Samson prayed to God.

■ Read Judges 16:29-30 to find out how God answered Samson's prayer.

Because Samson broke his promise to obey, God took his great strength away. When Samson saw that he was surrounded by Philistines, he was sure all he had to do was push them away. But with no strength, he was trapped!

The Philistines took him away, blinded him and then forced him to work in the prison mill, grinding grain into flour. Around and around Samson walked, day after day, pulling the large, circular grindstone over the grain.

It sounded like Samson's life was doomed to end in total failure! But God's love for Samson never stopped. The Bible doesn't say for sure, but perhaps during this time, Samson realized how he had failed as Israel's leader by disobeying God.

The Philistine rulers held a great feast in the temple to celebrate their false god, Dagon. Thousands of Philistines crowded into the temple and more crowded onto the roof. They drank lots of wine and then wanted to have some fun. So they called for Samson to come and entertain them. Maybe they wanted to see Samson perform some feats of strength. Or maybe they just wanted to make fun of this former leader of Israel.

When Samson pushed over the pillars, the roof and walls of the temple crashed down, killing all the Philistines in the temple, including ALL the rulers of the Philistine cities, and Samson himself.

By ridding the land of the Philistine rulers, Samson gave the people of Israel a chance to overcome the Philistines.

Conclusion

Samson's life was full of wrong actions. One result of his sin was the loss of his strength. And he also lost his sight. But God still loved Samson despite his sinful mistakes, and He heard Samson's prayer. Psalm 51:1-2 is an example of a prayer we can pray when we sin and need God's help just as Samson needed God's help. (Read verses aloud.) When Samson was ready to do what God wanted him to do, God returned Samson's special gift of strength. Samson gave up his life to put God's plan into action and help His people.

All of us fail and make wrong choices in serving God. Because of God's love and forgiveness, however, we can learn from what we've done wrong. If we ask Him, God will help us learn from our sinful mistakes and serve Him. (Pray with students, thanking God for His promise of forgiveness and help to learn from our mistakes and serve Him. Talk with interested students about becoming members of God's family, referring to "Leading a Student to Christ" on pp. 10-11.)

Get Going ■ 20-30 minutes

Action: Describe how we can serve God better by learning from our sinful mistakes.

Distribute Get Real (p.140) to students. Invite students to tell or write answers to the questions. End the discussion by completing Get Connected with students. (Optional: Students complete page at home.)

Get Real

- What are some things kids today could learn from Samson's mistake?

- When are some times that kids your age might choose to do wrong things? What are some better choices someone might make in situations like these?

- How do people usually feel after they have sinned?

- Why is it important to learn from our sinful actions?

- What can kids your age do to keep from sinning in the same ways over and over?

- What have you learned about ways you can serve God?

GET TO KNOW

"Have mercy on me, O God, according to your unfailing love; according to your great compassion blot out my transgressions. Wash away all my iniquity and cleanse me from my sin."
Psalm 51:1-2

Get Connected

Think about a time you have sinned. How did that sin keep you from serving God—loving and obeying Him? Pray and thank God for His helping you to learn from your sinful mistakes. Ask His help to continue to learn to serve Him better.

Make It Right

Get Started ■ 5-15 minutes

Action: Discover ways to make things right after doing wrong.

What's Wrong?

What You Need

A variety of classroom objects (pencil and pencil sharpener, books, trash can, posters, chairs, etc.), pencils, paper.

What You Do

1. Make 8 to 10 items in your classroom "wrong": books upside down on shelf, trash can upside down, posters sideways, chair on end, eraser end of pencil placed in sharpener, etc. You may also wear a sweater or coat that is buttoned wrong, wear two different earrings or shoes, etc.

2. Instruct students to find what's wrong in your classroom and silently write their observations on sheets of paper. After several minutes, group students together to discuss their observations. Ask, **How many wrong things did you find in our room?**

3. As students tell what they observed, volunteers may correct the wrong things. Then ask the questions below.

■ **It's pretty easy to make these wrong things right again. How easy is it to make right the wrong actions we do?**

■ **When are some times kids your age might fail to obey God?**

■ **What do you expect someone to do when he or she has wronged you in some way?**

■ **What does God expect you to do when you do something wrong? Is it hard or easy to do these things?**

4. Conclude the activity by saying,

■ **Making things right with people we've wronged is called restitution.**

■ **As we study about a man in Bible times who made right his wrong actions, think about whether it was hard or easy for him to make restitution.**

Bonus Idea

Bring a video camera. Invite a volunteer to play the role of a talk-show host and interview students, asking one or more of the above questions. Videotape the interview, and play the tape back for students to see.

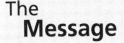

The Message

God wants us to make right the things we have done wrong.

The Bible Basis

Luke 19:1-10

Zacchaeus realized that following Jesus meant making right the things he had done wrong.

The Scripture

"Therefore, if anyone is in Christ, he is a new creation; the old has gone, the new has come!"
2 Corinthians 5:17

Get It Together ■ 20-30 minutes

Action: Realize that accepting God's love and forgiveness encourages us to make right what we have done wrong.

Luke 19:1-10

What You Need

Bibles.

What You Do

Lead students to read and discuss the Bible verses listed. Extend the discussion with the questions and comments provided.

Introduction

When have you not been able to see something because your view was blocked? In today's Bible story, Zacchaeus was a short man who wanted to see above the crowds who gathered around Jesus. Let's explore why Zacchaeus wanted to see Jesus.

Zacchaeus's Job

■ Read Luke 19:1-2. What do you learn about Zacchaeus in these verses?

■ What do you think the people around Zacchaeus felt or said about him?

Zacchaeus was a tax collector. Tax collectors were Jewish people who had agreed to work for the hated Romans by collecting money from the Jewish people to give to their Roman oppressors. To make matters worse, anything the tax collectors charged above the set tax amount, they got to keep for themselves as payment for their services. There was a suggested amount, but most tax collectors were in the position to collect more than what was fair without anybody knowing about it.

The Jewish people thought of tax collectors as robbers and traitors! Zacchaeus was not just ANY tax collector—he was a CHIEF tax collector. And he was probably rich enough to buy anything he wanted.

Zacchaeus's Plan

■ Read Luke 19:3-4 to find out why Zacchaeus could not see Jesus? What would you have done to get through the crowd if you were Zacchaeus?

■ What might the people have thought about Zacchaeus wanting to see Jesus?

Zacchaeus was so eager to see Jesus, he wouldn't let his size stop him. And he did not care if people thought badly about him. Seeing Jesus was all that mattered!

Jesus' Invitation

■ Read Luke 19:5-6. When Jesus saw Zacchaeus, what did He do and say that probably surprised Zacchaeus?

■ How did Zacchaeus respond to Jesus' words?

■ How does Luke 19:7 describe what the people in the crowd thought?

Zacchaeus was overwhelmed by the realization of Jesus' love. He probably had a hard time believing that Jesus wanted to come to his house—despite all the wrong things he had done.

The people called him a sinner and wondered why Zacchaeus, a man no one wanted to be around, was selected to host the most popular man in town! The people of the town were shocked! They probably thought that Jesus didn't KNOW about this man and that he didn't understand what an awful SINNER Zacchaeus was.

Zacchaeus's New Life

■ What did Jesus' love and forgiveness make Zacchaeus want to do? Read Luke 19:8.

■ What did Zacchaeus discover about Jesus that the crowd of people didn't know?

■ In Luke 19:9 what did Jesus say that showed He had forgiven Zacchaeus?

Zacchaeus was so grateful for Jesus' forgiveness that he wanted to repair the damage his sins had caused. Zacchaeus wanted to show by his actions that he was now a follower of Jesus!

Zaccaheus understood that Jesus was willing to forgive him for all his sins. Zacchaeus learned that to BE His follower, a person must ACT like His follower. Jesus explained that He had come to Earth to find people just like Zacchaeus and bring them into God's family.

Conclusion

Zacchaeus was so grateful for Jesus' acceptance and forgiveness that he decided to change his ways, even though it cost him something. To show his love and gratitude to Jesus, Zacchaeus promised to turn away from doing wrong and to put right what he had done wrong. Just as 2 Corinthians 5:17 tells us that we become a new creation when we follow Jesus, Zacchaeus made new choices when he decided to follow Jesus. (Read verse aloud.)

God's acceptance and forgiveness are for us, too. When we've done wrong, no matter how much others might dislike us or be mad at us because of our actions, God offers us forgiveness. Jesus' love for Zacchaeus caused Zacchaeus to make right his wrong actions. We can do that, too. Some of our sins and failures with others are easy to correct and make right. Some are not. But when we accept God's offer of love and forgiveness, we can show His love to others by doing our best to make right the situations in which we have sinned. (Pray with students, thanking God for His forgiveness when we ask Him. Then talk with interested students about becoming members of God's family, referring to "Leading a Student to Christ" on pp. 10-11.)

Get Going ■ 20-30 minutes

Action: Identify ways to make restitution for situations in which we have sinned.

Distribute Get Real (p. 144) to students. Invite students to tell or write answers to the questions. End the discussion by completing Get Connected with students. (Optional: Students complete page at home.)

Get Real

- What are situations in which kids your age fail to obey God and need God's forgiveness?

- How many different ways of making restitution can you think of?

- Is it always possible to make right the situations in which we've sinned? Why or why not?

- If you have done something wrong to someone recently, how might you make the situation right again, or make restitution?

GET TO KNOW

"Therefore, if anyone is in Christ, he is a new creation; the old has gone, the new has come!"
2 Corinthians 5:17

Get Connected

Think about a situation in which you can make restitution. Ask God to help you do this. Thank God that you can ask Him for forgiveness and that He promises to answer your prayer.

A Fresh Start

Get Started ■ 5-15 minutes

Action: Discover what it means to make a fresh start.

Clean It Up

What You Need

Water, measuring cup, several clear glasses, food coloring, bleach, rubber gloves, cookie sheet, spoon, white construction paper, eyedroppers, markers (nonpermanent), paper towels.

What You Do

1. Invite students to take turns participating in one or more of these experiments in which something with color is made clear. (Note: Carefully supervise students using bleach. Students wear rubber gloves when using bleach. Measure and pour bleach over a cookie sheet to catch any drips.)

■ Place one cup water in a clear glass and add three drops of blue food coloring. Add one-half cup of bleach. Stir and let stand. The water will become clear.

■ Place several drops of red food coloring onto white construction paper. Use eyedropper to place several drops of bleach onto the red food coloring. The red color will disappear.

■ Draw on white construction paper with markers. Use eyedropper to place several drops of bleach onto the drawing. Drawings will disappear.

2. As students work, comment,

■ **Using the bleach makes a dramatic difference in the color. It's an example of a way something with color or dirt can be made clean, or pure, again.**

■ **How would you define the word "pure"?**

■ **What other ways of making things clean can you think of?**

3. Conclude the activity by saying,

■ **The Bible tells us that our sins are like a bright red color. They are really, really obvious. When God forgives us, the result is that the sin disappears.**

■ **In our Bible story today, we'll find out why a man needed to make a fresh start and what happened to him.**

Bonus Idea

Students form pairs. Pairs brainstorm situations when a child their age may need a fresh start. Students tell situations to the class, or draw cartoons of the situation and the fresh-start solution.

The Message

God's forgiveness means I can make a fresh start.

The Bible Basis

Luke 22:33-34,54-62; John 21:1-19

Jesus' love helped Peter make a fresh start as the leader of the Church.

The Scripture

"The Lord our God is merciful and forgiving, even though we have rebelled against him." Daniel 9:9

Get It Together ■ 20-30 minutes

Action: Realize that because of God's love, He forgives us and helps us start over.

Luke 22:33-34,54-62; John 21:1-19

What You Need

Bibles.

What You Do

Lead students to read and discuss the Bible verses listed. Extend the discussion with the questions and comments provided.

Introduction

What would you think if one of your best friends pretended not to know you? That is what one of Jesus' closest disciples, Peter, did. Let's find out how Jesus helped Peter make a fresh start after he told some lies.

Peter's Friendship with Jesus

■ What are some things you know about Peter?

■ What might you promise to do for a friend to show them know how much you cared about them? Read Luke 22:33 to see what Peter promised Jesus.

■ What did Jesus say about Peter in Luke 22:34? How do you think Peter felt when He heard Jesus' words?

Peter was one of Jesus' closest friends. Most people would say that Peter was very loyal. Peter was the first disciple to say that Jesus was the Messiah, God's Son. And it was obvious Peter loved Jesus very much.

Peter made this promise to Jesus toward the end of Jesus' life on Earth. Jesus had gathered His disciples around Him to celebrate the Passover. The Passover is an important feast celebrated by Jews every year as a reminder that God freed them from slavery in Egypt. In their conversation after the Passover feast, Peter said that he would NEVER deny Jesus, no matter what!

Jesus' prediction about Peter must have surprised everyone!

Peter's Denial

■ What happened after Jesus' arrest to make Jesus' prediction come true? Read Luke 22:54-60 to find out.

■ Why do you think Peter said he didn't know Jesus? When might kids your age be afraid to admit they're followers of Jesus?

■ In Luke 22:61-62, how does the Bible describe the interaction between Jesus and Peter?

■ What do you think Jesus was thinking about when He looked at Peter? How would you have felt if you were Peter?

Peter probably couldn't believe it had all happened so fast! The disciples and Jesus had been in a garden when soldiers had arrested Jesus and taken Him to a building in Jerusalem to be falsely accused of crimes that would lead to His death.

Because of his fear, Peter had denied three times that he knew Jesus and was His follower. And the last time he denied Jesus, Jesus was right there in the courtyard. Jesus was probably on the way to see Pilate.

Peter was no longer proud of himself as a close friend of Jesus. He was ashamed of himself as someone who had let Jesus down. Peter ran from the courtyard and cried.

Jesus' Love for Peter

■ If this story was all we knew about Peter's friendship with Jesus, it would be very

This story takes place after Jesus died on the cross and came back to life. Peter and some of the disciples had spent the night fishing, but they hadn't caught anything.

sad. But read in John 21:1 about a time Peter and Jesus saw each other. Where were they?

■ Read in John 21:3-6 about the surprising thing that happened to Peter and the other disciples.

■ Read John 21:7. Who was the man on shore? How do you think Peter felt about seeing Jesus again? What did Peter know about Jesus?

In the early morning, a man on shore talked to them and told them what to do to catch fish. Then they caught so many fish, they couldn't haul them all into their boat!

When Peter realized that Jesus was the man on the shore, he was so excited he jumped into the water because he was in such a hurry to see Jesus. Peter not only knew that Jesus had come back to life, but that Jesus loved him—no matter what.

A New Beginning for Peter

■ After Jesus, Peter and the other disciples had eaten breakfast together, Jesus asked Peter a question. Read John 21:15 to find the question and Peter's answer.

■ What did Jesus mean by saying "more than these"? What did Jesus mean by saying "Feed my lambs"?

■ Look at verses 16 and 17 to find how many times Jesus asked Peter the same question. Why might Jesus have asked the question three times?

■ What was the last instruction Jesus gave to Peter in John 21:19?

Jesus may have been asking if Peter loved Jesus more than the other disciples did, or Jesus may have been asking if Peter loved Jesus more than he loved fishing. When Jesus said, "Feed my lambs," He meant that Peter was to teach people the truth about who Jesus is and what He did.

Peter had said three times that he didn't know Jesus. Now Jesus was showing that He forgave Peter and was giving Peter the opportunity to express his love for Jesus three times.

"Follow Me"—these were some of the first words Jesus had spoken to Peter. Jesus had asked Peter to leave his fishing business and to follow Him. Now, Jesus was giving Peter a chance to start all over. "Follow Me," Jesus said, and Peter did. Peter became one of the leaders of the Early Church.

Conclusion

Peter may have thought that his failure would prevent him from being a leader in Jesus' Church. But Jesus loved Peter very much. Jesus helped Peter make a fresh start and gave him the job of being a leader in the Church.

Just as Jesus loved Peter and helped him make a fresh start, Jesus will help us start over when we have failed by disobeying God. That's the awesome promise we read in Daniel 9:9. (Read verse aloud.)

It's fun to think about what it would be like to completely start our lives over with new names, new friends and new places to live. We can't ever really do that, but God promises us that when we've failed by sinning and disobeying Him, He will help us start over with new actions and attitudes (see 2 Corinthians 5:17). When we ask for and receive God's forgiveness, He helps us love and obey Him. (Pray with students, thanking God for His forgiveness.)

Get Going ■ 20-30 minutes

Action: Ask for God's forgiveness, and plan ways to make a fresh start by obeying Him.

Distribute Get Real (p. 148) to students. Invite students to tell or write answers to the questions. End the discussion by completing Get Connected with students. (Optional: Students complete page at home.)

Get Real

■ What can we remember about God that will help us make a fresh start after we've done wrong?

■ What are some words or phrases that describe God's love and forgiveness? What are the results of God's forgiveness?

■ What are some situations in school in which kids your age might need to make a fresh start? At home? In a neighborhood? In a friendship?

■ What might make it hard to make a fresh start?

■ How can you help someone who is trying to make a fresh start?

■ What is something you need to ask God's forgiveness for?

GET TO KNOW

"The Lord our God is merciful and forgiving, even though we have rebelled against him."
Daniel 9:9

Get Connected

Take a moment to think about one way you need to ask God for forgiveness and then make a fresh start today. Ask God for strength to follow Him, and thank Him for Jesus, who helps you make a fresh start.

Trust in God

Get Started ■ 5-15 minutes

Action: Discover difficult situations that kids face.

Refuge Acrostic

What You Need

Paper, markers, children's music CD and player.

What You Do

1. Print the word "refuge" vertically down the middle of several sheets of paper. Print "protection" down the middle of other sheets of paper, making at least one paper for each student.

2. Give each student one of the papers you prepared and a marker. **When is a time kids your age might feel they need God's help and protection at school? In the neighborhood? On the school bus? At a soccer game?**

3. Students sit in a circle. Each student writes a situation that might seem difficult to kids, connecting the words to the letters already on the page (see sketch).

4. After several moments, begin playing music. Students pass papers around the circle as the music plays. When you stop the music, each student quickly writes another situation on the paper he or she is holding, continuing to connect the words to the letters already on the page. Repeat several times, giving students the opportunity to write a variety of situations on different papers.

5. Ask the following questions to lead students in discussing the words:

■ **What are some other words for "refuge"?**

■ **How do you think people feel when they don't have a refuge or someone to help them in a tough situation?**

■ **What are some news headlines or movies that might make people feel worried or hopeless? Why?**

■ **What are some other things that might make a kid your age feel worried?**

6. Invite students to tell what they wrote and why. Conclude the activity by saying,

■ **There are always going to be times when people feel that things are difficult, or even hopeless.**

■ **In our Bible study today, we'll find out how God helped someone in situations that seemed hopeless.**

Bonus Idea

To help students think of words for the acrostics, invite them to find and read definitions of the words "refuge" and "protection" in a dictionary.

The Message

Security does not come from circumstances but from God.

The Bible Basis

1 Kings 17:1-16; 18:4

In the middle of a famine, God provided food and water for Elijah, the widow and her son.

The Scripture

"Blessed is the man who trusts in the Lord, whose confidence is in him."
Jeremiah 17:7

Get It Together ■ 20-30 minutes

Action: Understand that we can trust God to take care of our needs in all circumstances.

1 Kings 17:1-16; 18:4

What You Need

Bibles.

What You Do

Lead students to read and discuss the Bible verses listed. Extend the discussion with the questions and comments provided.

Introduction

What are some things people depend on? Sometimes it is hard to know who to trust, or depend on. A man in Bible times named Elijah knew who he could depend on in any situation. Let's find out what happened to him.

A Big Problem

■ Read 1 Kings 17:1 to see if you can figure out what the big problem is in this Bible story.

■ What are the results of a drought?

■ Look back at 1 Kings 16:33 to find out why God had sent this drought.

Elijah, God's prophet, told the king of Israel God's message that a drought—a time when there would be no rain—was coming. When there's no rain, the crops don't grow. Even today, we hear about the terrible problems of hunger and sickness that occur when a drought happens in some countries. In a drought, especially a long drought, people start to feel very hopeless. While people in Israel knew how to use irrigation, they didn't have enough water stored for a drought, and they didn't have the technology to get water from other places.

A long time before, God had warned His people that if they didn't worship and obey Him, trouble would come. Now, King Ahab didn't seem to care about what God had said. King Ahab married a woman, Jezebel, who worshiped false gods. Ahab even built a temple for his wife's false gods! King Ahab and Queen Jezebel led the people of Israel to worship these false gods. As a result, the people of Israel would soon be in a hopeless situation—no water or food.

An Angry King and Queen

■ How do you think the king and queen felt about Elijah?

■ Read the first part of 1 Kings 18:4 to find out what Jezebel tried to do to all prophets who served the one true God.

Elijah was in trouble with Ahab and Jezebel. First of all, Elijah reminded the people what God would do if they worshiped other gods. And THEN Elijah offended the evil Queen Jezebel by saying that there would be no rain—even though her false god, Baal, was supposed to have power over the weather.

By the third year with no rain, the king and queen were furious with Elijah! Queen Jezebel was trying to kill Elijah and God's other prophets, too. Elijah needed some help—and he needed it fast!

A Place of Refuge

■ Where would you hide today if you were looking for a refuge? Let's find out how God provided security for Elijah in 1 Kings 17:2-3.

God told Elijah to go and hide. Elijah walked until he found the brook God had told him about. Elijah stayed there and drank water from the brook, but there wasn't any food!

God took care of Elijah in an unusual way. Ravens usually eat things they find that have already died. The people of Israel would NEVER touch a raven because

150

■ Read 1 Kings 17:6 to find out what God did to give Elijah water and food.

■ Where do you think the birds got the food?

A Widow's Hopelessness

■ When the brook dried up, read 1 Kings 17:9 to find out what God told Elijah to do and who would be ready to help him.

■ In verses 10-12, read what Elijah asked the widow and what she answered.

■ Why was giving Elijah a piece of bread hard for the widow to do?

■ Read 1 Kings 17:13-14 to find Elijah's response to the woman. What promise of God did Elijah tell her about?

■ In verses 15-16, what did the woman do and what were the results of her belief? Why do you think the woman believed what Elijah said?

they were considered unclean. It must have been strange for Elijah to get bread and meat from birds that no one would usually even touch! But it was the way GOD had decided to take care of Elijah. Elijah had plenty of food to eat and water to drink for about a year!

Elijah might have wondered why God told him to go to a town where almost everyone worshiped other gods. But Elijah obeyed God's instructions.

The widow did not have enough food to give ANY to a stranger. After she fixed this last meal for herself and her son, they would starve to death because there was no food left. What a hopeless situation!

God's message of hope came true. Every time the widow took flour from the jar, there was enough. Every time she poured oil from the jug, there was plenty. God took care of Elijah, and He took care of the woman and her son. In the middle of a hopeless situation, God provided food for three people, day after day.

Conclusion

God gave Elijah the security that he needed. Elijah discovered that his security did not come from his circumstances but from God. Elijah trusted God to be his refuge and care for him in every situation. Jeremiah 17:7 reminds us that we can have confidence in God just as Elijah did. (Read verse aloud.)

God's love for us today is the same as His love was for Elijah. God's love and security doesn't mean we'll never have any problems or never be in difficult situations. But God promises to care for us no matter what happens. He'll give us courage, and He will help us know what to do. We can trust in Him. (Pray with students, thanking God for His care and asking for His help in specific situations that students are concerned about.)

Get Going ■ 20-30 minutes

Action: Identify situations in which we need to trust in God and ask for His help.

Distribute Get Real (p. 152) to students. Invite students to tell or write answers to the questions. End the discussion by completing Get Connected with students. (Optional: Students complete page at home.)

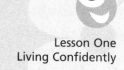

GET REAL

- When do kids your age need to trust in God's security?

- What are some ways we can show we are trusting in God?

- Why do some people choose not to trust in God?

- What can you do to remind yourself to trust in God when you need His help?

- How might God use other people to help you in situations when you feel worried or hopeless?

get to know

"Blessed is the man who trusts in the Lord, whose confidence is in him."
Jeremiah 17:7

GET CONNECTED

What is a situation in which you need to trust in God? Talk to God about how you need to depend on Him. Ask His help in knowing what to do. What action will you take this week to remind yourself to depend on God and trust in Him?

Handling Fear

Get Started ■ 5-15 minutes

Action: Compare the effects of different kinds of words.

Check Out the Comics

What You Need

Several pages of newspaper comics, scissors.

What You Do

1. Distribute newspaper comics. **Look through these pages to find comic strips that show a character talking to someone else.** Students cut out comic strips they find.

2. Students read and talk about comics. Ask the questions below.

■ **How did the words used by one character make the other character feel?**

■ **What are some examples of characters saying things that made another character feel afraid or worried?**

■ **What could the character have said so that the other character did not feel afraid or worried?**

■ **What are some examples of characters saying things that made another character feel encouraged?**

3. Students count the number of times they read encouraging words versus discouraging words. Students compare numbers and then tell what they think the effects would be if kids their age used discouraging words more often than encouraging words. **What might be some effects if we all used encouraging words more often?**

4. Conclude the activity by saying,

■ **Compare the words we've talked about with the words Paul used in the incredibly frightening situation in today's study.**

Bonus Idea

Look up websites of one or more of your favorite comic-strip artists and print out a number of comic strips to bring to class.

The Message

God's love reassures us.

The Bible Basis

Acts 21:27-36; 25:10-11; 27

Paul told his fellow travelers about his confidence in God's love, and all of them were kept safe during a shipwreck.

The Scripture

"Peace I leave with you; my peace I give you ...Do not let your hearts be troubled and do not be afraid." John 14:27

Get It Together ■ 20-30 minutes

Action: Conclude that God often shows His love by reassuring us of His presence in fearful situations and by helping us make wise decisions.

Acts 21:27-36; 25:10-11; 27

What You Need

Bibles.

What You Do

Lead students to read and discuss the Bible verses listed. Extend the discussion with the questions and comments provided.

Introduction

If you are playing in an important game, what would give you confidence? If you are taking an important test, what would give you confidence? Sometimes people say things to us that help us feel confident. Think of a time you felt afraid or discouraged and someone said or did something that helped you get through it. What effect did that person's words or actions have?

Paul was a powerful speaker. His words had helped many people learn about Jesus. Today we're going to discover the effect of Paul's words when some people needed confidence.

Paul's Final Journey

■ What do you know about the apostle Paul? How would you describe him? What do you remember about what happened to him? What kinds of troubles did he face?

■ After Paul was arrested and his request to go to Rome was granted, who was put in charge of Paul? Read Acts 27:1,3 to find out. How did this man treat Paul?

At first Paul (called Saul) had not believed in Jesus. But once he became a follower of Jesus, his life changed dramatically. Paul traveled as many places as he could, telling others about Jesus.

One day, after hearing Paul speak about how he became a follower of Jesus, a group of people started a riot because they were so upset by Paul's words. To make matters worse, Paul was arrested for starting the riot! Paul told his side of the story over and over again, but he still spent two years in prison waiting for officials to decide what to do with him. Finally, Paul, who was a Roman citizen, claimed his right to be tried in Rome before Caesar—the ruler of the entire Roman empire!

Julius was a centurion, which meant he was a Roman officer who was a commander of about 100 men. Julius assigned soldiers to watch over each prisoner. Two of Paul's friends, Aristarchus (ahr-ih-STAHR-kuhs) and Luke, signed up to travel with Paul.

Bad Weather Problems

■ To find out what happened during the trip, read Acts 27:7-8.

■ Read Acts 27:10 to find out what Paul said would happen if they kept traveling.

■ Even though this part of the journey started out good, a terrible situation developed. Read Acts 27:14-15,20 to find out what happened.

Paul and the other travelers on the ship might have been getting worried. It was not safe to cross the sea in wintertime, and winter was getting closer. Even though Paul faced danger in Rome, he desperately wanted to tell the good news about our Lord and friend, Jesus, to Caesar and the people in Rome!

Despite Paul's warning, Julius listened to the ship's owner and the ship's pilot instead. They wanted to keep going to Phoenix, only 40 miles (64 km) away. Phoenix had a safer port for the ship, and a large-enough city to provide housing for the 276 people on board.

As the hurricane-like winds hit, everyone was in a panic. The sailors couldn't see the sun or the stars, so they had NO idea where they were. The sailors even had

to tie ropes around the ship to keep the strong winds from blowing it apart. For nearly two weeks, they were bashed around in the storm, fighting just to keep the ship afloat.

Paul's Confidence in God

■ Then, one day, Paul got up to speak to everyone. Read Acts 27:21-26 to find out what Paul said. What did Paul say to remind everyone of God's help?

■ As the situation became more and more desperate, read Acts 27:33-36 to find what Paul did. How did Paul's actions make a difference in this frightening situation?

■ What was Paul's reason for choosing to trust God in the middle of a scary situation? What are some other choices he could have made?

■ Even when the shipwreck took place, read Acts 27:42-44 to find how God's promise of safety came true.

Paul's words calmed the people on the ship. He reminded them that even though things were very scary, God was with them, and this storm wasn't going to stop God's plans!

When everyone on the ship was exhausted, hungry and afraid, Paul again assured the people that God would take care of them. He insisted that they all eat, so they would have the strength to get to the island the next day. Paul prayed over the food, thanking God.

When the ship began breaking apart, the prisoners on the ship might have thought they could swim to shore. But the soldiers guarding the prisoners weren't so happy about this—they could be killed if they let a prisoner get away! So the soldiers decided to kill all the prisoners to make sure no one escaped! But Julius said no. He ordered everyone to jump overboard. Those who knew how to swim were to go first, and those who didn't know how to swim were to grab on to a piece of the ship and float to the land. Julius's plan worked! Just as Paul had said, every person from the ship made it safely to land!

Conclusion

Even though God did not keep Paul from having to go through the storm and the shipwreck, Paul knew that God loved him and would always be with him. When we are afraid, it can be hard to remember that God is with us and loves us. But we can choose to trust God and not be afraid like John 14:27 says. (Read verse aloud.) God shows His love in lots of ways, and He will help us make wise decisions when we ask for His help.

Sometimes God changes the situation we're in. Sometimes He gives us other people to be with us in hard times. Or as we talk to God about our fears, He helps us remember that we can trust Him. Because of His love for us, we can know that His promise that He will never leave us is true. (Lead students in prayer, thanking God for His love and His promise to never leave us.)

Get Going ■ 20-30 minutes

Action: Discuss fearful situations in which God can help us make wise decisions.

Distribute Get Real (p. 156) to students. Invite students to tell or write answers to the questions. End the discussion by completing Get Connected with students. (Optional: Students complete page at home.)

GET REAL

■ Why might it be hard to remember God's love when we're in a fearful situation?

■ What difficult or fearful situations might someone your age have to face?

■ How does knowing that God always loves us help us to make wise decisions?

■ How do many people make decisions when they are afraid? How does God want us to make decisions?

■ How can we prepare ourselves for times when we feel afraid?

get to know

"Peace I leave with you; my peace I give you ... Do not let your hearts be troubled and do not be afraid."
John 14:27

GET CONNECTED

What are some steps you can take when you need to make a decision—especially in a situation when you feel afraid of what might happen? Tell God when you need His help, and thank Him for always being with you and helping you.

My Future

Get Started ■ 5-15 minutes

Action: Identify typical situations that kids may face in the future.

Future Game

What You Need

Post-it Notes in three different colors, pens.

What You Do

1. Give each student three Post-it Notes, one of each color, and a pen. On one color Post-it Note, each student writes an occupation (lawyer, garbage collector, etc.). On another color Post-it Note, student writes a place (mall, Africa, etc.). On the third color Post-it Note, student writes an activity (skateboarding, eating tacos, etc.).

2. Students sit in a circle. Each student gives the Occupation Post-it Note to the person on his or her left, the Place Post-it Note to the person on his or her right and the Activity Post-it Note to any other person in the circle. (Each student ends with one Post-it Note of each color after trading.)

3. Students take turns using the words on their Post-it Notes to complete the following sentences: "In the future I will work as a (occupation) in (place). I will enjoy (activity)."

4. Ask the questions below.

■ **How many of these things are you likely to do in the future?**

■ **It's fun to think about what life might be like in the future. But what might happen in the future that might make people worry or feel afraid?**

■ **What might a kid your age think is scary about the future?**

■ **Sometimes the future can be exciting, and sometimes it can make us feel worried.**

5. Conclude the activity by saying,

■ **Today we are going to be talking about what God wants us to know as we think about the future.**

Bonus Idea

For a more active version of this activity, students stand in the middle of the room. At your signal, students begin quickly trading Post-it Notes, attempting to trade at least five times before you call time and have students complete the sentences. Repeat several times.

The Message

Face the future with confidence.

The Bible Basis

1 Samuel 17:40-50; 18:6-11; 26:7-11; 2 Samuel 17

David relied on God's presence throughout his life.

The Scripture

"I am the Lord, your God, who takes hold of your right hand and says to you, Do not fear; I will help you." Isaiah 41:13

Get It Together ■ 20-30 minutes

Action: Realize that knowing God is with us gives us confidence in facing future situations.

1 Samuel 17:40-50; 18:6-11; 26:7-11; 2 Samuel 17

What You Need

Bibles.

What You Do

Lead students to read and discuss the Bible verses listed. Extend the discussion with the questions and comments provided.

Introduction

What is something you really hope will happen in the future? What's something you DON'T want to have happen in the future? A man in Bible times had to face some very unexpected events in his future—and each time he discovered that God was with him and would help him. Let's find out what happened.

Face Up to a Giant

■ When David was probably still a young teenager, he ended up in a very scary situation. What do you remember about the time David fought the giant Goliath?

This is probably the most well-known story about David (see 1 Samuel 17:40-50). When David went to visit his brothers and bring them food from home, he surely never expected that there would be a giant in his future. But that's just what happened! Even when his enemies seemed to be much more powerful than him, David relied on God's help.

Hunted by a King

■ There was another time when something unexpected happened to David. The current king of Israel, King Saul, chased after David, hoping to kill him! Read 1 Samuel 26:7-11 to find out the choice David had to make.

■ What did David's friend Abishai want David to do? What did David choose to do?

■ Why did David choose not to kill King Saul? Was this a hard or easy choice for David? Why?

When David was a young man, he had been King Saul's faithful servant, but David was so successful that Saul became jealous and continually tried to kill David.

David could have killed Saul, and David's troubles would have been over! But David knew God didn't want him to kill God's chosen king. David didn't know how God was going to solve his problems with Saul in the future, but David was confident that if he obeyed God, God would take care of him. And sure enough, God kept David safe and later made David king when Saul died.

This wasn't the only time David's life was in danger! Later as Israel's king, David led his soldiers into battle many times. David knew what it was like to face death—not only his own, but also the death of people he loved.

Absalom's Plot

■ You might think that a king would not have any problems, but read in 2 Samuel 15:1-6 to find out how Absalom plotted against his father, King David.

■ Why might Absalom have wanted to turn people away from his father?

For many years, David had been a good king to his people. But one of David's sons, Absalom, had convinced people that David didn't care about them anymore. "He's too busy to listen to your problems, but I'll listen," Absalom kept saying. Many people believed Absalom and wanted to make Absalom their king instead of David.

Now David loved his son Absalom very much, so it must have been very painful to learn that Absalom wanted to destroy his own father! David didn't have enough men with him that day to win a battle. So David, the king, had to run away.

■ What did David do when he heard about Absalom's actions? How do you think David felt?

■ When David had run away, what did his supporters do to help David? Read 2 Samuel 17:27-29 to find out.

David's supporters brought him the things he needed to survive. God gave David what he needed through the generosity of others. Even though David had probably never expected that his son would turn against him in the future, David saw that God would take care of him.

Conclusion

David depended on God's presence in His life. God gave David the things he needed, taught him what was right to do, helped him when he faced danger and death, and protected him from his enemies. When David looked ahead to the future, he knew he could depend on God's presence in his life.

God doesn't promise that our lives will be perfect in the future—with no problems or upsets. Some kids worry that their parents will get sick, or be unable to pay their bills. Some kids worry about getting hurt or what will happen when they go to a new school. Through all these worries about the future, it's important to remember God's love for us. We can have confidence as we depend on God's promise to be with members of His family. (Read Isaiah 41:13 aloud. Pray with students, asking God to help us depend on Him with confidence. Talk with students about becoming members of God's family, following the guidelines in "Leading a Student to Christ" on pp. 10-11.)

Get Going ■ 20-30 minutes

Action: Plan ways to rely on God's presence in the future.

Distribute Get Real (p.160) to students. Invite students to tell or write answers to the questions. End the discussion by completing Get Connected with students. (Optional: Students complete page at home.)

GET REAL

- What are some of the good things God has given you or your family in the past?

- What do you know about God that can help you not worry about things that might happen in the future?

- What is another word for "confident"? How does a confident person act? How does confidence help a person who is worried about something?

- How can you show that you are relying on God's presence?

- When are some times kids your age need to rely on God's presence?

get to know

"I am the Lord, your God, who takes hold of your right hand and says to you, Do not fear; I will help you."
Isaiah 41:13

GET CONNECTED

Talk to God about any fears you have about the future. Ask His help in remembering His presence and in knowing right choices to make.

Tough Times

Get Started ■ 5-15 minutes

Action: List ways people may respond to trouble, or tough times.

Edible Answers

What You Need

Napkins, alphabet cereal.

What You Do

1. Students wash hands. Divide group into pairs. Give each pair a napkin and some alphabet cereal. (One cereal box provides enough letters for 20 to 25 students.)

2. Ask volunteers to describe some difficult situations that kids their age might face. (Students may describe situations dealing with friends, school, brothers and sisters, etc.) As each situation is described, ask, **If this happened to you, how would you feel? What would you do?**

3. Pairs spell out one-word answers with the alphabet cereal. If students want to give a longer answer, suggest they spell out one keyword of the answer and be prepared to tell about it.

4. Ask the questions below to guide students in discussing their answers together.

■ **How do kids your age sometimes handle hard things like these?**

■ **What are some other ways kids your age could handle these hard things?**

5. Students eat the alphabet cereal they used to spell answers. Conclude the activity by saying,

■ **Tough times can be hard to deal with and scary to talk about, but the Bible has a lot to say about how we can deal with trouble.**

■ **Today we are going to learn about how someone in the Bible handled some very tough times.**

Bonus Ideas

1. If students can't find the letters they need, students use *X*s and *Z*s to represent letters they don't have.

2. Instead of using alphabet cereal to spell out answers, students cut letters from magazines.

The Message

Trust God in tough times.

The Bible Basis

Genesis 37, 39

Even as a slave and a prisoner, Joseph showed faith and hope in God.

The Scripture

"God is our refuge and strength, an ever-present help in trouble."
Psalm 46:1

Get It Together ■ 20-30 minutes

Action: Understand that we can have confidence in God to help us get through difficult times.

Genesis 37; 39

What You Need

Bibles.

What You Do

Lead students to read and discuss the Bible verses listed. Extend the discussion with the questions and comments provided.

Introduction

What do you think a really good life would be like? Joseph was a young man who had a great life! But things didn't stay great for long.

Joseph's Troubles Begin

■ Read Genesis 37:2 to find out why Joseph's brothers didn't like him. What do you think Joseph might have said about his brothers?

■ Read Genesis 37:3 to find out what Joseph's dad gave him that caused more trouble between Joseph and his brothers.

■ How did the brothers feel about Joseph now? Read verse 4 to find out. How did the brothers treat Joseph?

■ What did Joseph dream in Genesis 37:5-7,9? How do you think the brothers felt now? Read Genesis 37:8 to find out.

Joseph was 17 years old when his troubles began. Joseph lived with his father, Jacob (also called Israel), and his brothers. They were shepherds. Joseph's brothers didn't like him when he gave their father a bad report about them.

Later, Joseph's father gave him a special robe that showed Joseph was his favorite. No wonder Joseph's brothers were jealous of Joseph!

Then, to make matters worse, Joseph told his brothers about his dreams that one day everyone in his family would bow down to him. Joseph's brothers DESPISED the idea of bowing down to their little brother! That was IT! They really couldn't stand him anymore! Even their father was irritated with Joseph for telling his dreams.

The Brothers Plot

■ Read Genesis 37:14 to find what Joseph's father told him to do.

■ If you had been Joseph's brothers, what would you have said when you saw him coming? Would you have felt the same way as Joseph's brothers? Why or why not?

■ Read Genesis 37:18-20 to see what Joseph's brothers said and did.

■ One brother was against the plot. Read verses 21-22 to find out about this brother's idea. Why do you think Reuben was different than the other brothers?

■ The Bible doesn't tell us how Joseph felt at this point in the story, but how do you think he might have felt?

When Joseph's father sent him to check on his brothers again, Joseph had trouble finding them. Eventually, Joseph traveled to Dothan and at last he could see his brothers in the distance.

When Joseph's brothers spotted him coming, they were not at all happy. "Here comes that dreamer!" they said to each other. They plotted to kill Joseph and throw him into a nearby cistern. A cistern was a pit for water storage. Their plan was to tell everyone that a fierce animal attacked and killed Joseph. They must have thought that this would be the end of Joseph!

Even though Reuben secretly hoped he could come back later and rescue Joseph, he didn't change the minds of his brothers. So the brothers threw Joseph into the pit.

A Brother Is Sold

■ Read Genesis 37:26-27 to discover the brothers' next plan!

■ Read Genesis 37:31-32 to find out how the brothers covered up what they had done with Joseph. In verses 33-34, how did their father respond?

■ How do you think the brothers might have felt when they saw how sad and upset their father was? Why do you think they did not tell the truth?

While Reuben was away, probably taking care of the sheep, and Joseph was stuck in the pit, the rest of the brothers sat down to a meal. As they were eating, along came a caravan of merchants. Their camels were loaded with spices to trade farther south in Egypt.

When Reuben returned, he was too late to rescue Joseph—Joseph was already on his way to Egypt to be sold as a slave!

Joseph Ends Up in Prison

■ Even though Joseph was sold as a slave, read Genesis 39:2 to find out why Joseph's tough times seemed to get better.

■ Read Genesis 39:5-6 to see how this worked out for Potiphar.

■ But suddenly life for Joseph took a turn for the worse! Read the lie that Potiphar's wife told about Joseph in Genesis 39:17-18.

■ Read Genesis 39:20-21 to find out what happened to Joseph and how Joseph's tough times turned out.

After Joseph had been sold as a slave to Potiphar, an Egyptian leader, everything Joseph did for Potiphar turned out great. God was with Joseph, helping him in everything he did. In fact, Potiphar put Joseph in charge of everything that he had!

Things looked pretty good for Joseph; unfortunately, Joseph looked too good to Potiphar's wife. She wanted Joseph to sleep with her! But Joseph refused. Potiphar's wife lied about Joseph, claiming that he had attacked her. Potiphar believed his wife's story and that's when things got tougher! Joseph was put in prison!

Even in prison, things turned out great for Joseph! The other prisoners respected him. The prison warden put him in charge of all the prisoners. He trusted Joseph because the Lord was with Joseph and gave him success in whatever he did.

Conclusion

With all the bad things that happened to him, Joseph could have decided that God really didn't care about him. Instead, Joseph continued to depend on God, even when he was in very difficult situations. Joseph was confident of God's love and presence. (Read Psalm 46:1 aloud.)

Just like Joseph, we need to ask for God's help and depend on Him to answer our prayers. Remembering the ways God helps us encourages us to be confident in Him. One reason God sent His Son, Jesus, to Earth was to be our example in doing what is right and depending on God's help. (Pray with students, asking God's help for us to continually depend on Him in good times and in tough times, which will lead to confidence in His love and presence.)

Get Going ■ 20-30 minutes

Action: Identify ways God helps us in tough times.

Distribute Get Real (p. 164) to students. Invite students to tell or write answers to the questions. End the discussion by completing Get Connected with students. (Optional: Students complete page at home.)

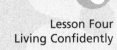

GET REAL

- When has God helped you or a family member get through a tough time?

- Think of a tough time, or problem, a kid your age might experience. How might God help with that problem?

- Why do you think it sometimes seems that God does not help?

- What problem, or tough time, do you need to ask God's help with?

- How might God use Christians to help other people who are having tough times?

get to know

"God is our refuge and strength, an ever-present help in trouble."
Psalm 46:1

GET CONNECTED

Think about a tough time you or someone you know is facing. Take a moment to talk to God about this time and ask for His help. Thank Him for always being with you.

God Is Good

Get Started ■ 5-15 minutes

Action: Discover times when something good has happened from something bad.

Actor Alert

What You Need

Index cards, pencils.

What You Do

1. On separate index cards, print the following bad situations kids might face: get picked last for the team, break your arm, catch a cold, lose a game, game gets rained out, wreck your bike, little brother bothers you, visit relatives you don't like and do homework. Shuffle cards together.

2. Divide group into pairs. Invite one pair to choose a card and act out the situation. Other students guess what the bad situation is. Then group thinks of one good thing that could result from it.

3. Repeat with another pair acting out a situation, but for the second situation, students think of two good things that could result. Continue to add more good things for each situation, listing them on the back of each card. (When group can no longer increase the list by one, start over with just one good thing for the next situation.)

4. Ask the questions below.

■ **When something bad first happens, how do you usually feel?**

■ **What might happen to change your feelings?**

■ **When has something happened to you that seemed bad at first but then turned out to be good or something good happened in spite of the situation?**

5. Conclude the activity by saying,

■ **In our Bible study today, look for ways good things happened in bad situations.**

Bonus Idea

Students may write additional situations on index cards.

The Message

God's ways are always good.

The Bible Basis

Genesis 39:21-23; 40—47:12; 50:19-20

God made something good from the difficult events in Joseph's life.

The Scripture

"We know that in all things God works for the good of those who love him." Romans 8:28

Get It Together ■ 20-30 minutes

Action: Understand that no matter what situation we are in, God can cause good to happen.

Genesis 39:21-23; 40—47:12; 50:19-20

What You Need

Bibles.

What You Do

Lead students to read and discuss the Bible verses listed. Extend the discussion with the questions and comments provided.

Introduction

What are some bad situations that might happen to kids today? What bad situations had Joseph faced in his life? His brothers had sold him as a slave, he had worked as a slave for Potiphar in Egypt, and THEN he was put in prison because of a lie Potiphar's wife had told! Does it sound like God was taking good care of Joseph? Why or why not? Let's find out.

Unusual Dreams

■ Read Genesis 40:1-5,8 to find out who was put in prison with Joseph, and what they wanted to know. What did Joseph say when he heard about their dreams?

■ Read Genesis 40:14-15,23 to find what Joseph asked the cupbearer to do when he left prison and what actually happened.

■ How do you think Joseph might have felt about God's protection and presence now? How would you have felt?

■ The Bible doesn't tell us what Joseph said or did, but look back at Genesis 39:21-23 to find a description of Joseph's time in prison.

Joseph realized that only God knew the meaning of dreams. With God's help, Joseph was able to tell these two what their dreams meant. The baker's dream meant that Pharaoh would order the baker to be killed. The cupbearer's dream meant that he would soon be released from prison and return to serve Pharaoh.

Joseph wanted to get out of prison, too, so he hoped the cupbearer would talk to Pharaoh and get Joseph released from prison.

In three days, both servants were taken from prison—the cupbearer to serve Pharaoh again and the baker to be hanged. But the cupbearer forgot all about Joseph. Joseph was stuck in prison for two more years!

Pharaoh's Dreams

■ After two years, Pharaoh had two surprising dreams. Read in Genesis 41:8 to find out what Pharaoh did.

■ Who finally talked to the king about Pharaoh? Read Genesis 41:9.

■ In Genesis 41:15-16, what did Pharaoh tell Joseph? And what did Joseph answer?

■ Read Genesis 41:39-40 to find out what good things God brought about from this bad situation in Joseph's life.

When all of the magicians and wise men came, none of them could interpret the dreams. When the cupbearer heard what had happened, he remembered Joseph! He told Pharaoh about how Joseph had interpreted his dreams two years before.

Pharaoh said to Joseph, "In my entire kingdom, no one can interpret my dreams. Is it true that you can interpret dreams?"

Despite the bad situations Joseph had been in, he was still confident of God's presence and help!

Pharaoh told Joseph his dreams. The dreams sounded confusing, but with God's help, Joseph told Pharaoh what these dreams meant: There would be seven years with plenty of food followed by seven years of famine (a time when there is not

enough food to eat). Joseph told Pharaoh to put someone in charge of collecting and storing a portion of every harvest for the next seven years, so there would be enough food to last through the years of famine.

Pharaoh was so impressed that he put Joseph in charge of Egypt. Only Pharaoh had more power than Joseph!

Joseph's Secret

■ Read Genesis 41:1-2 to find out how and why Joseph saw his brothers again.

■ Even though Joseph recognized his brothers when they came to ask for food, why do you think Joseph didn't tell his brothers who he was?

■ Read Genesis 45:3-5 to find what Joseph said when he finally let his brothers know who he was.

■ How did Joseph view what his brothers had done to him? Find out by reading Genesis 50:19-20.

■ How do you think Joseph's actions compare to how most people today would act?

When the famine came, the people in the land of Joseph's family soon ran out of food. So Joseph sent his sons to Egypt to buy food.

All but one of Joseph's brothers traveled to Egypt and met with Joseph. Joseph recognized them, but they didn't recognize him! To keep his identity hidden from his brothers, Joseph spoke Egyptian. He used an interpreter to talk to his brothers, who only spoke Hebrew.

Joseph decided to test his brothers to see if they had changed since the time they sold him as a slave. From all the tests Joseph gave, he learned that his brothers HAD changed. Now they were even willing to give up their freedom for each other! But finally, Joseph couldn't keep his identity a secret any longer.

Joseph completely forgave his brothers for selling him as a slave, and he invited his whole family to come and live with him in Egypt. Joseph was reunited with his father and brothers at last!

Conclusion

Joseph's life had an amazing ending—one only God would have caused! God made something good happen from the bad events in Joseph's life. Bad, unhappy things happen in our world because of sin and the ways in which people disobey God. God allows unpleasant things to happen to us, but because of His love and power, He causes all things to work together for good if we love Him and believe in Jesus Christ, His Son. (Read Romans 8:28 aloud.)

Sometimes we might find it hard to remember God's love and presence. We might feel as though God doesn't have any interest in our problems. Or we might feel as though our problems are too small or insignificant for God to care about. But not only does God promise to always be with us, He also wants to accomplish good things for us in every circumstance. No matter how WE feel, we can't change the fact that HE loves us and wants to show us His goodness. (Lead students in prayer, thanking God for His love and presence with us.)

Get Going ■ 20-30 minutes

Action: Discuss situations in which it is hard to recognize God's presence, and thank God for His love and goodness to us.

Distribute Get Real (p. 168) to students. Invite students to tell or write answers to the questions. End the discussion by completing Get Connected with students. (Optional: Students complete page at home.)

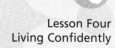

GET REAL

■ Think of a difficult situation a kid your age might experience. How might God make something good come from that situation?

■ How do you know that God wants what is good for you?

■ Why might it be hard to believe that something good can happen despite or because of a bad, or difficult, circumstance?

■ What do you know about God that will help you trust in His love for you in difficult times?

■ What can you do to show that you trust God to show His love and goodness to you?

get to know

"We know that in all things God works for the good of those who love him."
Romans 8:28

GET CONNECTED

What is something about which you are worried or afraid? What is a tough time you are facing? Talk to God about this situation, and ask Him to help you believe His promise to be with you and help you.

The Great Commission

Get Started ■ 5-15 minutes

Action: Discover a variety of ways to communicate with others.

Drawing Challenge

What You Need

Paper, pencils, erasers.

What You Do

1. Draw geometric figures on separate sheets of paper (see sketch). Make several drawings.

2. Group students into pairs, each pair sitting back-to-back. Show one partner of each pair one of the drawings you prepared. Student copies the drawing onto a sheet of paper. Then the student verbally tells his or her partner how to draw the figure, without letting the partner see the drawing. Student giving directions may not make any motions.

3. After completing the drawing, partners trade roles, giving instructions for a different figure. Continue activity as time permits.

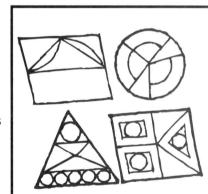

4. Group students together and ask the questions below.

■ **Was it hard or easy to communicate the directions for each drawing?**

■ **Was it harder to be the one telling the directions or to be the one trying to follow the directions?**

■ **When you were trying to communicate the directions, what did you have to do to make it easy for your partner to know what you meant?**

■ **What other ways of communicating would have made it easier to do the drawings?**

■ **What are some different ways of communicating with people?**

5. Conclude the activity by saying,

■ **All of these ways of communicating can be used to tell others about Jesus.**

■ **Let's discover how Jesus' first followers told others about Jesus.**

Bonus Idea

Search on the Internet and print pictures of different ways that people communicate with each other. Bring in pictures of a cell phone, computer, pen and paper, etc.

The Message

We can tell others about our hope in Jesus.

The Bible Basis

Matthew 28:16-20; John 20:30-31; Acts 2:42-45; Romans 10:14-15

Jesus commanded His followers to teach others in all nations about Him.

The Scripture

"Go and make disciples of all nations . . . teaching them to obey everything I have commanded you. And surely I am with you always, to the very end of the age."
Matthew 28:19-20

Get It Together ■ 20-30 minutes

Action: Realize that Jesus' followers can teach others about His uniqueness.

Matthew 28:16-20; John 20:30-31; Acts 2:42-45; Romans 10:14-15

What You Need

Bibles.

What You Do

Lead students to read and discuss the Bible verses listed. Extend the discussion with the questions and comments provided.

Introduction

What things might you say to your best friends if you had to move away? Jesus was leaving and He had something important to tell His closest friends. So He planned one last meeting with His 11 disciples on a mountain in Galilee. (Judas, the twelfth disciple, had killed himself after Jesus' crucifixion.) At the right time, all 11 disciples arrived at the mountain, ready to hear the important message Jesus had to tell them.

Jesus Gives a Command

■ Read Matthew 28:18. What was the first thing Jesus said to His disciples when He arrived?

■ What do you think was the special job Jesus wanted His disciples to do? Read Matthew 28:19.

■ Where did Jesus say the disciples should go to teach others?

If anyone had a doubt about who Jesus was, He cleared up those doubts right away. He was God's Son. He was the Messiah. And God had given Him authority over all of the world and heaven. The disciples could be sure everything Jesus had said was right and true.

The next part of Jesus' speech is called the Great Commission. A commission is a special command, or order, to perform.

Jesus had spent most of His time teaching in Galilee, Judea and Samaria. Now He was telling His disciples to preach to the people in ALL nations. During Jesus' time, that meant spreading the message a very long way. This would be a BIG job for a handful of disciples.

Jesus Makes a Promise

■ How would you feel if someone told you to tell the whole world about Jesus?

■ What promise did Jesus make to His disciples in Matthew 28:20?

■ We can also read about Jesus' command and promise in Acts 1:8. What does this verse say? How is this command and promise the same as what we read in Matthew 28? How is it different?

■ Read Acts 1:9-11 to find why the disciples were so surprised at what happened next.

No matter how hard the job might be, the disciples could have hope because Jesus would always be with them. They didn't have to do this big job alone! And Jesus promised to give them power by sending the Holy Spirit. Receiving the Holy Spirit meant that they would have God with them, helping them and giving them courage all the time.

The Bible says that after Jesus gave His final instructions, He was taken directly up into heaven in a cloud. The disciples stared at the sky in astonishment! After the angel's explanation, the disciples went back to Jerusalem.

Jesus' Followers Obey

■ What did Jesus' followers do to begin obeying Jesus' command? Read Acts 2:42-47 to find out.

■ If you had seen the actions of these people, what would you have learned about Jesus? What would you have learned about being a follower of Jesus?

■ What resulted from the actions of Jesus' followers? Read Acts 2:47 to find out.

The Bible does not tell us about what ALL of the disciples did after that, but from the book of Acts, we know what SOME of the disciples did to help others learn about Jesus. And the news about Jesus spread quickly!

Many people decided to follow Jesus because of the things Peter and the other disciples did and said. Because so many people became followers of Jesus, Peter and the other disciples organized the Early Church in Jerusalem. Peter taught the people of the church to care for each other as Jesus would care for them.

Other Disciples Obey

■ Read John 20:30-31 to find a way that one of Jesus' disciples obeyed the command to tell others about Jesus. What reason did John give for his writing?

■ What do you remember about Paul and the way he witnessed about Jesus?

■ Read Romans 10:14-15 to find some questions Paul asked that remind us why it's so important to tell others about Jesus.

■ Most people don't think of feet as being beautiful. But why did Paul say feet were beautiful?

The writers of the four Gospels, Matthew, Mark, Luke and John, helped others learn about Jesus in a different way. They are known for the books and letters they wrote telling the stories about Jesus.

The miracles John recorded were to help people understand who Jesus is and to encourage them to join God's family.

Paul was another famous early believer in Jesus. Paul also wrote letters about Jesus. Paul's letters tell us a lot about how to live as followers of Jesus. But Paul also did something else as a way of teaching others about Jesus.

Paul was a missionary who traveled from place to place, spreading the news about Jesus. More and more people became followers of Jesus, and they told even more people.

Conclusion

The Great Commission to tell others about Jesus wasn't just for the original disciples. It is for everyone who believes in Jesus. (Read Matthew 28:19-20 aloud). When we tell the good news about Jesus, we make it possible for others to experience the hope and joy that knowing Jesus brings.

There are lots of ways we can teach others about the hope we have in Jesus. We can tell stories about how Jesus has helped us, write letters, sing songs or draw pictures. One of the best ways to help others learn about Jesus is by showing His love to others in our actions. In all these ways we can be witnesses about Jesus.

When we think about helping others learn about Jesus, we might feel afraid or we might think we really don't know what to say. The promise Jesus gave to always be with His disciples as they told people about Him is a promise we can depend on, too. (Pray with students, thanking God for people who have told them about Jesus. Talk with interested students about becoming members of God's family, referring to "Leading a Student to Christ" on pp. 10-11.)

Get Going ■ 20-30 minutes

Action: Plan ways to teach others about the hope Jesus offers.

Distribute Get Real (p. 172) to students. Invite students to tell or write answers to the questions. End the discussion by completing Get Connected with students. (Optional: Students complete page at home.)

GET REAL

■ What are some of the different ways in which you've learned about Jesus?

■ Do you think it's harder to act like a Christian, showing God's love to others, or to talk about what it means to be a Christian? Why? Why do you think it might be important to do both?

■ What's something you can do this week to help someone else learn about the hope Jesus gives us?

■ What are some ways you can help others learn what you know about Jesus?

Get to Know

"Go and make disciples of all nations ... teaching them to obey everything I have commanded you. And surely I am with you always, to the very end of the age."
Matthew 28:19-20

Get Connected

Think about one way you could tell a friend something you know about Jesus or a way Jesus has helped you. Ask God's help in being ready to tell about Jesus.

Taking Action

Get Started ■ 5-15 minutes

Action: Discover situations in which actions may speak louder than words.

What You Need

Index cards, markers.

What You Do

1. On separate index cards, print the following words or phrases: "Stop," "Be quiet," "I'm lost," "Hurry up," "I'm impatient," "I'm hungry," "Don't know," "Slow down," "Fire!" "Emergency!" "I'm sick," "I'm confused" and "I can't find my keys."

2. Invite a volunteer to secretly choose a card. Volunteer attempts to get other students to guess his or her word or phrase by pantomiming, or acting out, the word or phrase. (Optional: Students create their own cards as time permits.)

3. Repeat several times with students choosing different words each time. Ask the questions below.

■ **How did you know what the word or phrase was?**

■ **What are some other things you can learn about a person by watching the way he or she acts?**

■ **How can you tell if someone is really your friend?**

■ **What are some other actions that people often use to communicate with others?**

4. Conclude the activity by saying,

■ **Try to find out what some of the characters in our Bible study were really like by noticing their actions.**

Bonus Idea

On an index card, each student writes a positive nickname he or she would like to have. Then student lists several actions he or she could take to become known by that name.

The Message

Meeting needs can open the door for sharing faith.

The Bible Basis

Acts 3—4:22

Peter's healing of the lame man at the Temple gave Peter the opportunity to tell about Jesus.

The Scripture

"Let your light shine before men, that they may see your good deeds and praise your Father in heaven." Matthew 5:16

Get It Together ■ 20-30 minutes

Action: Realize that when we act in ways that show our love and obedience for God, we are witnesses for Jesus.

Acts 3—4:22

What You Need

Bibles.

What You Do

Lead students to read and discuss the Bible verses listed. Extend the discussion with the questions and comments provided.

Introduction

What are some things people can do to make a difference for good in our world? What are some important things that kids your age have done? Jesus wanted His disciples to do some important things with their actions and words.

A Blind Beggar

■ Read Acts 3:1-2 to find out who two of Jesus' disciples met on their way to the Temple.

■ In verse 3 what did the man ask the disciples to give him?

■ When has anyone asked you or someone in your family for money? How did you feel about the request?

■ Read in Acts 3:6-7 the surprising thing that Peter and John did.

■ If you had never been able to walk and suddenly you could walk, what's the first thing you'd do? Where would you go? What did the crippled man do? Read verse 8.

A beggar was brought to the Beautiful gate of the Temple in Jerusalem. This man, who was over 40 years old, had been born crippled. Every day he was brought to this gate to beg. It was a good place for begging, because many people had to walk by this gate on their way to worship God and many people felt that giving money to a poor man would please God.

When the crippled man called out for help, the disciples turned and looked the crippled man straight in the eyes. This surprised him. Usually people just ignored him or, without looking at him, gave him coins and hurried on. But these men were different!

Although Peter and John might have wanted to give the man money, they didn't have any. Peter and John gave the man something even more valuable than money—the ability to walk!

A Wonderful Witness

■ Read Acts 3:9-11 to find out what the people who saw the miracle did.

■ In Acts 3:13,15-16, what did Peter say as he witnessed about Jesus? What made the people ready to listen to what Peter had to say?

■ After telling what the Old Testament prophets had said would happen to Jesus, and that these prophecies had come true, what did Peter tell the people to do? Read Acts 3:19.

Since it was prayer time, there were many other people at the Temple, too. The people were amazed at what they had seen! They all knew this man. For a long time, he'd been at the Temple, begging. Now he was walking! And jumping! And praising God! Of course the people wanted to know how this wonderful thing had happened. A large crowd gathered around Peter and John.

This was too good an opportunity to miss! Peter's act of faith and kindness had given him a chance to tell about Jesus. Peter didn't want people to think he had some sort of magical power, so the first thing he said was, "Why are you surprised? Do you think we healed this man with our own powers? It was God, who raised Jesus from the dead, who did this miracle!" Peter told the crowd who Jesus was.

Many people must have been very shocked to hear that a man they thought was a criminal was responsible for this great miracle!

Peter told the people to repent—to turn away from sin and seek to know and obey God. Peter went on to tell the people that Jesus was the One who fulfilled the promises God had made to His people through Abraham, Moses and David.

174

Peter and John's Obedience

■ Even though they had done nothing wrong, what trouble resulted from Peter and John witnessing about Jesus? Read Acts 4:2-3.

■ In verse four, what wonderful things resulted from their witnessing?

■ How might Peter and John have felt after being arrested, but at the same time realizing how many people had believed the good news?

■ Read Acts 4:7 to find out what the Sanhedrin asked them while they were under arrest.

■ What do you think Peter and John said when the Sanhedrin let them go but warned them not to talk about Jesus? Read Acts 4:19-20 to find out.

The crowd was excited about what they heard! With all the excitement and noise, the religious leaders and the captain of the Temple guard soon came over to investigate what was happening. When they heard what Peter and John were saying about Jesus, they arrested Peter and John on the spot.

When the Sanhedrin asked Peter and John where their power came from, Peter and John could have played it safe. "We don't really know," they might have said. But Peter and John were so convinced of the truth of what they were saying, they told the story of Jesus again!

Even when the Sanhedrin warned Peter and John not to speak about Jesus anymore, Peter and John were bold in saying they would continue to obey God.

Conclusion

Peter's actions AND words were a witness of his faith in Jesus. Matthew 5:16 tells us what we can do so that others can see our faith in Jesus. (Read Matthew 5:16 aloud.) Because Peter and John noticed the crippled man and chose to care for him, the man was healed through their faith in Jesus' power. As a result of this miracle that only God could do, Peter had the opportunity to tell about Jesus to many people.

Our right actions show our love for God. Sometimes our right actions can result in opportunities to talk about who Jesus is and His love for us. However, if we say we love Jesus but our actions are unloving, most people won't even listen to our words. Every day we are in situations in which our actions can make a difference in someone's willingness to listen to what we say about Jesus and what we say about our faith in Him. (Lead students in prayer, asking God's help in showing their faith by their actions.)

Get Going ■ 20-30 minutes

Action: Identify and discuss situations in which we may act in ways that help others learn about Jesus.

Distribute Get Real (p. 176) to students. Invite students to tell or write answers to the questions. End the discussion by completing Get Connected with students. (Optional: Students complete page at home.)

GET REAL

■ How might your actions and words help someone learn about Jesus? How might they keep someone from learning about Jesus?

■ When is a time kids your age might say they want to love and obey God but act in a way that's different?

■ When might your right actions—honesty, fairness, friendliness—give you an opportunity to talk about Jesus?

■ Why do Christians want others to learn about Jesus?

■ What would you think of someone who told others about Jesus but never helped them with things they needed?

■ What kinds of things can kids your age do to help others learn about Jesus?

Get to Know

"Let your light shine before men, that they may see your good deeds and praise your Father in heaven."
Matthew 5:16

GET CONNECTED

Think about some ways your actions as followers of Jesus can teach others about Jesus. Ask God to help you this week act as a follower of Jesus so that others can learn about Jesus from your words and actions.

Know and Tell the Good News

Get Started ◼ 5-15 minutes

Action: Discover things that need to be explained before they can be understood.

The Definition

What You Need

Bible, dictionary, slips of paper, pencils.

What You Do

1. Find and mark several unusual words in the dictionary.

2. Distribute paper and pencils.

3. Pronounce and spell an unusual word from the dictionary.

4. Each student makes up one definition that sounds as if it might be correct and writes it on a slip of paper. On another slip of paper, you write the correct definition using words your students will understand.

5. Collect the definitions. Shuffle them together and then read them ail aloud, including the correct definition. Students attempt to guess the correct definition. Repeat with other words as time allows.

◼ **Why did you choose the definition that you did?**

◼ **What are some ways you can find out what this word really means?**

◼ **How do you feel when you don't understand something?**

◼ **When have you had a hard time understanding something in the Bible?**

6. Conclude the activity by saying,

◼ **It's important to understand something in order to be able to explain it to someone else. Someone in our Bible study today needed something explained. See if you can figure out a good way to explain it to him.**

Bonus Idea

Ahead of time, prepare several wrong definitions for each word. Read your wrong definitions along with definitions that students create.

The **Message**

Be ready to explain God's Word.

The **Bible Basis**

Acts 8:4-6,26-40

Philip explained God's Word to the Ethiopian who accepted the good news of Jesus with joy.

The **Scripture**

"Always be prepared to give an answer to everyone who asks you to give the reason for the hope that you have."
1 Peter 3:15

Get It Together ■ 20-30 minutes

Action: Realize that we can help others learn about Jesus by explaining God's Word to them.

Acts 8:4-6,26-40

What You Need

Bibles.

What You Do

Lead students to read and discuss the Bible verses listed. Extend the discussion with the questions and comments provided.

Introduction

What are some jobs that kids your age might have? What skills would you need to do that job? Today we'll talk about a job Jesus wants us to be able to do.

Philip was a follower of Jesus, and he was willing to do jobs that needed to be done in his church. One of Philip's jobs had been to help make sure everyone had enough food to eat. (See Acts 6:1-6.) The Bible tells us that Philip was chosen for this job because he was wise. How do you think he became wise? He became wise by studying God's Word and doing what it says. When it was time for Philip's next job, he was ready!

Philip's Witness in Samaria

■ Read Acts 8:4-5 to find out what Philip did. Look back at verse 1 to see why Philip had gone to Samaria.

■ In Acts 8:6-7 read why people paid attention to what Philip said.

■ What was the result of these miracles?

People had begun persecuting Christians in Jerusalem, the city where Philip lived. So the Christians scattered. Philip was one of those Christians who left Jerusalem.

God performed many miracles through Philip. The miracles amazed people! They wanted to know more! When they came to Philip, they heard the good news about Jesus! Many people in Samaria believed what they heard from Philip and began to follow Jesus, too.

An Ethiopian's Question

■ Read Acts 8:26-27 to find out where God sent Philip next and who Philip saw coming down this road.

■ Who was this man? Why had he been to Jerusalem?

■ How many of you like to read while you are traveling? Read verse 28 to find out what this Ethiopian man was reading.

■ Read the question Philip asked in Acts 8:30. What did the Ethiopian answer in verse 31?

It must have surprised Philip when an ANGEL came to him and said, "Go to the southbound road—the one that goes from Jerusalem to Gaza." Philip might have wondered why God wanted him to go somewhere else, when things were going so well where he was. But he immediately obeyed these new instructions.

This man was from Ethiopia and was an important official to the queen of Ethiopia. A eunuch is a man who is physically unable to become a father. In Bible times, the country of Ethiopia was located south of Egypt along the Red Sea and included the country now called Sudan. This important official was in charge of all the queen's money! Because this man had been to Jerusalem to worship God, we know that he must have wanted to love and obey God.

This Ethiopian official was reading a scroll as his chariot rolled right past Philip. Suddenly the Holy Spirit said to Philip, "Catch up with that chariot and STAY with it!" So Philip did. And then Philip had to keep running just to keep up with the chariot!

The official was reading aloud from the Old Testament book of Isaiah. Because the Ethiopian didn't understand what he was reading, he stopped his chariot and invited Philip to ride with him. Philip was probably glad he didn't have to keep running! The two men continued talking.

The Good News

■ Read Acts 8:32-34 to find out what puzzled the Ethiopian official.

■ Who do you think this passage is talking about? What do you think Philip might have said to answer the Ethiopian's question? Read verse 35 to see what Philip said.

■ Look at Acts 8:36 to see what the Ethiopian wanted to do.

■ How does Acts 8:39 describe the feelings of the Ethiopian after his baptism?

■ Why do people like the Ethiopian think that hearing the good news about Jesus is worth celebrating?

Philip had studied the Old Testament. He knew this passage was about Jesus. So when the man asked, Philip was prepared to explain this passage and tell the good news about Jesus.

The Ethiopian believed everything that Philip told him about Jesus. The Ethiopian wanted to be baptized to show that he believed Jesus was the Messiah God had sent. So right then and there Philip baptized the Ethiopian official. (A person is baptized to show he or she is a member of God's family.)

God took Philip to the city of Azotus (ah-ZOH-tuhs), and the Ethiopian man never saw Philip again. But he continued on his way, thanking God for loving him and bringing him into God's family.

After THAT incredible day, Philip continued to explain God's Word to people and to tell the good news about Jesus in towns all the way from Azotus to Caesarea.

Conclusion

Philip was willing to obey what God told him to do—even if it meant running fast enough to catch up to a chariot! Philip had taken the time to learn about God's Word. He was ready to explain verses from God's Word and help someone become a member of God's family just as 1 Peter 3:15 says. (Read verse aloud.)

Sometimes we might think that only pastors or teachers at church need to understand what the Bible says. But they can't be everywhere! God wants ALL His followers to help others learn about Jesus. If we don't take the time to read, ask questions about and understand God's Word, we won't be ready to explain it. Some people may not want to hear about how knowing God can help us, but many people will. It's exciting to think about the opportunities you'll have now and as you grow older to explain God's Word to others. (Pray with students, asking God to give them a desire to know God's Word and asking that He would help them understand and be able to explain the good news to others.)

Get Going ■ 20-30 minutes

Action: Identify and discuss Bible verses that we can use to explain the gospel to others.

Distribute Get Real (p. 180) to students. Invite students to tell or write answers to the questions. End the discussion by completing Get Connected with students. (Optional: Students complete page at home.)

GET REAL

■ When has someone explained a Bible verse to you?

■ Why do you think kids your age might need someone to explain parts of God's Word to them? Why might it be hard for people to understand the Bible?

■ What are some ways you can learn more about God's Word?

■ What are some things in the Bible kids your age might have questions about?

■ What are some things kids your age could do to become better prepared to answer questions about the gospel?

Get to Know

"Always be prepared to give an answer to everyone who asks you to give the reason for the hope that you have."
1 Peter 3:15

GET CONNECTED

What is one Bible verse that you want to remember and talk to your friends about? Ask God to help you be ready to talk to others about the Bible and the good news of Jesus.

Witness with Love and Respect

Get Started ■ 5-15 minutes

Action: Discover misunderstandings that may occur between people of different cultures.

Word Guess Relay

What You Need

Masking tape, large sheets of paper, markers.

What You Do

1. Use masking tape to make a start line on one side of your classroom. Tape large sheets of paper to wall opposite the start line. Place markers near paper.

2. Divide group into two teams. Teams line up behind start line. At your signal, first two students run to the papers. Whisper a different word from 1 John 3:18 to each student ("not," "love," "words," "tongue," "actions," "and," "in," "truth").

3. Students draw pictures, without using any letters or numbers, to get others students on their teams to guess the words. As soon as someone on the team calls out the correct word, student runs back to his or her team and the next student runs to the paper to draw clues for another word. Continue until all the students on one team have had a turn.

4. Ask the questions below.

■ **Which clues did you misunderstand at first?**

■ **When is a time something you've said has been misunderstood by someone else?**

■ **What are some words or phrases you use that people from other countries might not understand?**

■ **What are some things that make it difficult to communicate with people from other cultures?**

5. Conclude the activity by saying,

■ **Even when we're speaking the same language, what we say can be misunderstood.**

■ **When we talk to people from other countries or people who are used to speaking in a different language, misunderstandings can also occur.**

■ **In our study today, find out what Paul, one of Jesus' followers, had to do so that the people he was talking to could understand about Jesus.**

Bonus Idea

Instead of drawing clues, lead students to play a game like Charades in which they pantomime actions to try to get their teammates to guess the words.

The Message

Show respect when sharing your faith.

The Bible Basis

Acts 17:16-34

Paul showed respect to the people of Athens when he preached to them in the marketplace.

The Scripture

"Let us not love with words or tongue but with actions and in truth."
1 John 3:18

Get It Together ■ 20-30 minutes

Action: Realize that respectfully witnessing to others requires knowing and understanding their culture.

Acts 17:16-34

What You Need

Bibles.

What You Do

Lead students to read and discuss the Bible verses listed. Extend the discussion with the questions and comments provided.

Introduction

What is a city you would like to visit? What would you like to do there? Paul had grown up in the city of Jerusalem, studying about the Hebrew faith and culture. But after Paul became one of Jesus' followers, he began traveling to lots of different cities. On one trip, Paul came to the Greek city of Athens. At that time, Athens was the center of learning in the world and had the best university. People came to Athens from everywhere to hear the latest ideas.

Paul's Visit to Athens

■ Read Acts 17:16 to find out what Paul noticed about Athens and how he felt about what he saw. Why do you think Paul felt this way?

■ Where does Acts 17:17 say Paul went? How does the Bible describe what Paul did?

When Paul arrived in Athens, he noticed all the idols there. Historians think that there were almost more idols than people! Idols were statues of gods worshiped by people for the powers the people thought they had.

Paul wanted these people to know the one true God and not waste their lives trusting in false gods.

Paul had learned what was important to the Athenians, so he was prepared to talk to these people about God in a way that they would understand.

Paul didn't make fun of what the Athenians believed; nor did he just spend his time preaching. He also took time to listen to what the Jews and Greeks who loved God had to say about their beliefs.

Paul's Teaching in Athens

■ Read Acts 17:18 to find the names of two popular Greek belief systems, or philosophies.

■ Read verse 20 to find out why the people in Athens wanted to hear more about Paul's teachings.

Stoicism taught that the wiser you became, the less you were affected by pleasure and pain. Epicureanism taught that the best thing in life was to be happy. Stoic and Epicurean philosophers debated with Paul about Jesus' resurrection from the dead.

Because the people in Athens were so interested in learning about new ideas, they wanted to bring Paul to the Areopagus (ahr-ee-OHP-ah-guhs).

Historians have found that the members of the Areopagus were very intelligent people who decided whether or not a teacher's ideas were true and whether or not the teacher could teach in Athens. They took their work very seriously and were well respected. Paul recognized this meeting as an important opportunity to tell about Jesus.

Paul's Respectful Words and Actions

- How do you think Paul felt when he came before this group of important leaders?
- Discover the first thing Paul said to the council in Acts 17:22-23.
- Once Paul had their attention, who did he begin talking about in verse 24?

Because Paul understood the different religions and philosophies practiced in Athens, he was able to speak in a way that interested the council. He didn't criticize them for worshiping idols. He even started his conversation with a compliment!

Then Paul described who God is—the one true God who made heaven and Earth and how He is far superior to the idols the Athenians worshiped. In his speech, Paul even quoted some Greek poetry to help his listeners learn about God. "God is ALIVE!" Paul said. "God knows you worshiped idols instead of Him because you didn't know He existed. But God wants you to know Him. He wants you to worship Him."

The Council's Response

- Read Acts 17:32 to find out how the council members reacted to the news about Jesus' resurrection.
- Read Acts 17:34 to find out what the other response to Paul was.
- How would you describe the way Paul witnessed to the people in Athens?
- How do you think they would have responded if he hadn't taken time to understand them and show respect for their culture?

The Greeks thought that a person's soul would live forever, so the idea of the resurrection of the body seemed ridiculous to some of them. Those council members made fun of Paul. But others in the council wanted him to come talk to them again.

After listening to Paul's witness about Jesus, several people accepted the good news about Jesus and believed in the one true God. Some scholars believe that Dionysius (di-oh-NI-sees), one of the members of the Areopagus who had believed what Paul said about Jesus, later became a Christian leader in Athens.

Conclusion

Paul demonstrated that respecting people involves learning what they believe and value. Paul chose to show his love for Jesus through his actions. (Read 1 John 3:18 aloud.) By taking an interest in what mattered to the Athenians, Paul earned an opportunity to tell them about Jesus. Paul spoke about Jesus in ways they understood.

Every day we have opportunities to talk with lots of different people. As we get to know them, we probably won't always agree with their beliefs about God and Jesus. Even when we disagree, however, we can always show respect. Because God loves and sent His Son to die for every person, all people deserve our respect. God can help us use what we learn about others to talk about Jesus in a way that makes sense to them. (Pray with the students that God would help them love and respect people from other cultures in order to witness effectively to them.)

Get Going ■ 20-30 minutes

Action: Discuss ways to share our faith in God, connecting the gospel to the cultures of people today.

Distribute Get Real (p. 184) to students. Invite students to tell or write answers to the questions. End the discussion by completing Get Connected with students. (Optional: Students complete page at home.)

GET REAL

■ What do kids your age think is important? How can you use these interests to tell about Jesus so that kids will understand?

■ Who are some people you know from different cultures or countries? How are they different from you? How are they the same? How can you tell them about Jesus in a way that they will understand?

■ Why is showing respect important?

■ How can you show respect to someone when you disagree with what he or she believes about God and Jesus? What can you say? How can you act?

■ What can you say or do to be respectful if someone tells you that what you believe is wrong?

Get to Know

"Let us not love with words or tongue but with actions and in truth."
1 John 3:18

GET CONNECTED

Who is someone you would like to tell about Jesus? What is important to him or her? What can you do or say to show the person what you believe about Jesus? Ask God to help you show respect and love to others as you tell about Jesus.

Teach Us to Pray

Get Started ■ 5-15 minutes

Action: Discover that talking with others helps build relationships.

Who's There?

What You Need

Self-adhesive labels, pen.

What You Do

1. Make at least one label for each student by printing each of these categories of people on separate labels: "mom," "dad," "doctor," "teacher," "friend," "police officer," "firefighter," "coach," "brother," "sister," "grandma" and "grandpa." Each category may be used more than once.

2. Place a label on the back of each student without revealing the word on the label. Each student tries to guess the word on his or her label by asking others yes-or-no questions. For example, a student might ask, "Am I someone you see every day?" "Do you see me at school?"

3. After several minutes, gather students. Reveal any labels students did not guess. Then ask the questions below.

■ **How often do you talk to the type of person on your label?**

■ **Why do you talk to your parents? Your friends?**

■ **Why would you talk to the doctor? Your teacher? A police officer?**

■ **Of all these different kinds of people, who do you know the best? Why?**

4. Conclude the activity by saying,

■ **God wants us to get to know Him, too. Praying to God is a good way to do that.**

■ **Today we're going to find out some ways that Jesus showed how important prayer is.**

Bonus Idea

Put more than one label on each student's back.

The Message

God wants us to talk to Him.

The Bible Basis

Mark 1:35-38; 6:45-46; Luke 6:12-13; 11:1-13

Jesus showed the importance of prayer by taking time to pray and by teaching His disciples to pray.

The Scripture

"Devote yourselves to prayer, being watchful and thankful." Colossians 4:2

Get It Together ■ 20-30 minutes

Action: Understand that just as Jesus needed time to pray, we also need to spend time talking with God.

Mark 1:35-38; 6:45-46; Luke 6:12-13; 11:1-13

What You Need

Bibles.

What You Do

Lead students to read and discuss the Bible verses listed. Extend the discussion with the questions and comments provided.

Introduction

When have you had a really busy day? What did you do? How did you feel at the end of the day? Let's find out about what happened after a busy day in Jesus' life.

Jesus and His disciples had gone to sleep after a really full day. From morning to night, Jesus had taught and healed people. Usually after we've had a busy day and evening, we like to sleep in the next morning. That's probably what Jesus' disciples, Simon, Andrew, James and John wanted to do.

Jesus Is Missing

■ Who do you think was missing when the disciples woke up? Read Mark 1:35 to find out.

■ What was Jesus doing so early in the morning? What does this action help you learn about Jesus? What do you think Jesus would have prayed about?

While it was still dark, Jesus had gone off by Himself to talk to God. We don't know what Jesus prayed about. He may have been talking to God, His heavenly Father, about the plans God had for Him. Or maybe Jesus was asking God for strength to go on helping people.

After Simon and the other disciples realized Jesus was gone, they went looking for Him. The Bible doesn't tell us how the disciples went about looking for Jesus, but probably each disciple said he'd look in a different place.

Disciples Find Jesus

■ Read Mark 1:36-37 to learn what the disciples said when they finally found Jesus.

■ In Mark 1:38, what does Jesus say He wanted to do next?

The disciples must have been surprised to discover that Jesus was by Himself—praying!

Jesus' reply to the disciples gives us a clue about how talking to God must have helped Jesus. After talking to God, Jesus was ready to travel to another town to keep on teaching and healing.

Jesus Prays All Night

■ Read Luke 6:12-13 to find out about another time Jesus prayed. How long had Jesus been praying?

■ What did Jesus do after spending a whole night in prayer?

■ Why do you think prayer was so important to Jesus?

Several other times, the Bible tells about Jesus teaching His disciples about the importance of prayer. And several other times, the Bible tells about Jesus going away by Himself to pray.

It seems as though no matter how busy He was, Jesus made time to pray and talk to God.

Jesus Teaches About Prayer

■ To help His followers learn more about prayer, Jesus told two stories. (Divide class into two groups. Ask one group to read Luke 11:5-8. Ask the other group to read Luke 11:11-13.) Who needed something in these stories? Who gave what was needed?

■ In what ways were the neighbor and the father acting like God? What do these stories teach about why we should pray?

■ What do you learn about how God answers prayer?

■ Read Luke 11:9 to find the words Jesus used to describe prayer.

■ What did Jesus say would be the results if we pray, asking for and then looking for God's help?

Jesus is not saying that God is like a sleepy neighbor who does not want to be bothered by our problems or like a parent who gives the wrong thing to a child. Instead, verse 13 clearly shows that He is telling us how MUCH more than a neighbor or even a parent God wants to give us what we need.

In between these two stories, Jesus gave some instructions about prayer. He used three different words to describe what we do when we pray. Jesus used the words "ask," "seek" and "knock" to help us understand what we do when we pray. "Seek" means the same as "to look for." "Knock" gives us a picture of what to do even when our way seems to be blocked.

Conclusion

You might think that because Jesus was God's Son, He didn't really have to pray. But if God's own Son regularly spent time praying, think how much more important it is for us to pray! We can devote ourselves to prayer just as Jesus did. (Read Colossians 4:2 aloud.) God loves us like a perfect parent would love his or her child. Because of this love, God wants us to talk with Him—getting to know Him, thanking Him and asking for His help.

We all have different prayer habits. Some of you may pray with your family every day— maybe before meals or when you're getting ready to go to bed. Some of you may only pray when you come to church or Sunday School. Some of you may remember to pray when you need God's help at school or in a game. God loves all of us, and He wants us to talk with Him often about the things that are important to us. Praying to God will help us get to know Him better and live in ways that show His love to others. (Lead students in prayer, thanking God for the ability to talk with Him in prayer.)

Get Going ■ 20-30 minutes

Action: Identify situations about which we can pray, and plan ways to make talking with God a priority.

Distribute Get Real (p. 188) to students. Invite students to tell or write answers to the questions. End the discussion by completing Get Connected with students. (Optional: Students complete page at home.)

Get Real

■ Why do you think God wants us to pray? How does praying help us? How does getting to know God as a member of His family help us?

■ Why might it be good to pray at the beginning of each day? At the end of the day? What might you say to God at those times? When else might you want to pray to God?

■ What can you do when you don't feel like praying or you don't know what to say? How can you remind yourself of God's presence and interest in your life?

■ What might happen when people don't take time to pray? Why?

■ What causes you to feel like you don't want to pray? What can you tell God about those feelings?

Get to Know

"Devote yourselves to prayer, being watchful and thankful."
Colossians 4:2

Get Connected

Think about one way you plan to focus more on prayer during the coming week. Plan one new time you will pray this week. Pray and ask God to help you make prayer more of a priority in your life.

A Song of Praise

Get Started ■ 5-15 minutes

Action: Discover what makes us want to show praise and honor.

Praise Frame

What You Need

A variety of old magazines, stopwatch or clock with second hand; optional—scissors.

What You Do

1. Divide group into pairs. Give each pair one or more old magazines.

2. At your signal, students begin hunting through magazines to find and tear out pictures of or words describing powerful things God made. (Optional: Students cut out individual letters to spell words they want to use.) After 30 seconds, call time and invite students to show what they found.

3. Repeat with other things for students to find pictures or descriptions of in magazines (very small things God made, complicated things God made, things that make people happy, things in our world that help people, etc.).

4. Several minutes before time is up, ask the questions below.

■ **How many different items did you find? What was your favorite?**

■ **What's something you didn't find that you praise God for making?**

■ **Because God made these awesome things, or made it possible for us to have these things, what do we learn about what He is like?**

■ **What words would you use to describe God?**

5. Conclude the activity by saying,

■ **Today we'll find out more about God's greatness and how someone in Bible times described and praised God.**

Bonus Idea

If you use magazines that you do not want to become destroyed, provide Post-it Notes for students to attach to pages with pictures or descriptions they find.

The Message

God loves us and wants us to express our love for Him.

The Bible Basis

Luke 1:26-56

Mary expressed honor and worship to God in her song of praise.

The Scripture

"Praise be to the name of God for ever and ever; wisdom and power are his." Daniel 2:20

Get It Together ■ 20-30 minutes

Action: Realize that awareness of God's greatness motivates us to express love for Him.

Luke 1:26-56

What You Need

Bibles.

What You Do

Lead students to read and discuss the Bible verses listed. Extend the discussion with the questions and comments provided.

Introduction

What is a song you like to listen to or sing? Included in the Bible is a story about a well-known song sung by Mary, Jesus' mother. Mary was a young woman who lived in Nazareth. She was engaged to be married to Joseph. Both Joseph and Mary were descendants of a famous Old Testament king, King David.

An Angel's Visit

■ Who was Mary's famous visitor? Read Luke 1:28 to find what the angel said about Mary. What do you think Mary must have been like?

■ How did Mary react to what the angel told her about her future? Read Luke 1:31-34.

■ Read Luke 1:36 to find out what else the angel said would happen. Read verse 37 to find out why the angel said these seemingly impossible things could happen.

■ What did Mary say to the angel in Luke 1:38? What do you learn about Mary from her words?

■ When Mary went to see her relative Elizabeth, what word did Elizabeth use to describe Mary and the child she would have? Read Luke 1:42,45.

Two times the angel said that God was pleased with Mary.

Since Mary wasn't married to Joseph yet, she wanted the angel to tell her how she would be able to have a baby. The angel told Mary that God's power would cause Jesus to be born. And that wasn't the ONLY way God's power would be shown.

A woman who everyone thought was too old to have a baby—Mary's cousin, Elizabeth—was going to have a baby.

When Elizabeth said that Mary and her child were "blessed," she meant that God had done good things for them and was showing great kindness to them.

Mary's Song

■ If you had been Mary, how might you have felt about these surprising events? Would you have been excited? Scared? Worried? Why?

The Bible tells us how Mary felt. She felt such love and worship for God that she sang a song of praise to Him.

■ Read Luke 1:46-49 to find what names Mary used when she sang about God. What do you learn about God's characteristics from these names?

■ Mary also sang about some of the things God has done. What did Mary say about God in Luke 1:49? How did God's action make Mary feel about Him?

Mary recognized that God was the one true, powerful God who offered salvation to her and all people.

Mary might have been worried or afraid about what was going to happen in her life. But she realized that the mighty God cared about her and had shown His love to her by choosing her to be the mother of the Messiah.

God's Mercy and Power

■ In Luke 1:50, what characteristic of God is shown to those who love and obey Him?

■ If you wanted to describe someone who is very powerful, what would you say?

■ Read the first part of Luke 1:51 to find what Mary said about God's power. What do you think this means?

■ Several other symbols are used in Luke 1:53. What are they?

Mercy is kindness and love shown to a person who doesn't deserve it. That's how God treats us—with mercy!

Mary described God's power in an unusual way. Since God is a spirit, and doesn't have a body like you or me, the words "his arm" are a symbol of His strength and power.

Mary wasn't saying that God was only concerned about making sure people have enough food to eat but that God would answer the deepest needs of people who really wanted to get to know Him.

Conclusion

Mary's song of praise is full of reasons to worship God. Another word for "worship" is "adoration." "Adoration" is the first word in the prayer-reminder word "ACTS." "ACTS" stands for Adoration, Confession, Thanksgiving and Supplication. When we adore something or someone, we love and are devoted to the thing or the person. One of the things we can do when we pray is to adore, or worship, God. When we remember the ways in which God has shown His greatness and His love, we want to worship Him. (Read Daniel 2:20 aloud.)

Sometimes it might be easy to take God's greatness for granted, not really taking the time to think about what He is like. But as we get to know about God and understand what He is like, we discover more and more reasons to praise and worship Him. Not only has God shown His power and greatness by creating the world and all its wonders, but He also shows His love to each of us personally. (Pray with students, praising God for His love.)

Get Going ■ 20-30 minutes

Action: Identify reasons to honor God and praise Him in prayer.

Distribute Get Real (p. 192) to students. Invite students to tell or write answers to the questions. End the discussion by completing Get Connected with students. (Optional: Students complete page at home.)

Get Real

■ When you honor someone, what do you do? How can you honor God in your prayers?

■ What things has God done that we can praise Him for? What do you know about God's character that we can praise Him for?

■ Why does God want us to praise Him?

■ When are some times you have praised God in the past? What did you praise Him for? What can you praise God for right now?

■ What's something you see every day that God made? What's an unusual thing God made?

■ In what way has God helped you or your family in the last week? In the last year?

Get to Know

"Praise be to the name of God for ever and ever; wisdom and power are his."
Daniel 2:20

Get Connected

What do you want to praise and honor God for? Tell Him why You think He is so great, and ask His help in continuing to praise Him during the week.

Confess Your Sins

Get Started ■ 5-15 minutes

Action: Discover what "humble" means.

Music Freeze

What You Need

Marker, large sheet of paper, music CD and player.

What You Do

1. Brainstorm a list of emotions (happy, cheerful, energetic, sad, excited, humble, proud, shy, sluggish, etc.) with students and write list on a large sheet of paper.

2. Play music as students move around the room. When you pause the music, call out an emotion from the list. All students freeze in place, showing that emotion. Invite one or two volunteers to quickly identify other students who are showing the emotion in interesting ways. Repeat several times with new emotions from the list, making sure to end with "humble."

3. After several rounds, ask the questions below.

■ **Which of these emotions was the most fun to act out? The easiest? The hardest?**

■ **What do you think "humble" or "doing something humbly" means?**

■ **Do you think it's good or bad to be humble? Why?**

■ **Do you think it's hard or easy to be humble? Why?**

4. Conclude the activity by saying,

■ **This activity helped us think about what being humble means.**

■ **In our Bible study, we'll find out why it's important to be humble—especially when we're talking to God.**

Bonus Idea

Videotape or take photos of kids showing different emotions. Show the video or display the pictures in your classroom or post video or still pictures, with parent permission, on your church's website.

The Message

Confession is more than saying, "I'm sorry."

The Bible Basis

Nehemiah 1—9

After rebuilding the walls of Jerusalem, the Israelites humbly asked God's forgiveness for their sin and promised to obey.

The Scripture

"If we confess our sins, he is faithful and just and will forgive us our sins and purify us from unrighteousness."

1 John 1:9

Get It Together ■ 20-30 minutes

Action: Understand that when we confess our sins, we recognize how we have disobeyed, and we humbly acknowledge God's holiness.

Nehemiah 1—9

What You Need

Bibles.

What You Do

Lead students to read and discuss the Bible verses listed. Extend the discussion with the questions and comments provided.

Introduction

Do most people think it's a good idea or a bad idea to be humble? Why? People are sometimes afraid that showing humility might make them appear weak or helpless. But let's look at what the amazing results were when a man in Bible times was humble.

Long before Jesus was alive, most of the Israelites had been taken away from the land of Israel to live as captives in other lands. Only a few had remained in Jerusalem, now a city in ruins. But among the captives living in Babylon was a leader named Nehemiah.

Nehemiah's Prayer

■ Find in Nehemiah 2:3-5 what Nehemiah said and what he did.

■ What do you think Nehemiah said to God? What did Nehemiah ask the king?

As a result of Nehemiah's conversation with the king, Nehemiah returned to Jerusalem and led the Israelites in rebuilding the walls and gates of the city.

Nehemiah Rebuilds the Walls

■ What did Nehemiah do when the enemies of the Israelites tried to stop the rebuilding of the walls of the city? Read Nehemiah 4:4,9 to find out.

The rebuilding job didn't go very smoothly. Some enemies of the Israelites tried to discourage the builders by yelling insults at them and threatening violence. So Nehemiah prayed, asking God to deal with the problem of these enemies. Several more times as the enemies tried to stop the rebuilding, Nehemiah prayed to God and God helped Nehemiah know what to do to keep the workers safe.

God's Law Is Read

■ Finally the walls had been rebuilt. As part of their celebration, the Israelites read from the Book of the Law. What was their response in Nehemiah 8:9?

■ What did Nehemiah say in Nehemiah 8:10,12 that encouraged the Israelites?

The Book of the Law was the first five books of the Old Testament. When the people heard the law, they started to cry because they realized they had not been following God's laws.

The people realized that because they now knew God's Word, they really had reason to celebrate. And they celebrated for seven days!

The Israelites Confess Their Sins

■ It's clear that Nehemiah was used to praying about everything! And he encouraged the Israelites to pray, too. How do you think a prayer of confession usually sounds? What might most people say when they're asking God to forgive their sins?

■ Read the prayer in Nehemiah 9:5-6 to see how the people began their prayer. What did they say about God?

■ What else did the Israelites say in Nehemiah 9:16-17?

■ What attitude did the ancestors of the Israelites have toward God?

■ What did their attitude result in? How did God treat them despite their sins?

■ How was the attitude of these Israelites different than the attitude of their ancestors?

Usually, when we're confessing our sins, we tell God we're sorry we've done something wrong. But Nehemiah and the Israelites told God about the wrong things they AND their ancestors had done! In fact, the Bible says the Israelites prayed for over three hours.

The Israelites adored God and began their prayer by describing the many, many ways in which God had shown His greatness and perfection.

The Israelites not only knew that they and their ancestors had sinned by disobeying God, but they also knew that God was far mightier and greater than they. Instead of being arrogant, or overly proud, of their accomplishment in rebuilding the walls, the people were truly humble before God!

The Israelites summed up their prayer of confession by saying, "In all the events of our lives, you've been faithful and perfect. We're the ones who have done wrong!" Then the Israelites went on to promise their faithful obedience to God in the days to come.

Conclusion

"Confession" is the second word in the prayer reminder, "ACTS." Confessing our sins to God is more than just saying "I'm sorry." It means agreeing with God about our sins. It also means knowing that God is perfect, holy and without sin. Knowing these two things—our sinfulness and God's perfection—helps us pray to God with a humble attitude. Then we know that because of His love for us, God forgives us and makes it possible for us to show our love and obedience to Him. (Read 1 John 1:9 aloud.)

Because we're human and imperfect, we will always struggle with sin. The apostle Paul, who wrote many of the books in the New Testament, often talked about his struggle with sin. He said that even though he wanted to do good, he often found himself doing wrong. But Paul went on to say that members of God's family don't have to give up and keep on sinning or live in fear of being punished for their sins. God's forgiveness, provided through the death of Jesus on the cross, takes away our sin. As God's children, we can ask His forgiveness and help in obeying Him. (See Romans 7:15—8:2.) Invite students to talk with you about salvation, asking questions they may have about confession of sins. (Refer to the "Leading a Student to Christ" article on pp. 10-11 for guidelines in talking with students.)

Get Going ■ 20-30 minutes

Action: Tell situations in which we often sin, and describe the results of confessing our sins.

Distribute Get Real (p. 196) to students. Invite students to tell or write answers to the questions. End the discussion by completing Get Connected with students. (Optional: Students complete page at home.)

Get Real

■ What is sin? What are some specific ways that kids your age might sin at school? At home?

■ Does confession help or hurt you? How? How does it feel to confess what you've done wrong and then be forgiven for it? What can you do after you've confessed a sin?

■ Have you ever been in a situation where you had to admit you had done wrong to another person? How did you feel? What was the result?

■ How is your attitude important in confession? What kind of attitude do we need to have when we confess our sins to God?

Get to Know

"If we confess our sins, he is faithful and just and will forgive us our sins and purify us from unrighteousness."
1 John 1:9

Get Connected

Because no one is perfect, there will be times when you sin. If there is a sin you need to confess, now is a good time to do that. Then remember that God's promise of forgiveness will help you live each day as a follower of Jesus.

A Grateful Heart

Get Started ■ 5-15 minutes

Action: Discover reasons to say "Thank you."

Clues, Clues

What You Need

Nothing.

What You Do

1. Give three clues for something or someone you're thankful for, trying to stump the group.

2. As a group, students have three tries to guess the item or person. If students cannot guess the item, give one more clue, this time making it easy for the students to guess.

3. Repeat the game as time permits, with students giving clues to the whole group, or divide group into pairs or trios to play the game.

4. Several minutes before time is up, talk with students about the items or people they were thankful for.

■ **When was a time you were especially thankful for this item? Why? When have you not felt thankful? How does complaining get in the way of being thankful?**

■ **How many different ways of expressing thankfulness to others can you think of?**

■ **What are some reasons it's good to be a grateful person?**

■ **What is something a friend or family member has done for you that made you feel REALLY thankful?**

5. Conclude the activity by saying,

■ **Compare your grateful feelings to the feelings of the people in our Bible study today.**

Bonus Idea

Display various props to help students guess what you are thankful for.

The 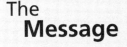 Message

Give thanks with a grateful heart.

The Bible Basis

Judges 4—5

Deborah and Barak thanked God for His help in defeating Sisera and his army.

The Scripture

"Give thanks to the Lord, for he is good. His love endures forever."
Psalm 136:1

Get It Together ■ 20-30 minutes

Action: Understand that thanking God for all He does is a natural expression of our love for Him.

Judges 4—5

What You Need

Bibles.

What You Do

Lead students to read and discuss the Bible verses listed. Extend the discussion with the questions and comments provided.

Introduction

When is it easy to be thankful? When is it hard to be thankful? Long ago, two people named Deborah and Barak sang a song, or prayer, of thankfulness. We can read this prayer in Judges 5. But Judges 4 tells us the exciting story of why they were thankful. Let's find out what happened.

A Cry for Help

■ What does Judges 4:1 say was the reason for the Israelites' troubles?

■ Read Judges 4:3 to find out what the Israelites did.

Because of their disobedience to God, the Israelites were in big trouble. Living in small villages had become so dangerous that people moved away to large, walled cities for safety. But even in these large cities, the people didn't have enough weapons to defend themselves.

God allowed the Israelites to be ruled by a cruel enemy named Jabin. The commander of his army was named Sisera.

After 20 years of disobeying God, the Israelites came to their senses and did the wise thing. At last, the Israelites realized that God was the only One who could come to their rescue. God's plan involved a woman named Deborah.

A Plan from God

■ What do you learn about Deborah by reading Judges 4:4-5?

■ What do you learn in Judges 4:6-7 about God's plans for defeating Sisera?

■ Read Judges 4:8-9 to find out Barak's answer to God's plan and Deborah's response.

Besides being a prophetess, one who gave God's messages to His people the Israelites, Deborah was also the judge who ruled in Israel. If people couldn't settle a quarrel, they would go to Deborah, tell her about their quarrel and let her decide who was right. Deborah was a very wise woman and her wisdom came from God.

Deborah not only told Barak exactly what God planned for him to do, but she told Barak that God had promised to give the victory to Barak!

Barak, however, probably knew about the strong iron chariots that Sisera's army owned. The idea of leading the frightened Israelites into battle against this fierce army must have been more than a little scary. So Barak agreed to lead the battle, but ONLY if Deborah would go with him. Deborah agreed, but told Barak that the credit for the victory would then go to a woman.

A Song of Thanks

■ How many men does Judges 4:10 say gathered with Deborah and Barak?

■ Read Judges 4:15-16 to see how the battle turned out.

■ After the battle, Deborah and Barak thanked God in a song. Read part of the song in Judges 5:20-21. What else do you learn about this battle?

■ Read Judges 5:3 to see how Deborah and Barak responded at the end of the battle.

Sisera's scouts and spies would have told him about these 10,000 Israelite soldiers preparing for a battle. Not feeling any fear, Sisera gathered up his 900 iron chariots and all his soldiers. The battle was ready to begin! Just as God had promised, the Israelites were victorious.

We learn quite a bit more about how that victory took place as we read what Deborah and Barak thanked God for. Deborah and Barak were so amazed at God's help in defeating Sisera that their grateful feelings were naturally expressed in a song of praise.

This poetic language indicates that God used nature itself to fight against Sisera. Here's how: evidently, Sisera chose the flat ground next to a river as his battle-ground. That kind of an area is called the floodplain. Here, Sisera thought his soldiers in their chariots would have lots of room for fighting.

But he didn't plan on one important thing: Sisera did not know that the mighty God of the Israelites would send a huge rainstorm, overflowing the banks of the river and making Sisera's battleground a sea of mud. The iron chariots got stuck in the mud! Sisera and his soldiers ran for their lives, but were all killed. The battle was over!

With God's mighty victory, it's no wonder that Deborah and Barak sang such a song of praise and thanksgiving to God!

Conclusion

God does many good things for us every day. It is often easy to ignore what He does or think that we deserve good things. When we stop to consider the ways in which God helps us and the things He provides for us, we want to express our thanks. "Thanksgiving" is the third word in the prayer-reminder word, "ACTS."

God tells us to give thanks, not because it makes Him feel good, but because He knows that when we remember how good He is to us, we can get to know Him better and trust Him more the next time we need His help. (Read Psalm 136:1 aloud. Lead students in prayer, thanking God for who He is.)

Get Going ■ 20-30 minutes

Action: List ways God helps us and thank God for His goodness.

Distribute Get Real (p. 200) to students. Invite students to tell or write answers to the questions. End the discussion by completing Get Connected with students. (Optional: Students complete page at home.)

Get Real

■ What are some reasons people today have for thanking God?

■ What can you do to help you remember to thank God more often?

■ What difference do you think thanking God will make in your life? Why?

■ Why might some people usually be grateful? Ungrateful?

■ What are you thankful for? What has God given you? How has He helped you? How has He helped your family?

■ What are some things that help people in difficult circum-stances to trust and thank God for His goodness? Why do you think thankfulness is important for people in dif-ficult circumstances?

Get to Know

"Give thanks to the Lord, for he is good. His love endures forever."
Psalm 136:1

Get Connected

Even if you have lots of problems in your life, you still have reasons to thank God. Think of reasons you have for thanking God. Tell God what you are thankful for.

Ask the Lord

Get Started ■ 5-15 minutes

Action: Discover ways of making and answering requests.

Mother, May I?

What You Need

Index cards, markers, two bags.

What You Do

1. Lead students in brainstorming categories of people (mom, dad, teacher, principal, coach, friend, baby, king, queen, TV star, star basketball player, grandma), writing each category on a separate index card. (Optional: Print people cards and question cards [see below] before class.)

2. Then brainstorm questions people often ask ("May I have some money?" "Where's the rest room?" "What was I supposed to do for homework?" "How are you?" "What's your favorite sport?" "What do you want to watch on TV?" "Want to play a game?" "May I have something to eat?"), writing each on a separate index card as well. Put people cards in one bag and question cards in another bag.

3. Select a card from each bag. One student asks the question to another student who answers the question as though he or she is a (king). Continue activity with different volunteers and different cards. Ask the questions below.

■ **How would you describe the way a king answers? A TV star? A friend? A mom or dad?**

■ **Which of these might be similar to the way in which God answers prayer?**

4. Conclude the activity by saying,

■ **Today we are going to talk about the kinds of things people ask God for and how He answers prayer.**

Bonus Ideas

1. Videotape students asking and answering questions. Play back video before discussing the activity.

2. Provide costumes and props for students to use as they act as different people and answer questions.

The Message

Tell your worries to God.

The Bible Basis

1 Samuel 1—2:10

Hannah prayed to God about her worries, and God answered her prayer.

The Scripture

"Do not be anxious about anything, but in everything, by prayer and petition, with thanksgiving, present your requests to God." Philippians 4:6

Get It Together ■ 20-30 minutes

Action: Realize that God always hears and answers the requests of those who love Him.

1 Samuel 1—2:10

What You Need

Bibles.

What You Do

Lead students to read and discuss the Bible verses listed. Extend the discussion with the questions and comments provided.

Introduction

What are some things little kids often ask for? What do parents often ask for? In our Bible study today, God heard and answered the prayers of a woman named Hannah.

Hannah's Problem

■ What do you remember about Hannah?

■ Find Hannah's problem in 1 Samuel 1:2.

■ Read 1 Samuel 1:6 to find out who made Hannah's problem worse.

■ Read 1 Samuel 1:6-7 to find out what Peninnah did to Hannah.

Hannah was in a situation that must have seemed pretty hopeless to her. And no matter how much she worried about this situation, it didn't go away. Not having any children might not seem like much of a problem to you, but in Bible times it was a BIG problem. In Bible times, if a woman didn't have any children, she often felt worthless. Women without children also felt that God was withholding His love and blessings from them.

To make Hannah's problem worse, another person refused to be quiet about the problem. Peninnah and Hannah were both wives of the same man, Elkanah. (In Old Testament times, some men had more than one wife.)

Peninnah was jealous of Hannah because Elkanah loved her very much. All during the year, but especially at the time when Elkanah and his family participated in a religious celebration, Peninnah made fun of Hannah.

Hannah's Request

■ How does the Bible describe Hannah's feelings about this situation? Read 1 Samuel 1:10.

■ After Hannah asked God for a son and talked to Eli the chief priest, how does 1 Samuel 1:18 describe Hannah's feelings?

■ Do you think Hannah knew how God would answer her prayer?

Peninnah teased Hannah so much that she cried and cried. Finally Hannah could not stand it any longer. She went to the Tabernacle (the place of worship for the Israelites) and asked God for a son, promising to give this son to serve the Lord all his life.

After praying to God and letting Him know just how sad and upset she was, Hannah was confident that God had listened to her request. Finally she could stop crying and worrying.

God's Answer

■ Some time later, God answered Hannah's prayer by giving her a son, Samuel. Read 1 Samuel 1:20 to find out what Samuel's name means.

■ What did Hannah say about God? Read 1 Samuel 2:2.

Samuel's name sounds like the Hebrew for "heard of God." Hannah wanted everyone to know that God had heard her prayers and that Samuel was an answer to prayer!

When Samuel was older, Hannah took him to the Tabernacle. It was time to keep her promise and give Samuel back to God. She arranged with Eli, the chief priest, for Samuel to stay at the Tabernacle and learn to become a priest. Once again, Hannah prayed to God. But this time her prayer was one of happiness and praise! Hannah knew that God was the only One able to answer her requests!

Conclusion

What are the kinds of things people today ask God for? Sometimes we ask God to help us do well on a test or get better when we're sick. Sometimes our prayers are for other people—like when a friend or a grandparent is sick. Another word which means the same as asking for something is "supplication." It's the last word in the prayer reminder "ACTS." When we, as members of God's family, ask God for ANYTHING, whether large or small, we can believe He listens to our prayers. (Read Philippians 4:6 aloud).

We've probably all had the experience of asking God for something and He answered our prayers by giving us what we asked for, like what happened with Hannah. But we've also probably all had the experience of having God say no when we asked for something. At those times, we might feel like God didn't hear our prayers at all! God understands when we feel that way. What we need to remember about talking to God is that He ALWAYS hears our prayers, He ALWAYS answers our prayers, and He ALWAYS loves us. Because God knows everything about us, He knows what will be best for us. So whether God says yes, no, later or "I have something better" in answer to our prayers, we can always depend on Him to do what's right. (Lead students in prayer, thanking God for hearing our requests and doing what is best in every situation.)

Get Going ■ 20-30 minutes

Action: Discuss ways God answers prayer, and ask God's help with problems.

Distribute Get Real (p. 204) to students. Invite students to tell or write answers to the questions. End the discussion by completing Get Connected with students. (Optional: Students complete page at home.)

Get Real

■ What are different ways God answers prayer? Why might God answer prayer in these ways?

■ Why is it best to talk to God about your worries? How does praying help if God doesn't always do what you want?

■ Why do you think God wants you to ask Him for help?

■ What is something you have asked God for recently? How did God answer your prayer? How do you feel about the way God answered your prayer?

■ What reasons might God have for not answering the way you want Him to?

Get to Know

"Do not be anxious about anything, but in everything, by prayer and petition, with thanksgiving, present your requests to God."
Philippians 4:6

Get Connected

Tell a prayer request to a friend. Ask a friend what his or her prayer request is. Then pray for your friend. Thank God for hearing and caring about your friend's concerns.

Here I Am, Lord

Get Started ■ 5-15 minutes

Action: Identify tasks people use their abilities to do and rate them as hard or easy.

Hard or Easy?

What You Need

Markers, 10 to 12 paper lunch bags, beans, pennies.

What You Do

1. As students arrive, ask them to print on separate bags tasks requiring a variety of abilities (play video game, hit home run, design web page, play in recital, plan birthday party, draw picture, etc.). Give each student a handful of beans and pennies. Students evaluate each task by placing beans in bags to indicate tasks they think are hard, and by placing pennies in bags to indicate tasks they think are easy.

2. Students count the number of beans and pennies in each bag, recording the number on the bags. Ask the questions below.

■ **Which task got the most votes for being hard? Easy?**

■ **Why might people disagree about whether or not a task was hard?**

■ **What are some other tasks, or jobs, you do? Are they hard or easy? Why?**

■ **How do you feel when you have to do something you're not good at or have never done before?**

3. Conclude the activity by saying,

■ **When we are faced with new or hard tasks, it's easy to worry about them.**

■ **In our Bible study today, compare your feelings about hard tasks with the feelings of a man in Bible times who was given a task to do.**

Bonus Idea

After students complete the activity, invite them to use a graphing program on a computer to generate different kinds of charts to represent the data they gathered.

The Message

Because God made me and is with me, I can do the good things He asks me to do.

The Bible Basis

Exodus 3—4:17,27-31

When Moses didn't feel he was able to complete a hard task, God reassured Him of His presence and help.

The Scripture

"For we are God's workmanship, created in Christ Jesus to do good works." Ephesians 2:10

Get It Together ■ 20-30 minutes

Action: Understand that because God knows and loves us, He will help us do what He asks.

Exodus 3—4:17,27-31

What You Need

Bibles.

What You Do

Lead students to read and discuss the Bible verses listed. Extend the discussion with the questions and comments provided.

Introduction

When have you seen something unusual? Some unusual things have natural explanations behind them. In today's story, an unusual thing happened that could have only come from God.

For 40 years, Moses' job had been as a sheepherder in the desert. One particular day, however, Moses was on an isolated mountain. He spotted a bush that seemed to be on fire. Most bushes burn up when they catch on fire, but this bush just kept burning!

God's Voice

■ When Moses walked closer to the bush to see the strange sight, read Exodus 3:4 to find out whose voice he heard. What did Moses reply? Then read Exodus 3:5 to find what God said next.

■ What did God tell Moses? Read Exodus 3:7. What do you think it was like to be a slave?

This ground was holy because God was present. When Moses learned it was really God that he was talking to, Moses turned and hid his face.

The Israelites had been slaves of the pharaoh of Egypt for a long time, quite possibly building some of the pyramids. These slaves had no rights. They had to work when their masters said to and do ANYTHING their masters told them to. They could be beaten or killed if they refused, or even if they made a mistake.

God's Command

■ When God told Moses to go back to Egypt and free His people, read Exodus 3:11 to find out what Moses said to God. If you were Moses, what would you have said to God?

■ What did God answer? Read Exodus 3:12.

■ Read Exodus 3:14 to find out what else God said when Moses was still worried.

Moses told God he was a nobody. Moses said, "Why should I be the one to go to Pharaoh and tell him to let the slaves go free?" (Pharaoh is an Egyptian royal title, not a person's name.)

God said that Moses was going to be successful and promised that Moses would meet with God on that very same mountain after Moses had accomplished his task. GOD was going to make sure Moses was successful!

Because Moses was so worried, he asked, "What if the leaders of the Israelites want to know who actually sent me? What if they want to know Your name?" God's answer meant that He is truly God, the only God who exists and does exactly what He declares.

God's Power

■ Read Exodus 4:2-5 to discover the first thing God told Moses to do.

■ Read about the second thing God told Moses to do in Exodus 4:6-7.

■ What was the third way in which God told Moses to demonstrate God's power? Read Exodus 4:9 to find out.

God had a solution for Moses' doubts. God told Moses about three amazing ways in which he could show God's power to the Egyptians. Moses usually used his staff for herding sheep. But now God said that Moses could use his staff to prove that the one true God had actually appeared to him.

If the people STILL didn't believe God had sent Moses, God told Moses to show His power in a second way. Leprosy was a horrible disease. Moses must have been relieved when his hand was healed!

The Egyptians believed that the Nile River was a god. If, by God's power, Moses changed the water of this river into blood, it would show Pharaoh and the rest of the Egyptians, as well as the Israelites, that Moses' God was more powerful than the Egyptians' gods and that He was the one true God.

God's Help

■ What did Moses say now about the job God had told him to do? Read what he said in Exodus 4:10.

■ What did God say to Moses? Read Exodus 4:11-12. What did God say about Himself? How would He help Moses?

■ When Moses STILL wasn't convinced, what do you think God's reaction was? Read the beginning of Exodus 4:14.

■ Read Exodus 4:29-31 to find out what happened when Moses and Aaron talked to the Israelites.

Moses had no trouble talking to God, but he was still really worried about talking to Pharaoh! Once more, God had a solution.

Because God was the one who created people, God said that by His power He would help Moses know what to say!

The Bible says that despite God's anger, He had loved and had chosen Moses, so He solved this problem, too. God told Moses that his brother, Aaron, could help him. Aaron could speak for Moses. Together, they could lead the people out of Egypt.

The people were so glad to hear God would rescue them from slavery that they worshiped God right there!

Conclusion

God knows, better than anyone else, what we are really like. In God's eyes, we can't pretend to be better than we really are or worse than we really are. Because God made us, He knows what we're good at and He knows what we're not so good at. He won't ever ask or expect us to do something we can't really do. With His help, we know that we can do even the hardest task He asks us to do because we are His workmanship, as Ephesians 2:10 says. (Read verse aloud.)

As you're growing and learning, you'll discover more of the special abilities God has given you. Making you wonderfully unique is one way God shows His love for you. Because God promises to be with members of His family, just like He promised to be with Moses, God will help you as you learn about the abilities He has given you. (Pray with students, asking God to help them trust Him; and then talk with interested students about salvation, referring to the "Leading a Student to Christ" article on p. 10-11.)

Get Going ■ 20-30 minutes

Action: Describe the abilities God has given us, and thank God for His presence.

Distribute Get Real (p. 208) to students. Invite students to tell or write answers to the questions. End the discussion by completing Get Connected with students. (Optional: Students complete page at home.)

GET REAL

- What's something you've learned to do better than you used to do?

- How do our attitudes make a difference when we do something?

- What are some things you're good at and enjoy doing? Some things you're not good at and don't enjoy doing?

- What are some ways you can find out what your abilities are?

- What are some of the things you know God wants you to do with your abilities?

Get to Know
"For we are God's workmanship, created in Christ Jesus to do good works."
Ephesians 2:10

Get Connected

Think about an ability you have that you could use for God. What is an ability you would like to develop? Ask God to help you use your abilities in ways that show your love and obedience to God.

Serve with God's Strength

Get Started ■ 5-15 minutes

Action: Discover abilities that are needed in leaders.

Job Wanted Ads

What You Need

Large sheet of butcher paper, tape, marker, employment classified section from several newspapers.

What You Do

1. Tape butcher paper to wall. Draw a line to divide paper in half.

2. Distribute newspaper sections. Students look through listings to find interesting jobs and descriptions of the skills, or abilities, necessary for those jobs. Students list each job on the left half of the paper and abilities needed for that job on the right. Ask the questions below.

■ **What are some jobs that interest you?**

■ **What are some of the abilities wanted in these advertisements? What abilities does a computer programmer need? A sales manager? A mechanic?**

■ **If you were hiring a schoolteacher, what abilities would you require? A nurse? A banker?**

■ **Which of these jobs would need leadership abilities? Why?**

■ **What is a good leader like?**

3. Add the word "leader" to the list of jobs. Students tell abilities someone would need in order to lead a group of people and list those abilities on the right half of the paper.

4. Conclude the activity by saying,

■ **The abilities that God looks for in a leader are often different from what the world looks for in a leader.**

■ **We may not all become leaders of big groups of people, but all of us can use our abilities to lead others to follow God.**

■ **Today we'll look at a person God wanted to become a leader of Israel. Let's see how this person responded.**

Bonus Idea

Provide paper and markers. Divide class into pairs. Each pair writes an ad for a job they would like, listing the skills, or abilities, they would need for it. The ad could be for a real job or for a made-up one.

The Message

God can achieve great things through unlikely people.

The Bible Basis

Judges 6:1-35

God sent an angel to Gideon to give him the important task of leading the Israelites against the Midianites.

The Scripture

"If anyone serves, he should do it with the strength God provides, so that in all things God may be praised through Jesus Christ." 1 Peter 3:10

Get It Together ■ 20-30 minutes

Action: Realize that to accomplish tasks that benefit others God chooses people who obey and depend on Him.

Judges 6:1-35

What You Need

Bibles.

What You Do

Lead students to read and discuss the Bible verses listed. Extend the discussion with the questions and comments provided.

Introduction

Why do you think that a person might hide? An Israelite named Gideon was hiding while he was doing a job for his family. His job was threshing grain. That means he was stomping on the grain to break it loose from the hulls. When the hulls and grain were tossed up into the air, the lighter hulls (called chaff) would blow away, leaving the heavier grain. Threshing was usually done by animals on a threshing floor. Threshing floors were flat open places on hillsides where there were good breezes.

But no animals were helping Gideon thresh. And Gideon was not threshing his grain on a threshing floor. Instead he was all by himself, stomping his grain down in a rock pit, where grapes were usually stomped on by people making wine. It was not too easy for Gideon to thresh the wheat in a winepress, but Gideon had his reasons!

Gideon's Fear

■ Read Judges 6:3-4 to find out why Gideon was hiding.

■ Who found Gideon and what did he call Gideon in Judges 6:12? Why was the phrase "mighty warrior" a surprising description of Gideon?

■ Gideon wanted to know why there was so much trouble from the Midianites if God was with them. Read Judges 6:10 to find the reason.

Gideon hoped that if he stayed hidden in the winepress, the Midianites wouldn't see him and steal his grain. But much to Gideon's surprise, someone DID find him while he was working.

When Gideon heard the phrase "mighty warrior" he thought that the angel could not be talking to him!

As Gideon had grown up, he had probably heard lots of stories about how God helped the Israelites in the past. But now, the Israelites were worshiping false gods, and God allowed their enemies to conquer them so that the Israelites would learn to follow His ways.

Gideon's Worries

■ When the angel told Gideon he was to save Israel from the Midianites, what reasons did Gideon give for why he felt he could not lead Israel? Read Judges 6:15 to find out.

■ Read Judges 6:16 to find out what the angel said that made Gideon wonder if he was really talking to the Lord.

The leaders of the most powerful, influential families became the leaders of the nation, and Gideon's family was NOT very important. Gideon was also the youngest in his family. And in an Israelite family, younger sons were NEVER leaders. Younger sons just had to obey their fathers or older brothers until they died!

At this point, Gideon must have wondered just WHOM he was talking to. *The Lord is with you!* thought Gideon. *The LORD? Was this GOD talking to him?*

Gideon's Test

■ Gideon was still so uncertain, that he asked the angel to do something special. Read in verse 17 what Gideon said.

■ When Gideon brought some meat and bread, what did the angel do to the meat and bread that showed He was God? Read Judges 6:20-21.

Gideon wanted the angel to do a miracle so that he could be certain that this was God talking to him.

When he returned, Gideon gave the meat and bread to the stranger. Even though the bread and meat were soaking wet from the broth, they burned up completely and nothing was left. Then the Lord disappeared.

Gideon's Assignment

■ Even though Gideon was still fearful, read in Judges 6:23 what God promised Gideon.

■ Was Gideon brave when He obeyed God's command? Read verse 27 to find out.

■ How would you describe Gideon?

■ Everyone in the town DID become angry at Gideon, but what did Gideon's father say in Judges 6:31 about who would punish Gideon for his actions?

God promised Gideon he would not die, and later that same night God spoke to Gideon again, giving Gideon his first assignment as a leader for God. God wanted Gideon to tear down his father's statues of the false gods, Baal and Asherah. God wanted Gideon to use the wood from those statues to make a special place to worship the one true God instead.

Now this was a risky job. If Gideon did what God asked, Gideon's father and neighbors would be angry. They might kill him! So Gideon did it at night. But he trusted God and obeyed Him.

Gideon's father told the crowd that if Baal really was a god, he could punish Gideon himself—without the crowd's help. The crowd thought this was a pretty good idea. That would show Gideon! The crowd even gave Gideon a nickname—"Jerub-Baal," which means, "Let Baal Fight."

In the meantime, Gideon prepared for his next assignment as a leader for God. With God's help, Gideon called together the men of his tribe, plus men from several other tribes, to fight against the large army that was gathering against them. The men came by the thousands, answering Gideon's challenge. (And Baal, of course, never did punish Gideon!)

Conclusion

Sometimes we might think that only the smartest, strongest or most popular kids can be leaders and use their abilities to serve God. But we can all lead, or influence, others to do good. God knows the unique abilities that each of us has. When we depend on God and obey Him, God can use our abilities to accomplish good things. Even when we don't feel very confident, or we're not sure what will happen, God is with us and gives us the courage we need. (Read 1 Peter 3:10 aloud. Pray with students, asking God to help them use their abilities for Him.)

Get Going ■ 20-30 minutes

Action: Plan ways to use abilities to serve God.

Distribute Get Real (p. 212) to students. Invite students to tell or write answers to the questions. End the discussion by completing Get Connected with students. (Optional: Students complete page at home.)

GET REAL

- When have you felt like you couldn't do something? When have you felt confident about doing something?

- When is a time you've used an ability, or skill, you have to help someone else?

- What are some situations in which you can use your abilities to serve God?

- How can you encourage someone else in using his or her abilities to serve God?

- How can knowing that God made you in wonderful ways help you believe that God will help you to serve Him?

Get to Know

"If anyone serves, he should do it with the strength God provides, so that in all things God may be praised through Jesus Christ."
1 Peter 3:10

Get Connected

What's one ability you have that you could use to help others? Thank God for your ability and ask His help in seeing opportunities to use it.

Rely on God's Strength

Get Started ■ 5-15 minutes

Action: Discover situations in which students may feel insecure about using their abilities.

Grab-bag Gab

What You Need

Marker, index cards, three lunch bags.

What You Do

1. Ask students to suggest names for kids (Lisa, Adam, etc.), worries kids might have about using their abilities (might make a mistake, other kids will laugh, etc.) and abilities kids might have (draw picture, play guitar, etc.). Write each suggested name, worry and ability on a separate index card. Place name cards in bag 1, worry cards in bag 2 and ability cards in bag 3.

2. One student chooses a card from each bag and uses the words on the cards to create a sentence about a situation in which kids find it hard to use their abilities. For example, Harry was afraid the kids would laugh at him for his ability to spell words. Student returns cards to bags. Continue activity with other students choosing cards and creating sentences. Ask the questions below.

■ **What are some abilities kids your age use at school? At home? At church? In a sport? In a hobby?**

■ **What helps you feel confident in using an ability?**

■ **What are some times kids your age might not want to use their abilities? Why?**

3. Conclude the activity by saying,

■ **Sometimes it is hard to believe we have the ability to accomplish something important.**

■ **Today we will learn about a man who led Israel. But even though he was chosen by God, he had a hard time believing in his ability to do what God wanted.**

Bonus Idea

Add more fun by playing music as students sit in a circle. Students pass bags randomly as the music plays. After a moment, stop the music. Students holding bags when the music stops remove cards. Students with cards work together to create a sentence.

The **Message**

God can help us exceed our capabilities.

The **Bible Basis**

Judges 6:33—7:25

God showed Gideon that His power won the battle against the Midianites.

The **Scripture**

"I can do everything through him who gives me strength."
Philippians 4:13

Get It Together ■ 20-30 minutes

Action: Understand that we need to trust God as we serve Him and use our abilities.

Judges 6:33—7:25

What You Need

Bibles.

What You Do

Lead students to read and discuss the Bible verses listed. Extend the discussion with the questions and comments provided.

Introduction

When was a time you tried something and you ended up doing better than you expected? Gideon discovered how God helped him to be a successful leader. The Israelites were being attacked by their enemies the Midianites, and God used Gideon to lead Israel against them.

The Proof

■ Before Gideon led the Israelites in battle, what did Gideon ask God to do? What was the result? Read Judges 6:37-38 to find out.

■ Read Judges 6:39-40 to find the result of the second way in which Gideon wanted God to prove Himself.

Gideon wanted to be really, REALLY sure God was with him. So Gideon asked God for some proof. God did exactly as Gideon asked! But, just in case he had made a mistake, Gideon decided to make another request of God.

When he put out another piece of fleece, Gideon asked God to make the ground around the fleece wet and keep the fleece dry.

When God gave Gideon proof of His promise to save Israel, Gideon was sure God WAS with him! Gideon could be the leader God had asked him to be.

The Army

■ Read Judges 7:2 to find out why God wanted Gideon to have a smaller army when he led the Israelites in battle against the Midianites.

■ What would you have thought about having a smaller army if you were Gideon?

■ How many men stayed with Gideon after he sent home everyone who was afraid to fight? How many left? Read Judges 7:3.

■ God told Gideon to make his army even smaller. But how many men did this leave to fight the Midianites? Read Judges 7:8.

Gideon had called together the men of his tribe to come and fight against the Midianites, as God had said to do. Thirty-two THOUSAND men were now gathered to fight the Midianites.

God wanted the Israelites to have a smaller army so that they would clearly see that they needed GOD'S help to be successful. If the Israelite army was too big, the Israelites might think they had won the battle on their own.

So God told Gideon to send home anyone who was afraid to fight. Now Gideon had an army of only about 10,000 men.

To make the army even smaller, God told Gideon to send all his men down to a stream to get water. Gideon carefully watched the men. Some put their faces down to the water and lapped up the water like dogs. Others scooped the water up and drank from their cupped hands.

"Gideon, send away the men who lapped up the water," God said. The few left were the ones God had chosen to follow His extraordinary plan. Gideon's army had decreased from 32,000 to only 300!

The Victory

■ What do you think weapons were like in Bible times? Read Judges 7:16 to find out what weapons Gideon gave his men.

■ Read Judges 7:20 to find out what Gideon and his men did with the strange weapons. What did the men shout?

■ Why do you think the Midianites were so upset by what they saw and heard? What did the Midianites do? Read Judges 7:21.

The trumpets were not like today's musical instruments. They were animal horns that made a sharp, shrill sound. The trumpets were usually blown by just a few men to let everyone in the army know it was time to attack. And usually only a few men in each section of an army would carry torches to help the others see where they were going. But in God's plan, each man had a trumpet and a torch hidden in a jar.

Gideon told his men to watch what he did and then do the same thing. Quietly, the 300 men sneaked up on the Midianite army.

The Midianites heard 300 trumpets blowing, the crashing of 300 clay jars breaking and saw themselves surrounded by 300 torches. They panicked! The Midianites probably assumed that they were only seeing and hearing a small portion of a much larger army.

Not only did the Midianites start to run away, but God caused the Midianites to become confused and they started attacking each other! Gideon's army had won by simply doing what God said to do!

Conclusion

Gideon learned that only with God's help could he successfully lead the Israelites against the Midianites. God used Gideon's obedient, trusting and willing attitude to do something that went far beyond Gideon's actual abilities. (Read Philippians 4:13 aloud.)

The Bible compares life to running a race (see 1 Corinthians 9:24). In this race, you'll have many opportunities to trust God as you learn new things and develop your abilities. Best of all, you can depend on God to help you do the good things He wants you to do. (Pray with students, asking God to help them trust Him at all times as they live for Him.)

Get Going ■ 20-30 minutes

Action: Describe situations in which we need to depend on God in using our abilities, and ask His help.

Distribute Get Real (p. 216) to students. Invite students to tell or write answers to the questions. End the discussion by completing Get Connected with students. (Optional: Students complete page at home.)

GET REAL

■ What might make a kid feel nervous or worried at school? At a soccer game? At a piano recital? What might kids your age do and say to ask for God's help in these situations?

■ When might someone worry about doing something that shows their obedience to God?

■ When have you realized that you really needed God's help more than you needed your own abilities?

■ How might God help you use your abilities?

■ What do you know about God that gives you confidence in Him?

Get to Know

"I can do everything through him who gives me strength."
Philippians 4:13

Get Connected

What is something you need to do this week? What ability has God given you to accomplish this goal? Remember that God is the One who made you and who gave you the abilities you have. Ask God to help you depend on Him to serve Him. Thank God for His help and love.

Parable of the Talents

Get Started ■ 5-15 minutes

Action: Compare and contrast ways people use their abilities.

Scavenger Hunt

What You Need

A variety of newspapers and news magazines, scissors.

What You Do

1. Students look through newspapers and magazines to find articles or pictures showing ways people have used or wasted their abilities. Challenge students to find at least two examples of each category.

2. Students tear or cut out articles and pictures; then they show and briefly describe their articles or pictures. Ask the questions below.

■ **What ability does the person in this article have?**

■ **How did the person use his or her ability?**

■ **What are the results of how this person has used his or her ability? What could the person have done instead?**

3. Conclude the activity by saying,

■ **Each of us chooses how we're going to use our abilities, too.**

■ **Three people in our Bible study today made choices about using their abilities. You can decide if you think they used their abilities in good ways or if they wasted them.**

Bonus Idea

As needed, preselect appropriate articles and cut them out for students to choose from and sort. Students tape or glue articles or pictures to a piece of mural or butcher paper. Keep the mural and add pictures of your students using their abilities in various activities.

The Message

Using our abilities pleases God and brings us joy.

The Bible Basis

Matthew 25:14-30

Two servants used their master's money to produce good results so that their master was pleased.

The Scripture

"Each of you should use whatever gift he has received to serve others."
1 Peter 4:10

Get It Together ■ 20-30 minutes

Action: Recognize very different results that come from using or not using the abilities God gives us.

Matthew 25:14-30

What You Need

Bibles.

What You Do

Lead students to read and discuss the Bible verses listed. Extend the discussion with the questions and comments provided.

Introduction

Tell about a time you were able to earn some money. Today we'll talk about two people who earned some money and another person who didn't.

The Parable of the Talents

■ In Bible times a word for "money" was "talent." What do we usually use the word "talent" for?

■ What do you remember about the parable of talents—a story Jesus told? Who are the characters in the parable? What did the master wants his servants to do?

■ What kind of servants do you think the master chose? Why might the man have trusted his servants to handle so much of his money?

■ Read Matthew 25:15. How do you think the man decided how much money to give each servant?

We use the word "talent" to refer to someone's ability or skill. In Bible times, however, the word "talent" didn't mean that at all. The word meant a large amount of money in the form of gold or silver coins.

The meaning of the word changed because of the story Jesus told. This parable tells about a man who left on a journey. Before he left, he told three of his servants to take care of his money. He certainly expected his servants to make MORE money for him.

It really wasn't unusual in Bible times for a master to leave his most trustworthy servants in charge of his property. This man was going on a very long journey. He wanted to make sure his money and property were well taken care of while he was gone.

The Three Servants

■ What was different about each of these servants? Read Matthew 25:16-18 and compare their actions and attitudes.

■ What do you think the first servant did to earn more money?

■ How do you think the second servant might have felt when he was given less money than the first servant?

■ Reread Matthew 25:18. How were the actions of the third servant different?

The man knew the abilities of his servants well. He gave each of them the amount of money he thought they could handle.

The first two servants knew what their master wanted them to do with the money: He wanted them to use it to make more money. He wanted them to invest it.

The Bible says the first two servants put their money to work. Perhaps the first servant bought a good field, grew grain and then sold the grain at the marketplace. Or maybe he bought a few sheep and used their wool to make clothes and blankets. Perhaps he bought spices from a traveling salesman and then packaged the spices and sold them in the marketplace for a profit. Whatever he did with the money, he probably also had to do some work himself. And he did! But he not only got back the money he had spent, he got back DOUBLE the amount.

The second servant could have been insulted that the master had only given him two talents when the other servant had been given five talents. But he didn't waste his time being jealous. He just went out and did the best he could with what he'd been given. Just like the first servant, his hard work paid off and he got back DOUBLE the amount of money he'd invested—four talents of gold for two!

The third servant was a fearful man. He wanted to play it safe. So he dug a hole and hid his money in the ground! Well, that was safe. There was no risk of losing it! And he didn't have to DO anything except wait around for his master to return.

The Results

■ Read Matthew 25:20-23. What did the first two servants earn and what did the master say and do for them?

■ Contrast this with how the third servant handled his task. Read Matthew 25:26-27. Why was the master angry with him?

The master was VERY pleased with what the first two servants had done. He was so pleased, in fact, that he put them in places of authority on his estate. The servants would enjoy his future wealth. And notice the master said exactly the same thing to both servants. It wasn't how much the servants had made that concerned the master, rather that they had been faithful with what they had been given.

The master had given the third servant a responsibility he KNEW the servant had the ability to handle. Yet the servant had wasted his ability and had done NOTHING.

Conclusion

This parable teaches us that the ways we use our abilities lead to very different results. People who use the abilities God gives them usually find they enjoy using them and get better and better at using them. (Read 1 Peter 4:10 aloud.) But those who don't use their abilities may find that they miss out on opportunities to truly experience the joy of using their abilities in serving God.

At some time or another we've probably all acted like the third servant and missed an opportunity to use an ability to serve God. We might have felt nervous about using an ability; or maybe we felt lazy, and using or learning the ability just seemed like too much work! God promises to forgive us if we've been wasting our abilities, and He'll help us enjoy serving Him with the things we're good at. Then we won't miss out on all the good things God has planned for us. (Lead students in prayer, asking God to help them use every ability and opportunity they are given.)

Get Going ■ 20-30 minutes

Action: List reasons we sometimes waste abilities, and plan ways to use our abilities to serve God.

Distribute Get Real (p. 220) to students. Invite students to tell or write answers to the questions. End the discussion by completing Get Connected with students. (Optional: Students complete page at home.)

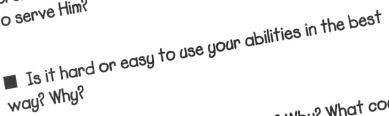

- How does knowing the way God made you make a difference when you think of wasting or using your abilities to serve Him?

- Is it hard or easy to use your abilities in the best way? Why?

- How might a kid waste an ability? Why? What could the person do differently?

- How have you already enjoyed using your abilities in good ways to serve God? What's another way you can use that ability this week? What might result?

- What can you do if you realize you've been wasting an ability?

Get to Know

"Each of you should use whatever gift he has received to serve others."
1 Peter 4:10

Get Connected

Think about one way you can use a talent, ability, or skill to serve God. Ask God to help you follow through with your plans to serve Him.

Index of Bible Lessons

Bible Study Index

Genesis 2 • The Problem of Sin 13

Genesis 3:1-19 • The Problem of Sin..................13

Genesis 12:1-5 • God's Faithfulness..................125

Genesis 15:1-7 • God's Faithfulness..................125

Genesis 21:1-7 • God's Faithfulness..................125

Genesis 27:1-45 • Live Honestly 41

Genesis 37 • Tough Times 161

Genesis 39 • Tough Times 161

Genesis 39:21-23 • God Is Good 165

Genesis 40—47:12 • God Is Good..................165

Genesis 50:19-20 • God Is Good 165

Exodus 3—4:17,27-31 • Here I Am, Lord..................205

Exodus 6—12:42 • Ever-Present Power..................129

Exodus 20:8-20 • Love Is God's Law..................97

Leviticus 9 • The Sin Solution 17

Leviticus 16: 21-22 • The Sin Solution..................17

Judges 4—5 • A Grateful Heart 197

Judges 6:1-35 • Serve with God's Strength..................209

Judges 6:33—7:25 • Rely on God's Strength..................213

Judges 16:4-31 • Learn from Your Sin..................137

1 Samuel 1—2:10 • Ask the Lord 201

1 Samuel 15:1-29 • Obey All the Way..................29

1 Samuel 17:40-50 • My Future..................157

1 Samuel 18:1-16 • Faithful Friends..................37

1 Samuel 18:6-11 • My Future..................157

1 Samuel 19 • Faithful Friends..................37

1 Samuel 20 • Faithful Friends..................37

1 Samuel 26:7-11 • My Future..................157

2 Samuel 1; 9 • Faithful Friends 37

2 Samuel 17 • My Future..................157

1 Kings 3:4-28 • Depend on God's Wisdom..................33

1 Kings 4:29-34 • Depend on God's Wisdom..................33

1 Kings 16:29-33 • The Only True God..................121

1 Kings 17:1 • The Only True God 121

1 Kings 17:1-16 • Trust in God..................149

1 Kings 18:4 • Trust in God..................149

1 Kings 18:7-46 • The Only True God..................121

2 Kings 22—23:30 • Doers of the Word..................81

Nehemiah 1—9 • Confess Your Sins..................193

Jeremiah 31:3,17; 36:1-32 • Everlasting Love..................133

Daniel 6 • Faithful Habits..................101

Matthew 4:11 • The Great Temptation..................85

Matthew 12:9-14 • Love Is God's Law..................97

Matthew 18:1-4,15-16 • Be Angry, But Sin Not..................53

Matthew 18:21-35 • The Gift of Forgiveness 57

Matthew 21:12-16 • Love and Pray for God's Family 109

Matthew 25:14-30 • The Parable of the Talents 217

Matthew 28:16-20 • The Great Commission 169

Mark 1:35-38 • Teach Us to Pray 185

Mark 3:1-6 • Love Is God's Law 97

Mark 4:1-20 • The Fruit of God's Word 89

Mark 6:45-46 • Teach Us to Pray 185

Mark 9:33-37 • Be Angry, But Sin Not 53

Luke 1:26-56 • A Song of Praise 189

Luke 2:22-40 • Light in a Sinful World 21

Luke 6:6-11 • Love Is God's Law 97

Luke 6:12-13 • Teach Us to Pray 185

Luke 9:46-48 • Be Angry, But Sin Not 53

Luke 10:25-37 • Who's Your Neighbor? 45

Luke 11:1-13 • Teach Us to Pray 185

Luke 12:13-21 • Get to Know God.............................25

Luke 19:1-10 • Make It Right...................................141

Luke 22:33-34,54-62 • A Fresh Start 145

John 3:1-21 • Hungry for Goodness............................93

John 4:4-42 • Living Water 61

John 6:1-15,25-51 • Bread of Life 65

John 10:1-30 • The Good Shepherd 69

John 12:12-15 • The Way 73

John 14:1-14 • The Way 73

John 15:1-17 • The Vine 77

John 18:1—20:31 • The Vine 77

John 20:30-31 • The Great Commission 169

John 21:1-19 • A Fresh Start 145

Acts 1:4-5; 2 • One Spirit 113

Acts 2:42-45 • The Great Commission 169

Acts 3—4:22 • Taking Action 173

Acts 8:3 • Accept Each Other 117

Acts 8:46,26-40 • Know and Tell the Good News 177

Acts 9:1-31 • Accept Each Other 117

Acts 17:16-34 • Witness with Love and Respect............181

Acts 21:27-36 • Handling Fear 153

Acts 25:10-11 • Handling Fear 153

Acts 27 • Handling Fear 153

Romans 3:23 • The Problem of Sin.............................13

Romans 5:12 • The Problem of Sin.............................13

Romans 6:23 • The Problem of Sin.............................13

Romans 10:14-15 • The Great Commission 169

Hebrews 7:23-28 • The Sin Solution............................17

Hebrews 10:1-4 • The Sin Solution.............................17

Hebrews 11—12:3 • Faith That Leads to Obedience 105

James 3:2-12 • Tongue Control 49

Bible Verse Index

Deuteronomy 5:32 • Faithful Habits............................101

Psalm 36:5 • God's Faithfulness................................125

Psalm 46:1 • Tough Times 161

Psalm 51:1-2 • Learn from Your Sin 137

Psalm 77:12-13 • The Only True God 121

Psalm 77:14 • Ever-Present Power 129

Psalm 119:10 • Obey All the Way 29

Psalm 119:10 • Hungry for Goodness 93

Psalm 119:11 • The Great Temptation..............................85

Psalm 119:60 • Faith That Leads to Obedience...............105

Psalm 119:127 • Doers of the Word..................................81

Psalm 136:1 • A Grateful Heart......................................197

Psalm 145:8 • Everlasting Love......................................133

Proverbs 3:5-6 • Depend on God's Wisdom 33

Proverbs 29:11 • Be Angry, But Sin Not 53

Isaiah 41:13 • My Future 157

Jeremiah 17:7 • Trust in God..149

Daniel 2:20 • A Song of Praise.......................................189

Daniel 9:9 • A Fresh Start..145

Matthew 5:16 • Taking Action 173

Matthew 6:20 • Get to Know God....................................25

Matthew 21:13 • Love and Pray for God's Family 109

Matthew 28:19-20 • The Great Commission..................169

Luke 10:27 • Who's Your Neighbor?.................................45

Luke 10:27 • Love Is God's Law 97

John 4:14 • Living Water 61

John 6:35 • Bread of Life 65

John 10:11 • The Good Shepherd....................................69

John 14:6 • The Way..73

John 14:27 • Handling Fear...153

John 15:5 • The Vine 77

Acts 10:43 • Light in a Sinful World................................21

Romans 6:23 • The Problem of Sin..................................13

Romans 8:28 • God Is Good 165

Romans 15:7 • Accept Each Other 117

1 Corinthians 12:27 • One Spirit....................................113

1 Corinthians 13:4-5 • Live Honestly 41

2 Corinthians 5:17 • Make It Right 141

Ephesians 2:10 • Here I Am, Lord...................................205

Philippians 2:4 • Faithful Friends....................................37

Philippians 4:6 • Ask the Lord.......................................201

Philippians 4:13 • Rely on God's Strength 213

Colossians 3:13 • The Gift of Forgiveness 57

Colossians 4:2 • Teach Us to Pray 185

James 1:19 • Tongue Control 49

James 1:22 • The Fruit of God's Word 89

1 Peter 3:10 • Serve with God's Strength........................209

1 Peter 3:15 • Know and Tell the Good News...............177

1 Peter 4:10 • Parable of the Talents..............................217

1 John 1:9 • Confess Your Sins.......................................193

1 John 3:16 • The Sin Solution 17

1 John 3:18 • Witness with Love and Respect 181

More Great Resources from Gospel Light

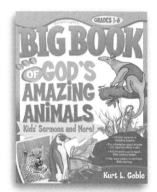

The Big Book of God's Amazing Animals
This book includes 52 lessons about a variety of animals that will intrigue kids, such as dolphins, penguins, koala bears, whales and condors. Each lesson relates facts about the featured animal to a particular Bible verse. As kids learn about fascinating animals that God created, they'll also learn about Him and how He wants them to live.
ISBN 08307.37146

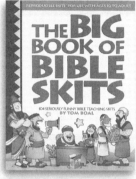

The Big Book of Bible Skits
Tom Boal

104 seriously funny Bible-teaching skits. Each skit comes with Bible background, performance tips, prop suggestions, discussion questions and more. Ages 10 to adult. Reproducible.
ISBN 08307.19164

The Really Big Book of Kids' Sermons and Object Talks with CD-ROM
This reproducible resource for children's pastors is packed with 156 sermons (one a week for three years) that are organized by topics such as friendship, prayer, salvation and more. Each sermon includes an object talk using a household object, discussion questions, prayer and optional information for older children. Reproducible.
ISBN 08307.36573

The Big Book of Volunteer Appreciation Ideas
Joyce Tepfer

This reproducible book is packed with 100 great thank-you ideas for teachers, volunteers and helpers in any children's ministry program. An invaluable resource for showing your gratitude!
ISBN 08307.33094

The Big Book of Christian Growth
Discipling made easy! 306 discussion cards based on Bible passages, and 75 games and activities for preteens. Reproducible.
ISBN 08307.25865

The Big Book of Bible Skills
Active games that teach a variety of Bible skills (book order, major divisions of the Bible, location references, key themes). Ages 8 to 12. Reproducible.
ISBN 08307.23463

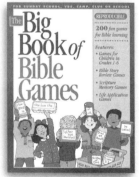

The Big Book of Bible Games
200 fun, active games to review Bible stories and verses and to apply Bible truths to everyday life. For ages 6 to 12. Reproducible.
ISBN 08307.18214

The Big Book of Bible Games #2
150 active games—balloon games, creative team relays, human bowling, and more—that combine physical activity with Bible learning. Games are arranged by Bible theme and include discussion questions. For grades 1 to 6. Reproducible.
ISBN 08307.30532

To order, visit your local Christian bookstore or www.gospellight.com

Gospel Light
God's Word for a Kid's World!™